A FAITH
FOR ALL SEASONS

T0097099

A FAITH
FOR ALL SEASONS

Islam and the Challenge of
the Modern World

Shabbir Akhtar

Ivan R. Dee • Publisher • Chicago

Library of Congress Cataloging-in-Publication Data:
Akhtar, Shabbir, 1960–
A faith for all seasons : Islam and the challenge of the modern
world / Shabbir Akhtar. — 1st American ed.
p.   cm.
Includes bibliographical references and index.
ISBN 0-929587-54-5 (cloth : acid-free paper) —
ISBN 0-929587-63-4 (pbk. : acid-free paper)
1. Islam—20th century. I. Title.
BP163.A417   1991
297—dc20   90-24786

To F.H. – companion on the straight path.

Contents

Preface   vii

Acknowledgments   ix

Part 1: The Age of Innocence

1 The Fateful Vision   3

2 A Change of Masters   24

3 'Poetry from Heaven'   39

4 The Silence of Allah   77

Part 2: The Virtues of Heresy

5 The Wisdom of the Fool   89

6 The Brave New World   114

7 The Kingdom of God   129

8 The Riddle of Man   143

Part 3: Modernity and Beyond

9 Choice and Destiny   165

10 The Road to Mecca   202

Notes   215

Index   246

Preface

Once upon a time, it was said: 'Islam is the best religion with the worst followers.' After Rushdie, many say: 'Islam is the worst religion with the worst followers.' Certainly, there can be no greater proof of the current intellectual paralysis among the followers of Muhammad than their complete failure to respond adequately to the many challenges of secular modernity.

Modern Muslims are, as a group of people, embarrassingly unreflective: it were as though Allah had done all the thinking for his devotees. Friedrich Nietzsche's acid comment on his compatriots in *Twilight of the Idols* also applies with peculiar justice to the Muslim communities of the modern world: 'The Germans – once they were called the nation of thinkers: do they still think at all?' After developing a great rational philosophical tradition, the adherents of Islam have lapsed into an intellectual lethargy that has already lasted half a millennium.

Although there is no lack of religious apologists or religious theoreticians in Islam, they have altogether failed to offer any principled and thoughtful response to modernity. Owing to an absence of sceptical and liberal influences, itself traceable to the lack of an extant philosophical tradition, few Muslims have even recognised the threats of secularity and ideological pluralism that our current circumstance brings in its train. Many a Muslim writer prefers to pretend that modernity poses a challenge solely to Christian convictions: it is merely a local threat to an impotent faith domesticated within an aggressively materialistic culture.

I argue in these pages that nothing could, in fact, be further from the truth. In seeking to repossess the legacy of Muhammad for the needs of the modern age, Muslims must recognise and answer the challenges of secularity and religious pluralism. The beginning of the fifteenth century of Islam marks the end of their age of innocence. Can Muslims, then, show their modern critics that Islam supplies its votaries with a faith for all seasons?

This book makes many large claims. But my principal aim has been simply to counsel Muslims to be reflective, to be intellectually honest enough to face frankly and conscientiously the tribunal of secular reason and to do so within faithful parameters. I offer no facile solutions to admittedly complex worries, nor do I deny that the details of the solutions that I do offer may legitimately be seen as mistaken or implausible. (One occupational privilege, not always noted, of working in philosophy is that one's mistakes are of little consequence since very few people of influence are likely to be misled by them.)

I do not criticise Islam in the manner of some unsympathetic Christian and Marxist thinkers who assume that it is essentially a false religion with a dangerous political potential. Nor do I defend Islam root and branch in the manner of most Muslim apologists. It cannot be expected that a book which serves the interests of neither camp will entirely escape criticism. But it can be hoped that some impartial students of Islam will see something worthwhile in these pages.

I am a Muslim and have neither reason nor motive to conceal this fact. But I am neither pretentious nor ambitious enough – is ambition itself a species of pretension? – to have acquired a sense of religious mission in writing this book. In setting limits to my task, I have laid aside many significant religious concerns – concerns which have failed to find a place in a primarily philosophical contribution. Those anxious to read somewhat more committed works should consult my other writings.

It is natural to feel pleasure in the accomplishment of complex designs that may confer intellectual kudos on Islam. But one should have no illusions as to the worth of purely intellectual endeavours. Religions are never saved by mental efforts alone. As it happens, Islam, as a relatively young and strikingly vigorous faith, is not in urgent need of being rescued from the ravages of hostile ideologies. But its future lies ultimately in the sacrifices of the believing society – ordinary men and women who are capable of patience in the hour of trial and mercy in the hour of triumph. The thinker has here a relatively modest role to play.

A remark now, in another vein, about something I would have preferred not to have had to say. While all authorship is of its nature a personal and demanding vocation, writing this book has been a peculiarly lonely and difficult task – and not merely for the usual narrowly intellectual reasons. Since it is considered in bad taste to mention those who may have plagued one's labours, suffice it to say that I have not found many allies in contemporary Islam or Christianity for most of the views and aspirations expressed here.

SHABBIR AKHTAR

Acknowledgments

The author and the publishers are grateful to the following for permission to quote from copyright sources:

Unwin Hyman Ltd for two quotations from Arthur Arberry's *The Koran Interpreted*; BBC Enterprises Ltd for one quotation from Don Cupitt's *The Sea of Faith*; David Higham Associates for two quotations from Dylan Thomas *The Poems*, published by J M Dent.

A FAITH
FOR ALL SEASONS

Part 1
THE AGE OF
INNOCENCE

1

The Fateful Vision

I

It was the habit of a certain Muhammad ibn Abdullah to meditate alone for a month at Mount Hira in western Arabia. One night, towards the end of Ramadan, when the seventh century of the Common Era had reached a tenth of its span, the angel Gabriel, tradition relates, disturbed the solitude of this ageing Arabian and ordered him to recite some words. These words, held sacred by subsequent Muslim tradition,[1] were destined to transform not only Muhammad's Arabia but indeed the course of universal history.

Some years after Gabriel's visit, the Arabian iconoclast began to preach the new monotheistic faith to his pagan compatriots in Mecca. Most of them rejected it. A small motley band did, however, respond enthusiastically to the Prophet's call. There followed many dark hours of persecution and ostracism; Muhammad's ministry had fallen on decidedly evil days.

To any impartial observer situated in early-seventh-century Arabia, it would have seemed that nothing would become of the new faith. Although the Jews had been for some time expecting a Messiah and the pagan Arabs badly stood in need of a prophet, most of Muhammad's contemporaries initially disbelieved in the message he had brought. And although there were some influential conversions to the new cause, pagan opposition and animus grew steadily. In the event, Muhammad's ministry remained immersed in a sea of troubles for some thirteen years.

And then, suddenly, the tide turned. A small group of men from the northerly city of Yathrib, later renamed Medina, endorsed the Arabian Prophet's mission. They invited him and his small band of devoted if dispossessed disciples to seek asylum in their metropolis. Muhammad accepted the invitation and in A.D. 622, after negotiating the terms of settlement for his followers, he fled his native city to seek refuge in Medina – an event which marks the beginning of the Islamic era.

The move to Medina was not a flight into exiled frustration. The new location provided the conditions that served to celebrate Muhammad's mission. Within a decade, the newcomer had established an autonomous political community in the form of a theocratic state bearing allegiance to 'Allah and His Apostle'. The prophet-statesman taught the details of the new religion to the growing crowd of neophytes. Having subdued internal and external opposition to his ministry and having engaged his Meccan opponents in a few decisive battles, he eventually re-entered, in triumph and without bloodshed, the city which had once rejected him.

At the time of his death in A.D. 632 (10 A.H.),[2] Muhammad was the ruler of an Arabia united under the banner of the Crescent. Within one century, his followers, fired with the febrile enthusiasm of the new faith, scored a series of spectacular military victories which humbled two major empires. As the new religion spread, the Muslims became masters of a vast kingdom stretching from the Pyrenees in the West to the borders of China in the East. Along with the peoples they conquered, the Muslims proceeded to create a civilisation whose better aspects may fairly be ranked among the glories of the human record.

II

The message vouchsafed to Muhammad by his supernatural visitor on that fateful night in 610 today retains the loyalty of about a fifth of the human race. The modern disciples of the Arabian Prophet see themselves as inheritors of the Abrahamic tradition. For Muslims, the prophetic tradition effectively begins with Abraham[3] before branching off into the two separate sacred histories of the descendants of Isaac and Ishmael respectively. The former history traces the vicissitudes of the favoured House of Israel: a series of Hebrew Patriarchs – including Moses, David and Solomon – culminating in the appearance of Jesus the Messiah in first-century Palestine. The Ishmaelite line finds its terminus in Muhammad – the Gentile messenger who arose among 'the common folk' (K:62:2).[4] The appearance of the Arabian Prophet is seen by Muslims as the last major event in sacred monotheistic history.[5] His ministry is interpreted as having unified the two branches of sacred lineage, stabilised and completed the Abrahamic religious edifice, and thereby completed God's favour on mankind.

The content of Muhammad's preaching was, like that of his prophetic predecessors, uncompromisingly monotheistic. There exists, he told his Meccan detractors, a remarkable being – Allah[6] – who both created and continues to sustain the universe and all that is in it, including man. Allah created the world in six 'days';[7] altogether there are seven earths arranged vertically on top of one another with a corresponding set of seven heavens arranged on top of the earths. The lowest of the heavens is our sky, the highest is Eden. He also created Adam from dust; subsequently he created Adam's consort and thereby the entire monogenetic human race.

Allah is metaphysically perfect: eternal, omniscient, independent of his creation, indeed omnipotent. Above all, he is unique, having no partner in his divinity and allowing no one any share in the sovereignty of the created order. While transcendent to the natural world, he remains active in it and is deeply concerned to make moral demands on his human subjects. He expects worship, voluntary submission to his dictates, and virtuous conduct. Although Allah is merciful and forbearing, he justly punishes or even destroys those who are disobedient to his righteous will.

Unfortunately, the record of human conduct has generally been deplorable: rich in vice and poor in virtue. In the colourful catalogue of mortal ills, one is especially prevalent: the age-old failure to accord to Allah the exclusive worship which is his right and our duty. At a momentous assembly held before their earthly sojourn began, the souls of the Children of Adam had freely promised allegiance to their unique creator (K:7:172). Many, however, subsequently failed to keep this primal promise.

Part of the reason for this failure is men's heedlessness (*ghaflah*). But that is not the whole story. A supreme evil being, Satan, wishes to encourage disloyalty to Allah. Satan had indeed originally questioned the divine decision to appoint Adam as a vicegerent on earth on behalf of his creator (K:2:30ff). The angels had all temporarily evinced doubts about the wisdom of the divine proposal but only Satan had insisted on its foolishness.[8] Expelled from Heaven, Satan swore enmity to Adam and his kin. Indeed, he tempted Adam and his consort to eat a forbidden fruit which led to their expulsion from Eden (K:2:35).

Allah forgave Adam and promised guidance and education for him and his progeny (K:2:37–8). Apart from Adam – who was himself a minor prophet – Allah has despatched a series of messengers, including some Arabian figures before the advent of Muhammad, all bearing (a few insignificant details apart) the same message. In this way, men have been continually reminded of their original treaty of exclusive loyalty to their creator. For all their lapses into idolatry (Arabic, *shirk*) and sin, belief in the uniquely true divinity and a virtuous disposition remain their human birthright. Having been doubly fortified against the machinations of Satan – that is, on account of their conscience and the heavenly reminders – they have only themselves to blame for their waywardness.

Although Allah has inspired countless prophets, rejection dominates the human response. The pattern of mortal history is painfully simple. A messenger arises within every community counselling his people to eschew idolatry in favour of their monotheistic heritage. Typically, his audience perversely disregard the warning; they impiously mock the messenger's religious credentials and ignore his threats about divine retribution. Suddenly, without further notice, the community is destroyed in some peculiarly dramatic fashion at the hands of an outraged deity. The prophet and those few who took heed are miraculously rescued. Nothing remains of the sinful society except ruins and a grim reminder for later generations. Indeed, Muhammad's contemporaries had seen some of the signs of Allah's wrath in the pathetic ruins found towards the north of the peninsula – bygone communities that had once flourished providing a welcome halt for the weary traveller.

Fortunately, not all nations had rejected the divine summons to appear before the sacred tribunal. In particular the Jews, and later the Christians, had embraced the message from Allah. Although the message had been faithfully delivered in the first instance, these communities subsequently misinterpreted or wilfully distorted it. Despite the Almighty's disappointing experiment with these two groups of errant theists, he decided to bestow the gift of revealed guidance yet again – albeit on another community. Allah's latest choice settled on the Arabs.

The Arabs certainly stood in need of guidance. While Allah's previous interventions in human history had influenced large tracts of the Levant and the Near Mediterranean, the pagan tribes of the Hejaz had remained noticeably indifferent. They had continued to live in sin and error in a period of Arab history called *al-jahilliyyah* (the age of ignorance).[9] Now, however, as a society newly blessed with a scripture, they had the honour of receiving Allah's final and conclusive message – the Arabic Koran[10] – the handing down of which marked the close of the age of revelation.

At a time known only to Allah, human history will terminate – giving way to the terrors that herald the Last Day. The débâcle will be complete: the earth pulverised, the mountains ground to fine dust and the sky split asunder. With remarkable ease, Muhammad's Lord will resurrect all the descendants of Adam. Fearful and expectant, they will stand silently before their creator as the divine assizes commence.

Apart from martyrs for the cause of Islam – who will gain, without reckoning, immediate entrance into Paradise – all other men must wait their turn as their deeds are weighed and assessed in the balance. Those who welcomed the heavenly despatches and attempted to live in a manner pleasing to the Deity may, by his grace, be allowed to enter Eden and partake of its delights for eternity. As for those who neglected the heavenly warnings and gave free rein to their own whims and passions – such must taste, for as long as Allah pleases, the unspeakable torments of Gehenna.

III

This is the Islamic *Lebenswelt*. It is a disturbing and suggestive view of the world and of our place in it. Whether coherent or not, whether true or false, it has guided, and continues to guide, the lives of countless millions for one and a half millennia. It is a powerful vision with ambiguous potentialities, having inspired, on the one hand, lives displaying selfless devotion to noble if austere ideals, and on the other, appalling obscurantism and restriction of human sympathies.

A few significant details apart, the Muslim vision is identical with the vision of Judaism and Christianity, Islam's ethical monotheistic predecessors. This theistic outlook is no longer fashionable in the advanced industrialised communities of the western world and their satellites and colonies. Belief in the existence of a divine being has been held with extraordinary tenacity from antiquity down to the Age of Reason. Ever since the European Enlightenment, however, it has become a genuine question whether or not belief in the God of the Christians and Jews, and indeed of the Muslims, is intellectually defensible or even morally necessary. Many modern thinkers believe that recent advances in secular scientific and rational thought have exposed much of the monotheistic tradition to be making claims that are embarrassingly fantastic and indeed barely credible, if not wholly false. In effect, the Near Eastern religions of revelation are no longer seen as offering a metaphysically plausible world-view for modern enlightened man.

Theism is currently facing an unprecedented crisis in urbanised society. There has been a mass leakage from the vessel of belief: the Christian communities increasingly face apostasy, and the exodus from strictly orthodox Judaism is not inconsiderable. In the case of Islam, although the number of defiantly orthodox exceptions remains surprisingly large, the secular attitudes that inform modern intellectual and popular culture have certainly influenced many members of the sizeable Muslim communities now settled in western lands.[11]

Islam has, like Roman Catholicism, continued to keep the mass of its adherents on a relatively exacting plane of moral and religious obligation. But there are signs of lapse and confusion within orthodox religious communities. In the case of Islam, while there are no unambiguous indications of any imminent crisis, the uniform socio-moral discipline in Muslim lands is internally disturbed by many ferments. To be sure, on the level of external observance, there is no cause for alarm. But beneath the surface the perceptive observer can discern all the familiar paradoxes of a great religious civilisation in the throes of secularity. Thus, despite the recently acquired reputation for a confident self-assertiveness that fabulous wealth can bring in its train, significant numbers of Muslims secretly continue to extol foreign exemplars. A conscientious religiosity must necessarily walk uneasily alongside all the familiar anarchies of desire and a free-ranging caprice.

The whole chaos is the natural result of a central revolt in which an age-old orthodoxy of intellect, taste and behaviour, once enforced by the power of eschatological agitations and the implicit sanction of public opinion, is beginning to be despised. Of course, the leader of many a revivalist movement calls for a return to the pristine Islam of the first Muslims. Throughout the history of Islam there have been countless attempts to restore the purity of the faith by curing it of any contamination by profane values. And such attempts continue. But no perceptive spectator could ignore the conspicuous tendency, in many modern Muslim lands, to imitate non-Islamic exemplars, in particular those of western culture – the culture that, for better or for worse, dictates the mental fashion throughout much of the modern world.

I cannot of course paint the whole picture; generalisations in the sociology of Islam are often belied by the rebellious facts. In the tumultuous Middle East itself – Islam's land of origin – orthodoxy seems to have been reasserting itself in the 1980s after a brief flirtation with the West in the previous decades. Muslims have sobered up after the 'Westoxication' of the 1960s and 1970s. (The term 'Westoxication' – or *Gharb-zadehgui* – was coined by the Iranian writer Jalal al-Ahmad to denote the tendency of Muslim intellectuals to flirt with western ideas and ideals at the expense of the Arabic-Islamic traditions of thought and scholarship.) Muslims still feel the charms of that old temptress who has not changed her ways for well over a millennium. Thus, Khomeini had no shortage of martyrs for the Shi'ite cause; and a blind Sheikh Kishk's hellfire-filled sermons, anachronistic to most modern Christian ears, still bring the Friday traffic to a halt outside ancient Cairo's overflowing Sunni mosques. Allah is certainly not dead.

The orthodox cast of mind is, however, undeniably perturbed, in its own way, by the increasing secularisation of many a traditionally Islamic society. Naturally, the worries are predominantly political in flavour. As the shibboleths of orthodoxy weaken, the religious intelligentsia renews its call for a return to the glorious past. Fanned by the memory of past western colonial excesses against the peoples of Islam, aided in part by current social grievances, the impulse to restore the past glory of Muhammad's faith is strongly and passionately felt by many Muslims. Many movements have recently arisen in uneasy defiance of the increasingly powerful semi-secular order. All aim at the triumphant monopoly of Islam; many stir up a temporary enthusiasm before ending up in the dustbin of history.

The golden age of Arabian imperialism is indeed dead and gone. In Muslim activist circles, there are all the signs of disillusionment with the historical order. Nostalgia and helpless rage together inform a complex mood which invites comparison with the mood of revisionist Marxism in the 1930s. Men like Herbert Marcuse, Theodor Adorno and Max Horkheimer – members of the so-called Frankfurt School, founded in the 1920s, now dismantled – were sitting and wondering: 'What has gone wrong with history?' 'When will the promise of revolution come to pass?' There is no shortage of questions in the Muslim camp: 'What has gone wrong with sacred history?' 'Has Allah perhaps withdrawn his favour from "the best nation ever brought forth" (K:3:110) among mankind – the nation whose power had once served to topple many a dynasty of rejectors?' 'Or is it all a repayment for our infidelity, for our refusal to accept that Allah is indeed greater (*Allah-u-akbar*)?'

IV

Whatever may be said concerning the causes of the current decline of Islam as a religious and political force, there is no denying the increasing threat of secularity. Secularity is becoming more and more pronounced even in the most traditional Muslim countries. Islam is in principle a theocratic doctrine in which all the details of secular existence, no matter how recalcitrant, are systematically subordinated to religious prescriptions. One reliable indication of the prevalence of secular norms is the creation, albeit unwittingly, of a recognisable ghetto for traditional religion amid a markedly secular structure of thought and behaviour. The isolation and subsequent attenuation of religion in this manner have become commonplace in the West. The same seems to be happening in Muslim lands, with the result that Islam is slowly beginning to have, like a diluted Christianity in the West, a reduced status in the daily life of believers. The laicisation of modern sensibilities in the West appears to be far more pronounced: it seems that men rarely remember God outside the context of the rites of passage – birth, marriage and death. But the religious ghetto (which is the normal preface to such pronounced secularity) has already been created even in Muslim lands. Thus, for example, social functions and television programmes, which are more or less wholly secular in content and impulse, continue to be burdened by a religious preamble that is recognisably unrelated to the rest of the agenda. The overall result, of course, is that men entertain a general religious view about the nature of life and the world – as a matter of religious obligation – but simultaneously entertain a secular view about daily life in practice. Religion leaves the public sector of practical experience only to retreat into the private sector of theoretical dogma.

There are features internal to Christianity which serve to account for the appearance of secularity in lands with a predominantly Christian heritage. Unlike Islam, Christianity has been marked by a religiously significant distinction between the sacred and the secular, between the goods that belong to God and those that belong to Caesar, or, on an institutional level, between the clergy and the laity. Such distinctions are – or rather should in principle be – foreign to Islam. In fact, of course, Islam has its clergy, the *'ulama*, a class of religious apologists. Historically, there was no clerical class in Islam, its present existence being, strictly speaking, an innovation.

Once secularity, as a specific matrix for intellectual and popular culture, becomes prevalent, however, it affects all religion: it threatens to plunge transcendent religion itself into a crisis. We are not here concerned to trace the history of the genesis of the secular revolt against Christianity. Our concern here is with the logical and conceptual worries that the prevalence of secularity could bring in its train. And these latter troubles are quite clearly a plague on all our houses. Thus, the Rev. Kenneth Cragg, one of the ablest Christian students of Islam, is surely right to counsel religious believers that 'wherever its incidence may most strongly fall, the burden of the secular condition is with us all'.[12]

The point has often enough been made, I trust, that ever since the rise of modern science and humanism, the influence of religion – its sovereignty over beliefs and institutions – has gradually been eroded. More specifically, cataclysmic changes have taken place in the West particularly as a result of the Industrial Revolution and the accompanying desecration, since roughly 1850, of a life lived close to Nature and her harmonies. The overall result of these changes has been the development of a new body of theory about the social causality of individual and corporate existence, about the bases of responsible social and personal life; new ways of thinking about human nature and its resources have found favour leading to the formation, in consequence, of new types of social and political organisation. In short, there is a new *Lebenswelt* available – an alternative way of making sense of life and its pressures.

The tradition of militant humanism, forged by men like Friedrich Nietzsche, Karl Marx, Ludwig Feuerbach and others in the nineteenth century, sought to challenge the religious ideal of a universe under benevolent supervision. The idea, the atheist warns us, of a morally responsible providence at work behind Nature is a legend that must be stripped of its fantasies. We are alone in this whole nasty affair that life is; there are no benign intentions in the cosmos. The metaphysical instinct that lies at the very root of religion – all religion – is, he argues, peculiarly prey to tragically mistaken if admittedly constructive illusions. The will to transcend the natural and the human is doomed to failure. We must end where we begin: in the human, all too human, predicament.

Now it is sanguine for a Muslim to suppose that this scepticism is properly directed only towards Christian convictions. For even supposing, for the sake of a case, that Islam has somewhat fewer scandals to the secular intellect than Christianity, it has at least one central scandal in common. The very category of the transcendent is being rejected as illusory. The challenge of secular modernity, then, cannot be merely a local challenge to the Christian faith. It is not some isolated heresy invented by western intellectuals seeking to tear themselves away from their traditional Christian roots; it is rather a challenge to monotheistic conviction as a whole, indeed to all transcendent religion. It is true of course that historically the challenge was first formulated in western Christian lands and remains to this day directed in the first instance largely towards Christians. But the flood of secularity could certainly engulf Muslims too. It would therefore be wise to take seriously the warning of some sympathetic critics of Islam. Thus the Rev. Don Cupitt, for all his mistaken views about Christianity, is surely right in his assessment of the dangers of modernity for all faiths including Islam. Cupitt warns:

> The slow process of secularization, the impact of science and then of biblical and historical criticism, the shift to an ever more man-centred outlook, the encounter with other faiths, and then finally the awesome and still incomplete transition to modernity – all this makes up a story which for Christians has extended over some three or four centuries. There are people in other traditions, and most notably in Islam, who say that the story is a purely Christian one that reflects only Christianity's weakness in controlling developments in its own culture and its failure to resist the corrosive effects of scepticism. They flatter themselves that they will be able to escape the fate that has overtaken Christianity, some Muslims even adding that they will be able to create an Islamic science free from the undercurrent of scepticism that has marked western science. They are, I fear, mistaken.[13]

How long can we Muslims, then, honestly believe that modernity is only someone else's problem?

V

Modernity is perhaps everyone's problem, a Muslim may retort, but *western* modernity surely is not. What are we to make of this? There are profound ideological complications caused by the fact, itself historical and sociological, that the sceptical mentality has largely been cultivated by the peoples of the western world. Muslims will naturally be suspicious of the application of western criteria of plausibility, truth and rationality to their dogmatic convictions – a circumstance aggravated by the by no means defunct rivalry between the Crescent and the Cross. Indeed many Muslims will see it as a particularly insidious form of intellectual imperialism whereby Eurocentric critiques attempt to pass for impartial analyses.

This is an influential suspicion nourished by many factors. It needs to be carefully identified at the very outset of our project and then partly allayed. That much of orientalist scholarship does, despite its pretensions to a lofty supra-ideological objectivity, bear clearly on its face the impress of partisan religious and cultural values is beyond reasonable dispute.[14] Furthermore, recent western scholarship has itself conclusively established that much of the orientalist literature produced in the past betrays not only misunderstandings but also deliberate misrepresentations of Islam.[15] More specifically, it is now widely recognised that many Christian and Jewish critics of Islam have, with a few commendably isolated exceptions, deliberately sought to distort the image of their religious rival. There are complex historical reasons for these polemical attacks and the story is a long one. It may, however, fairly be said that, in general, if recent orientalism has made genuine contributions to the study of Islam and the Arabs, a great deal of it in previous epochs has tended unjustly to malign the faith and its founder.[16] It is also worth noting in this context that the rise of genuinely impartial study of Islam has come with the increasingly secular bent of western society; as long as Latin Christianity cherished the ideal of the *corpus Christianum*, objective treatment of religious rivals was, to put it no more strongly, not seen as an important priority.[17]

The western treatment of Islam, then, is not being recommended as a model for imitation by religious thinkers. Such treatment has unarguably, through a combination of ignorance and prejudice, deeply hurt Muslim sensibilities, whether orthodox or liberal. But the history of Christianity's own encounter with modernity is, I believe, worthy of serious study by all students of religion. The fact is, of course, that Christianity, particularly Protestant Christianity, has confronted the cold and riddling gaze of secular modernity longer and more self-consciously than any other extant religious tradition.

Partly as an accident of history, European Christianity became the religious hinterland of the Enlightenment. A few centuries later, it encountered Marxist humanism as an independent secular force – a circumstance that effectively forced Christians to justify their religious claims in the face of militant alien challenge. In short, Christians have had to endure for a significantly long period of time the sceptical and liberal influences which the cultural milieu of Christianity has brought in its train – influences which have, as in the case of the Darwin affair, entailed the obligation to suffer heavy casualties in the religious camp.

The external critique of Christianity, however, was only the beginning of the long season of torment. Nineteenth-century Protestant thinkers themselves turned the full fury of critical biblical scholarship on Christian dogmatic convictions. Armed with the scholarly weapons of modern critical history, themselves the product of a secular if not heretical mentality, they went on to produce what may be described, without undue exaggeration, as possibly the finest essay in intellectual probity in the history of religious ideas.

Christian theology in the tradition of Protestant liberalism has been truly remarkable. It has been characterised by candour and openness in its dealings with secularity and modernity. Despite the traditional imposition of an internal religious veto on any self-criticism of the bases of revealed theology (a veto naturally imposed by strictly orthodox Christian authorities) many Christian writers have, with courage and insight, exposed their own deeply held religious convictions to the full light of secularity.[18] The historical traditions of the Christian faith, its scriptures, and its entire dogmatics have in the process been subjected to searching criticism both external and internal. Indeed, Christian theology has in recent years been distinguished by its willingness temporarily to deny and even partly to disown pietistic and apologetic motives in the larger interests of objectivity. This scholarly detachment, more at home in academic philosophy than in theology, has been cultivated by many thinkers in the Christian tradition.[19] And that is why Christian thought provides an instructive paradigm for other faiths entering the dangerous arena of modernity.

These remarks, especially the concluding one, are liable to misinterpretation. I am not saying that the history of Christianity's dealings with modernity is fully normative, that is, worthy of complete emulation by others. On the contrary, I argue, in the manner of many Thomists within the Christian tradition, that excessive capitulation to secularism is self-defeating and that many a Protestant writer has unwittingly sold his faith down the river. But I also argue, importantly, that the wish to avoid compartmentalising our understanding of reality as a whole – a wish expressed typically by liberal Christian thinkers – is fully justified. The point, of course, is that it is not necessary to go along with every twist and turn in the recent history of Christianity's commerce with its 'cultured critics' (to use Schleiermacher's apt phrase) in order to appreciate and indeed welcome its fundamental aim – namely, the attempt to serve an intellectual honesty while sincerely searching for truth, including religious truth. Let us not forget that Christianity is the only faith in the Semitic trio whose adherents still continue seriously to produce intellectual self-defence when challenged by the alien convictions of the contemporaneous age.[20]

One final word to conclude this section. The suggestion that Muslims should see the dealings of western Christianity with secularity as a paradigm will appear anathema to the orthodox Muslim mentality. After all, Christianity and Islam as missionary faiths have been for centuries staunch religious rivals for the allegiance of mankind. And, it may be added, the Crusades are not necessarily over in all parts of the world: Third World Christianity has daily battles with the Crescent. None of this need be denied. But our concern here is with western Christianity. And it is clear that western secularity is far more threatening to Islam than western Christianity. The secularity of the modern West is vigorous and self-confident; western culture has indeed, in recent years, to put it in Professor Kolakowski's striking phrase, 'canonised its own secularity'.[21] Western Christianity is becoming, on the other hand, something of an embattled sub-culture – a minority group, if you wish – under attack from several fronts.[22] Now, western secularity poses a serious threat not only to Christianity but, as I suggested earlier, to all the theistic faiths, indeed to all religious faith *simpliciter*. Would it not be sensible therefore for all members of the so-called western faiths – Judaism and her religious offspring – to put up a united intellectual front against western secularity? Would it not be wise to become partners in adversity, to tread the same path, if only for this part of the journey?

VI

I should say a little now about recent Islamic theology.[23] Although Islam is a proselytising religion currently under the threat of leakage, Muslim theology has in recent years been distinguished largely by its resolute refusal to take seriously the dangers of secular modernity. Of course, there have been attempts by Muslim scholars, especially in the last few decades, to diagnose what they have taken to be the madness of modernity. The basic claim here is all too familiar: modernity is the plague of western humanity. In making this claim, almost all the writers within the Muslim tradition have betrayed a total indifference to possibilities outside received religious norms; many have in addition been wholly dismissive of western criteria of rationality and plausibility as 'occidocentric' and in consequence suburban. Inevitably, the whole corpus of such literature from the Islamic camp, often by famous hands, is seen by the advocates of secularity as, in my view quite legitimately, straightforwardly question-begging in its fundamental assumptions. (Could it be that only a major modernist heretical movement could ever jolt us Muslims out of our complacency?)

At the risk of over-simplification, one could in this connection list as more or less in the same class the work of many Muslim writers of the latter half of this century, including famous exegetes,[24] theologians[25] and even 'philosophers'.[26] None has, in my opinion, been touched by modernity. Indeed even those Muslim thinkers who are influenced by western scholarship, settled in western lands and often at odds with their native Islamic culture, remain none the less insufficiently aware of the extent and radical nature of the modern sceptical challenge to theism.[27] Nor is this the full extent of the problem, daunting as it already is. The recent resurgence of Islam in Iran and the Middle East has led to the production of an unduly conservative, at times provocative, scholarship in which issues such as secularity and religious pluralism are dismissed with withering contempt as merely pseudo-problems.[28]

I exaggerate but not greatly. Muslim writers differ among themselves and not all are equally indifferent to the challenges of secularity, religious pluralism and the modern outlook.[29] But it would be difficult to find among them any who have fully taken to heart the western reservation about transcendent religion in the age of secular reason. The reader innocent of the ways of contemporary Islam may be forgiven for thinking that I am exaggerating the extent to which Muslims are indifferent to the verdict of secular scepticism. Be that as it may, it is fair to speculate that unless large numbers of reflective Muslims experience an *internal* scepticism about the Islamic outlook and, more broadly, about the theistic world-view in general, they are not likely to consider seriously the scepticism of modern western writers touched by modernity. (What may be required here is a kind of Islamic radicalism with the temper of a militant Islamic group in the Middle East, but with a very different content.)

The reasons for the Muslim reluctance to come to terms with modernity – in any sensible way – are not far to seek. Even a cursory glance in the right direction reveals a whole cluster of powerful if familiar religious reasons, of which two deserve a brief mention here although all receive fuller treatment in later chapters. First and foremost, Muslims are preoccupied with the guardianship of what they take to be the only extant fully revealed scripture, the Arabic Koran. Celebrating its remarkable freedom from textual corruption, they believe they can discern within its pages God's final and unalterable reminder to a wayward humanity. Indeed Muslims see modern Jews and Christians as being increasingly unfaithful to their own dogmatic traditions. In coming to terms with modernity, Muslims contend, Jewish and Christian theists have wrongly felt the need to reform the immutable word of God. Muslims, it is triumphantly concluded, can do without the dubious benefits of modernity.

Secondly, to turn to a consideration internal to Islam, the Muslim tradition has, since the earliest times, condemned all innovation in matters of religion as heretical. (The word for 'innovation' and for 'heresy' is, unfortunately, the same in Arabic: *bid'a*.) There was in the beginning a deeply religious reason for prohibiting innovation – a reason integrally linked to the nature of Muhammad's own mission. The Apostle's task, as someone commissioned with a sacred message from the eternal Deity, was to convey it to an ignorant people, not to indulge in personal fancies by taking the high road to theological adventurism. Subsequent generations of Muslims thought, naturally enough, that if it was right for Muhammad, the envoy of Allah, to content himself with Allah's revelation of the divine purpose, then surely it is only right that we, his followers, should do the same. Indeed, the argument has run, it is religiously salutary for believers to adhere scrupulously to the *sunna*, 'the beaten path', of the Prophet. Muslims should shun all deviations from the prophetic norm: they should avoid innovation (*bid'a*) – the opposite of *sunna*. And those who follow the example of Muhammad must recognise, the argument continues, that the sole purpose of human life is the ceaseless worship of Allah. This should use up the allegiance of every human faculty – including the mind. (Remember that Muhammad was no theologian, let alone a 'philosopher' in our sense of the word.) Life is short, he is said to have taught, and no one can afford to waste time. There is certainly no time for constructing speculative philosophies in a world labouring under the burden of divine judgement. The way to Heaven is to turn to the right – and go straight on. Isn't the Apostle of Allah the best of guides?

VII

These are legitimate religious concerns. But the challenge of secularity is not adequately answered simply by ignoring it. It is true of course that intellectual and religious problems, unlike brick walls, only confront those who, in part, choose to recognise them. But if Muslims continue to disengage themselves from importantly relevant issues (such as secularity), the consequences could be disastrous. Is it indeed wise for Muslims to pretend that Islam can be practised in total disregard of the current reservations about the truth of transcendent theism? Would it not be better for Muslims to seek a creative engagement with these doubts and hesitations? Given that Muslims have already faced modernity on the plane of western science and technology, should they not also, if only for the sake of consistency, face it on the level of religious conviction?

Conservative confidence in the Islamic tradition is no longer fully intact. Traditional Islam is in sorry decline; many in the educated classes are repelled by it. By refusing to address the problems that plague the modern mind, by displaying its total inability to harness and assimilate modernity, Islam is gradually losing control, as did the Christian Church some time ago, over the daily life of secularised believers. And it is unwise to take it for granted, incidentally, that this decline in influence is merely the inevitable darkness before the equally inevitable dawn of another truly Islamic age – as men return wholeheartedly to religion after seeing the error of their secular ways. To think thus, unfortunately, is merely to indulge in one of the many familiar fantasies of the apologetic imagination.

It has been of late a favourite habit of Muslim apologists to mock the eagerness of Christian apologists to come to terms with every new twist and turn of the secular dance. There is implicit in this, in my view, a perfectly absurd conceit. Surely, the Christian writers rightly wish to render their faith relevant to a self-consciously secular age; they rightly want to provide a faith that can anchor the deepest hopes and ambitions of modern humanity. Unless the theologian can find a creative mechanism – a metaphysic, a mode of thought – to express old insights, render them relevant, and compel new ones, theism will become effectively irrelevant even if it expresses eternal truths. It will at best be an ossified orthodoxy effectively in danger of extinction. Any mental lag in religious categories of thought, any suspicion that they are outdated, will naturally justify the secularist in his claim that traditional faith is today a superfluity. Remember that the authenticity of an ideology is not to be judged *a priori* but rather in relation to the capacity it has for overcoming the crises that life produces. Will we remain Muslims if Islam produces more crises than it overcomes?

It seems to me mistaken loyalty to Islam to think that its interests are best served by isolating it hermetically from the current of contemporary secular opinion. I have already made this point and will make it often, for it is important enough to bear repetition. Sooner or later Islam must, like its monotheistic rivals, face the tribunal of secular reason and patiently endure 'trial by modernity'. To the extent that Muslim thought remains entrenched within the fortress of dogma, secure in its provincialism, the critic is justified in his suspicion that Muslims secretly fear that Islam is incapable of surviving the ordinary rigours of rationalism – incapable of surviving 'trial by secular modernity'. Are Islam and its scripture, then, capable of patiently tolerating disciplined investigation? It is high time for us Muslims to raise our heads above the dogmatic parapet.

VIII

Islam as the historical community of Muhammad (*al-umma al-Muhammadiyya*)[30] has recently completed its fourteenth century. Some of the challenges it faces now are unlike any of those in previous epochs. Unfortunately, the Muslim community is, in general, poorly equipped for a confrontation with modernity. For one thing, classical Islam worries in tiresome detail about many issues which are today irrelevant. If this were merely a matter for modern patience, it would be harmless enough. But it impedes the formulation of characteristically modern worries. For another, the traditional interpretations of scripture and doctrine enjoy so prodigiously massive a prestige that even the posing of distinctively modern problems is rendered extremely difficult. Scholarly work can rarely proceed without the obligatory reference to a past master: the exegete casts a long shadow. And yet surely there are at the moment more pressing concerns on the agenda than those associated with, for example, grammatical peculiarities of the koranic diction or, to take another example, casuistical irritations about the morality of concubinage.

The fear of novelty is the beginning of every conservatism. Modernity gives a rough ride to those accustomed to paying homage only to the familiar. Muslim society has, owing to a lack of liberal and sceptical influences, been largely insulated from the dangers of secular criticism. Since there is no extant philosophical tradition in Islam, Muslims have, unlike those religious folk settled in the West, been largely spared the rigours of philosophical rationalism. In seeking therefore to repossess the legacy of Muhammad for the needs of the secular age – an age that is more hospitable to rational philosophy than to dogmatic theology – we need to be at once both loyal to the religious demands of the Islamic tradition and yet simultaneously responsive to the rational and critical pressures of the present.

What a far cry from speech to deed! The task may be impossible but it is necessary to attempt it – now. The beginning of the fifteenth century of the Islamic era marks for Muslims the limit of their age of innocence. We must recognise both the need for continuity with our specifically Muslim past, on the one hand, and the importance of creative change. To effect this delicate balance between two opposed but equally important demands is indeed no easy matter.

Islam, in its legitimate concern to maintain faithful continuity with its glorious past, has generally frowned on any kind of change or novelty. This has been at once both its strength and its weakness. It is a strength in so far as Islam is not plagued with the problem that potentially endangers every religion with historical foundations and which has pre-eminently endangered modern Protestant Christianity; a religion cut adrift from its historical moorings is likely to flounder for want of an anchor. The weakness of course is that Islam is likely to become an increasingly straitjacketed faith irrelevant to our modern aches and agonies. It may in time even cease to be a truly live option – for the educated classes.

We need to understand the nature and causes of the Islamic resistance to change, the reasons for the Muslim reluctance to engage with secularity or accept some of the changes which a programme of secularisation would bring in its train. Islam, like secular modernity, has a self-image strongly conducive to the assessment of itself as climactic, indeed ultimate. The Muslim religion is seen by Muslims as the last rung on the ladder of sacred history (or, rather, history *simpliciter* since all history is sacred, in some sense, for the believer); Islam, then, finalises all previous monotheistic history, thereby bringing to a climax the whole of the prophetic tradition[31] – indeed the historical process itself. Accordingly, the scripture of Islam contains within its literary fabric an impressive climax recruiting the Arabic language in the service of the prophetic vocation. Now, it is a major *motif* of argumentative apologetics in orthodox Islam (and what other kind of Islam is there?) that Muslims have, ever since the early seventh century, at best 'maintained' Islam and at worst debased it. They have not, indeed cannot, 'improve' it. Thus, there was pristine Islam in all its perfection in Muhammad's Arabia – a perfect gift of grace that had simply descended on a grateful community. This perfect Islam has, with the progress of time, been tarnished by Muslims but it maintains its religious momentum thanks largely to that first push by the brave and devout early guardians of the faith.

It cannot be expected that such a system of thought assigns any very ambitious or original doctrinal tasks to those who succeeded the first generation. The task of all Muslims who succeeded the early community is, it has been said, to preserve precisely this original pure Islam: to bring the early Muslim vision and the Muslim experience within the purview of every succeeding generation. Islam at any given period of its history is authentic only in so far as it resembles the original faith. That is why any deviation – by way of addition, deletion or other alteration – is *ipso facto* reprehensible. It amounts to innovation (*bid'a*); and the Muslim should tread forever on 'the beaten path' (*sunna*) already traversed by the Arabian Prophet. There is, it is often concluded, no room for development, change or radical reinterpretation of ancient doctrine.

This is an orthodox religious view held with remarkable tenacity – a view with which I have, in most moods, a lot of sympathy. Indeed, I argue in later pages that Muslims have shown, like Roman Catholics, a sound intuition in opposing certain characteristically modern ideas. But it is at the same time impossible to deny the need to achieve a contemporary dramatic impact – the need to render religious claims relevant to the daily existence of believers. Every historical religion needs to be concerned both with pedigree of doctrine *and* with contemporaneous relevance. It is true of course that no faith can be understood or practised outside its actual tradition and dogmatic context. But it is one thing to make every decision about the nature and demands of faith *begin* within the territory of received dogma; it is quite another to make sure these decisions *end* there. Any faith or ideology that loses the capacity to transcend the *de facto* loyalties of its first adherents is inexorably destined for the dustbin of history.

My own view, to anticipate later discussions, is that Islam is properly to be seen as a raw material entering the world from Heaven, waiting to be moulded and shaped, sometimes decisively and clearly, at other times in unspectacular and tortured ways – always to suit the innermost passions of a human nature at its best and, in doing so, aiming to display the glory of its creator. Islam, like its sister faiths, aims to seek the pleasure of God through the art – and it is an art – of individual and communal repentance, the art of learning how to be perpetually in the wrong, to echo a familiar religious sentiment, in the vicinity of a devastatingly pure Will. Islam is a guide to social and individual reproach for every age and community. It cannot therefore be the case that the details of the task of reproach – and it is a task – can be settled once and for all in some kind of supra-historical fixity of belief and dogma. The impulse that seeks an absolute immutability of dogma, itself sustained in a kind of paralytic crescendo, is bound to be frustrated. It is an error of some consequence to think of Islam as finished and ready, so to speak, once it has appeared on the mortal plane, the plane of human history. ('Early to blossom, early to wither' may well be as true of the genius of religious dogma as of the genius of human individuals.) It could be the case that the abiding concern with this kind of finality and climax, a concern which is at the root of Islamic anti-historicism, may now need to be abandoned just as it could be the case that our modern imitation of the prophetic consciousness (*imitatio Muhammadi*) may well lean more towards an imitation of the will to self-incrimination than towards an acceptance of every belief entertained by the early community. In short, each generation must learn afresh how to become worthy of the grace and mercy of God. But enough of these dark sayings for the moment.

IX

For a very long time, our thought in Islam has flowed without impediment along the deep-cut grooves of custom and tradition. This is no longer possible, given the increasing secularisation of modern sensibilities. The traditional vision of the world, being what it is because of Allah's free decree, is not defunct but it is no longer the only available outlook, even in conservative Muslim lands. In the past, many human beings more or less spontaneously believed that their experience was objectively grounded in an external cosmos under benevolent supervision. Naturally, they thought instinctively in terms of fate and destiny, in terms of preordained courses of existence. Of course, it is a fundamental feature of our intellectual condition in all ages that the questions and answers about the true purpose of life arise only within the framework of option and decision or, equivalently, of choice and reflection. But it is only within the pluralist cultures of the modern world that this fact has attained wide recognition. It is not surprising that fate and destiny have been largely replaced by choice and decision as central categories of thought in the contemporary world.

Our current circumstance marks for Muslims the end of an age of innocence. We do face a crisis, at least in the technical sense: we need to *choose* a direction, *decide* for ourselves. ('Crisis' comes from the Greek *krisis*, meaning decision, which itself derives from *krino* meaning to decide.) There is no choice but to choose. In that sense, we can no longer avoid the responsibility of decision, for even to adopt a received view is in effect to choose one option among others.[32] A major reason for the Muslim failure to appreciate the true nature of our predicament as choosers is of course the lack of an extant philosophical tradition in modern Islam: the awareness of choice is fostered by philosophy when it permeates culture. Be that as it may, the central question here is whether or not we can create a favourable crisis in our own situation. Can we make the right choice? Can we opt for the right 'heresy'?

The proposal for an open confrontation between traditional Islam and modern secularity admittedly carries with it many dangers. At the very least, it will lead to confusion and uncertainty, the usual concomitants of choice and decision. In a traditional society, there is typically very little uncertainty or confusion since there are few occasions for making complex decisions. The range of choice is very narrow. Any culture in which a blind conformity to inherited norms is required of its members will not witness any undue confusion. Indoctrination and religious evangelism will see to it that people are not confused too often. Indeed reflective free choice can hardly be maintained in those circumstances.

The luxury of free choice presupposes lack of clarity, hesitation and confusion. In religious parlance, this could lead to heresy, even apostasy. At the very least it could lead to increased variety and dissension in the household of faith. Men's religious commitment may weaken after sceptical encounters; some may experience their faith *as* faith, that is, as a commitment beyond the limits of rationally established certainty. Others may leave the household of faith or even convert to a rival religious vision, and so on. Unfortunately, there is no guarantee that genuinely free inquiry, conducted with due respect to religious as well as secular intellectual norms, will necessarily lead eventually to the adoption of an orthodox religious stance. The availability of choice presupposes the possibility of heresy, even apostasy and outright rejection.

The availability of religious freedom, then, effectively presupposes the need to countenance desertion from the scriptured society. Whether or not we Muslims should allow individuals in the Muslim community to exercise free reflective choice is, of course, itself a matter for considered judgement. And, of course, it is a matter of great moment. My own view – and I should say a little here for we shall not return to this theme in these pages – is that the potential risks inherent in the offer of religious freedom are worth taking. Why? Well, if there is a God, I would argue, it can be expected *a priori* that he wants a voluntary response born of genuine gratitude and humility themselves rooted in reflection and morally responsible choice. Seen in this light, heresy and even apostasy are morally more acceptable than any hypocritical attachment to orthodox opinion out of the fear of public sanctions. Fortunately, for us, we have the evidence of the Koran itself in favour of this view: 'there should be no compulsion in religion' (2:256).[33] Unfortunately, however, many learned authorities have sought to cancel this noble sentiment by finding verses within the sacred volume that favour the opposite opinion.

I am tempted to pursue this theme directly but I fear it would take us too far afield. Suffice it to say here that even in terms of a pragmatic (as opposed to a moral or religious) outlook, there is much to be said in favour of religious freedom.[34] Islam has today in its populous community a significant number of people who are its members by chance rather than by choice. Their orthodoxy is typically neither suspect nor enthusiastic, merely unreflective. It is a hallmark of their character that they speak in favour of Islam only when the West attacks it: at home they prefer accommodation to polemic. (It has always struck me as noteworthy that even lapsed Muslims, like lapsed Roman

Catholics, tend to dislike strongly any criticism of the legion they themselves have effectively deserted.) So, if we give notice to the lukewarm
and time-serving elements in the community (*umma*), we shall end up
with a residual believing group, no doubt very considerably reduced in
numbers if all the hypocrites took the notice seriously, but at least it
would be one community entertaining a single intensely shared vision.
Only such a group could then be purified of any remaining moral
unworth – the common burden of human nature even at its best.
Obviously, a group with a genuine love of faith and piety could resist
the ravages of alien ideologies far more successfully than a group whose
members are mostly indifferent, hypocritical in their allegiance and
readily 'selling out' to opposed convictions.

Islam is, of course, like medieval Christianity, profoundly opposed
to heresy and apostasy. According to some authorities at al-Azhar,
Islam's policy-making centre, apostasy is punishable by death.[35] A
missionary faith, with its political overtones, cannot naturally tolerate
leakage from the vessel of belief; indeed, it cannot turn a blind eye on
the heretic, the 'brother that walketh disorderly'.[36]

The religious fear of heresy, apostasy and social dismemberment is
fully justified and understandable. But the concern with intellectual
honesty must also claim our attention. We Muslims must attempt to
sustain our intellectual honesty both on the individual and the social
level. Can each of us, then, from his or her perspective, accept an
Islamic vision of the world and of our place in it? Can we, as a group
of people under the joint tutelage of the Muslim scripture and the
Islamic tradition, enter a new era with a secure sense of our destiny
and direction? Can we avoid a retreat from modern integrity while
simultaneously resisting the temptation to relax a traditional conscience? Can each of us sincerely claim to be practising a faith that
suffices us amid all the rebellious vagaries of birth and biography,
reason and scepticism? In short, is our Islam a faith for all seasons?

X

I am not unaware of those who, from within Islamic circles, think all this
is unduly alarmist, that only someone unduly impressed with western
modernity and modern intellectual culture could cry wolf so often. This
is a familiar criticism and there is, to be fair, some force in it. Perhaps,
the orthodox mentality will never feel the impulse to uncertainty so
characteristic of modern pluralist culture. Perhaps, the majority of Muslims will never see modernity except as an epoch of peculiar chaos and
sinfulness in the human world – an epoch whose temptations are merely
different from or more widespread and powerful than those of bygone
ages. Certainly, Muslims have throughout the ages placed a sturdy trust
in the ultimate truth of Islam and have indeed in general been well-nigh

totally indifferent to the verdict of secular scepticism. A Muslim may well argue that Islam is as relevant today as it has always been – indeed more so. Secularity, it may be thought, is a striking proof of our need for religion, not an objection to it.

We may indeed mourn the advent of modernity as a titanic lapse from grace; or we may celebrate it as heralding the final emancipation of the human consciousness from the bondage of illusion. What we cannot reasonably do is to dismiss it as being unworthy of serious or sustained reflection. Unfortunately, the sentiment of triumph over secularity is widespread among Muslims: Islam can trample secularity under its feet. But the real task is to face secularity, take it seriously as a rival for the allegiance of modern man. To be sure, modernity as an epoch is, like all other historical epochs, a specific socio-historical phenomenon with discernible features, sustained by determinably specific social and political forces, and subject to the indifferent ravages of time. It too will pass away. But it is the era in which we happen to be living; and it is therefore our task to show that a faith which has always boasted its capacity to guide men squarely amid the hurly-burly of life can indeed survive 'trial by modernity'.

The paradigm shift from medievalism to modernity has in the West for the last two centuries brought confusion and uncertainty. But it was initiated at a time when Christendom was more or less politically stable. The House of Islam is today, by contrast, politically in a mess. And unfortunately, the urge for infallibility and unequivocal certainty, sometimes expressed in the desire for the apodictic affirmations of religious enthusiasm, is precisely at its strongest in times of political crisis and social change. I offer no facile solutions; the historicist temper has taken root too deeply for us to allow ourselves any such luxury. We have no right to the certainties of an age that has passed away. Nostalgia for the glorious past will have to do for now.

Finally, we live in an age of rapid and global change. Islam is, like every living faith, an ever-changing reality. A religious tradition cannot be frozen or arrested; the household of faith cannot, as it were, be closed temporarily for repair or reform. We must adapt it, change it, perhaps even eventually transform it, all within the flux of history. There is no extra-historical position from which men and women could have commerce with the tradition of their faith.

2

A Change of Masters

I

The author of the old revivalist song

> It was good enough for Moses
> It's good enough for me

was certainly no philosopher. Arguments from authority, whether religious or secular, have never been popular with the thinkers.

While seeking to undermine the authority of revealed dicta, sceptical thinkers in all ages, and particularly in this one, have simultaneously sought to justify reasoned reliance on the deliverances of impartial reflection. The mind must, the advocates of reason tell us, submit primarily to the authority of the reasonable, and only derivatively, if at all, to the authority of the revealed. If in the past Allah knew best, today it is the enlightened rationalist who knows best.

The issue of revealed authority conveniently includes within its compass three related problems, all elemental and all of which need to be broached in order to get our project off the ground. Although the entire trio will concern us throughout the book, it is best to outline the terrain at this initial stage. Our concerns are: (a) the religious ban on any critical or detached assessment of revealed claims, (b) the perennial question of the true office of reason in theology, and (c) the vexed and delicate problem of justifying the sceptical spirit of the inquiring mind in matters theological.

I begin with a brief examination of the rational philosophical tradition of Islam before describing and challenging, from a variety of angles, the operative theological veto on any internal criticism of the bases of revealed faith. This leads me on naturally to outline provisionally the role of independent reason in the interpretation of religious claims and finally, .in an all too tentative and inconclusive fashion, to run these issues to earth by commenting on the quality of the scholarly temper engaged in the objective study of faithful conviction in the liberal age.

II

Magic, and arguably poetry, are arts condemned by the author of the Koran (K:2:102; 26:224–6). Would academic philosophy of religion have escaped condemnation if the sacred volume had been revealed in a different age or in a different culture (like, say, Socrates' Greece)? It is a fascinating question; we cannot be sure of the answer. The religionists, however, have been sure of the answer for a long time. Ever since the first currents of Hellenic philosophy overwhelmed the simple literalism of the Muslim creed, Islamic orthodoxy has never ceased to frown on the unsettling power of philosophy to plague its labours. Philosophy, we are told, creates at worst unnecessary doubts and hesitations, and at best mere conjecture and confusion; scripture by contrast, it is said, offers assurances for Paradise. The orthodox view prevalent among Muslims, as among orthodox Jews and orthodox Christians, is as simple as it is familiar: there is neither the time nor the need for philosophy in a world under the burden of divine nemesis and blessed with the benefits of divine tuition. Doesn't the Book of Allah contain sufficient guidance and education for the faithful student?

Islamic orthodoxy has generally been content to condemn philosophy as futile. An unspeculative practical piety, largely unperturbed by philosophical or theological quarrels over free will or trancendence or whatever, merely saw philosophy as irrelevant. Fortunately, therefore, Muslim orthodoxy has not, a few shameful episodes apart, actively opposed philosophy as heretical. The early and medieval Muslim philosophers actually managed, despite the occasional persecution, to produce a relatively autonomous intellectual tradition free from religious domination.

The attempt to seek co-existence for the rational Hellenic elements and the faithful Islamic ones began as early as the ninth (third Islamic) century with Ya'qub al-Kindi and continued in the next century with the Neoplatonist Abu Nasr al-Farabi and his popularising disciple Ibn Sina (Avicenna). Somewhat later, the great theologian al-Ash'ari – justly called Islam's Aquinas – showed his Muslim contemporaries how Greek philosophy could be recruited in the service of dogmatic orthodoxy. Paralleling these developments, a suspicious Islamic orthodoxy encouraged conservative religious thinkers to demonstrate the impiety of excessive confidence in the prowess of philosophical reason.

Detail is inappropriate here but one major tussle between orthodoxy and the thinkers looms very large and should perhaps be briefly recorded as an instance of the everlasting skirmish between faith and reason. It will certainly give us an overall sense of the necessary tension between an authoritative faith and the inquiring mind which instinctively rebels against religious strictures. We know on the authority of the traditionist Abu Da'ud as-Sijistani that Muhammad promised his followers that in every century Allah would raise someone to revive the Islamic faith.[1] Sheikh Abu Hamid al-Ghazzali is identified by most learned authorities as the renewer (or reformer, if you like) for the sixth Muslim (twelfth Christian) century. This privilege is conferred on him largely because he is the author of three monumental works of scholarly piety: the anti-philosophical *The Incoherence of the Philosophers*, the pro-religious *The Revival of the Religious Sciences* and the passionately devotional *Deliverance from Error*. Many among the religious intelligentsia (*'ulama*) of the Middle Ages, and since, have thought that the great reformer had, aided no doubt by supernatural wisdom, successfully refuted all the philosophers who preceded him and, according to some religionists, more generously, all the additional philosophers who succeeded him.[2]

This judgement might well have been allowed to stand unchallenged had it not been for the appearance of a book, towards the end of the twelfth century, with the provocative title *The Incoherence of the Incoherence*. Its author was Ibn Rushd, better known in the West as Averröes, a philosopher destined to disturb not only Islamic but also medieval Christian orthodoxy. With Averröes on the field, the religious innings was over. But not for long. An outraged orthodoxy, angered partly by the philosophical attack on its great hero, exiled Averröes and ordered the destruction of his books. Though the great philosopher himself briefly regained, towards the end of his life, the favour of his co-religionists, his death at the close of the twelfth century marked the beginning of the end of the golden age of Islamic philosophy. Heaven had heard the prayers of the orthodox.[3]

III

The Devil is not alone in being able to quote the scriptures for his own use: the religionists can do it too. Although the Koran does not outlaw philosophy, as I noted earlier, it does contain verses which, given a playful ingenuity, in alliance with the liberty to overlook an occasional clause, can certainly be interpreted to possess a deeply anti-intellectual potential. In the Koran's longest (and perhaps most inaptly named) *surah*,[4] an incident is related the details of which could easily be recruited for orthodox service. The incident, suggestive though it is of the wider possibilities of the human potential for perversity, itself involves a simple clash between Moses and his community over the sacrifice of a yellow heifer. The notorious Children of Israel fabricate an unusually large number of objections and questions before eventually sacrificing the cow – and even then doing so with reluctance. The Koran relates this incident in surprisingly great detail giving us, in doing so, a picture of the laboured, indeed contrived, nature of the hesitations (K:2:67–72).

It does not require too much extrapolation or ingenuity, as scriptural exegesis goes, to see the relevance of this incident to the wider problem of the impiety of rational interrogation of religious imperatives. Men are doubters whose arrogant self-will makes them resist surrender to the will of Allah. They pretend to have sincere reservations, arguing that they wish to probe religious demands before agreeing to submission – all in the larger interests of intellectual integrity. But, it will be said, human beings deliberately introduce unnecessary complications and induce perverse doubts in order to seek release from duties they secretly acknowledge as binding. Philosophy, with its questioning bent, itself nourished on specious reasoning, is, it will be said, a monument to the mortal tendency to sinful perversity. Predictably, it is the discipline in which the Devil has always had his greatest following.[5]

IV

There are many religious objections to any philosophical approach to faith. In order to set limits to our task, we shall make contact with only a few of the central ones. There are in this area of our concern a large number of misunderstandings and confusions. In what follows I shall attempt to remove these misunderstandings while simultaneously identifying communities of sentiment and recording the ultimate differences between the religious and the philosophical approaches to religious faith.

I begin with the important if stock religious objection about the essential impiety of philosophical method when applied to revealed conviction. How can the philosopher judge the word of Allah – his Lord and our Lord? Muslim scholars have, from the earliest times, emphasised the Koran's role as final arbiter, as secreting a criterion (*furqan*; K:25:1; 3:4) for judgement – a role from which the sacred volume acquires one of its many honourable titles. Thus, revelation supplies, we are told, a supernatural verdict on man and all things natural or human, including human reason (*'aql*). God judges us; we do not judge God or his message. 'Isn't Allah,' asks the Koran rhetorically, 'the best of judges?' (K:95:8)

Allah is indeed the best of judges. It is of course true – indeed necessarily true – that what God says about us is superior in insight to what we may say about ourselves, our capacities, or about God. To say, however, that God's (alleged) revelation should be assessed by use of the normal methods of scrutiny is not to deny the ultimacy – or primacy (whichever sounds better) – of God's views. It is merely a comment on how to seek to determine what God's views actually are, and the recommendation is that we should use the only apparatus we possess, namely, the methods of reason. (Remember that rejecting the supremacy of *reason* here is one thing; rejecting the importance of

reasoning is quite another.) If the religionists have a privileged access
to God's truth such that they can legitimately dispense with the normal
amenities of reasoned reflection, they have yet to convince those other
than the converted.

Closely related to this objection is the extremely popular accusation
that reliance on reason in discussions of revealed claims is in effect
intellectually idolatrous. The philosopher commits *shirk*, to use the
Arabic term for idolatry. To obey the voice of reason rather than the
revealed commands of sacred scripture is, it will be said, out-and-out
idolatrous.

This is possibly the most irritating of all the religious objections to
rational or philosophical method. For surely, it is not as though, in the
manner of a Faust, one were to sell one's soul in exchange for knowledge, fully aware of the superior worth of preserving one's soul in order
to seek the pleasure of God. Our situation, especially in the modern
world, is hardly (or is hardly ever seen to be) that grandiose or even
that well-defined. At the very least, our alleged intellectual idolatry is
unintentional. We are simply ordinary folk caught up in some very
messy epistemological predicaments in an age of uncertainty. The perplexed man, seeking to know the truth about life before leaving a scene
where discordant cries of conflicting views assail him from all sides, is
forced to rely upon his intellectual apparatus, modest as that may indeed
be for his purpose. Without the discrimination that reason provides,
we cannot find our way out of the jungle. Without the aid of reason,
how is one to distinguish truth from falsehood – even revealed truth
from merely impressive-sounding untruth?

Nor is it as though one said, as a Nietzsche would in a defiant mood,
'God has his own opinions: I prefer my own.' The fact is of course that
one merely wishes to know what God's views really are. After we know
them, it is, for a reasonable man, no longer an open question whether
or not such views express an ultimate truth. In fine, accusations of
intellectual *shirk* are the outcome of confusing a sincere search for
(religious) truth – using reason as a tool – with the bad and self-
indulgent Faustian bargain that Jesus and the author of the Koran, in
strikingly similar ways, rightly condemn.[6]

V

At the funeral of the legendary Sheikh from al-Azhar who was credited
with having produced no fewer than 500 proofs of Allah's existence, a
pious old co-religionist is reputed to have remarked with pointed sarcasm that the Sheikh must have had at least 500 doubts about the
existence of Allah. An apocryphal story, perhaps, but it will serve to
introduce our theme.

Anti-intellectualism runs deep in religious thought. Nor is it just plain religious folk or even plain religious philosophers who are under its spell. In fact, no less sophisticated a philosopher than Professor Sir Karl Popper allows himself to remark, in his autobiography, that systematic theology and rational theorising about God are due to want of faith![7] A view with so distinguished an advocate should not be despised.

But whether we despise it or not, we need first to understand the claim being made. People of course engage in systematic theology and indeed in philosophy of religion for many different reasons. While it is relatively rare for an atheist to be interested in Christian or Islamic theology proper, there is no shortage of disbelieving philosophers of religion. Now, presumably, the group accused of lack of faith are the *believing* theologians (isn't a Christian theologian necessarily a Christian believer?) and *believing* philosophers of religion – and not those who reject faith altogether. The believing theologians would no doubt find the charge of lack of faith a curious one: after all they see themselves as professionally engaged in the service of their faith. Believing philosophers of religion may more plausibly be accused since part of their professional obligation *qua* philosophers requires them to suspend their religious commitments.

It is not easy to make the charge stick. As I understand it, it amounts to saying that unless believing thinkers and theologians were assailed by doubts about their religious convictions, they would not need the props of academic theology or philosophy in the dark hour of scepticism. But how is this an *accusation*, even if we accept the foregoing reasoning as sound? Why should it be seen as culpable in any case? Perhaps – and it is only a bare possibility – we could say that believing writers who suspend their religious convictions temporarily (in the interests of objectivity) are men of, if the expression be allowed, 'intermittent faith'.[8] They sometimes need to think and write like sceptics rather than as mosque- or church-going believers. But to be men of intermittent faith, in this sense, is not the same as being men 'of little faith', in the derogatory sense in which this expression is employed in scriptural writings. And it is certainly false to say that men of intermittent faith are men of no faith at all. For such a view would rule out the entire run of ordinary believers from the believing club leaving only a few of the seminal religious figures (who lived in the heat of active faith and piety day and night) to qualify as genuine believers. Almost all believers have their sceptical moments; the believing thinker or theologian merely seeks to cultivate some kinds of sceptical moods as a part of his professional obligation in order to be objective about his religious convictions.

As it happens, the religionist's initial reasoning is itself unsound, inspired as it is by a mistaken view about the nature of faith. It is often said by religious writers that once faith is proved or conclusively justified, it can no longer be an appropriate candidate for mere belief: one can only have faith where there is uncertainty. (How many a treatise, how many an ordinary conversation, in which this claim is made with routine conviction!) The Christian philosopher Terence Penelhum has questioned this popular assumption in a series of articles and books. Penelhum shows clearly and insightfully that faith can incorporate knowledge just as it can incorporate doubts.[9] Faith and knowledge, like faith and uncertainty, can co-exist in religious as in secular contexts. Thus, one can believe what one knows, have faith in what one knows; indeed one can even doubt what one knows or 'knows very well'. The success of Penelhum's case implies that the classical dichotomy between faith and knowledge, endorsed by such writers as St Thomas Aquinas and by many Muslim and Jewish religious thinkers, is actually untenable. It is indeed very surprising that theists should have seen faith as being incompatible with knowledge. After all, many of the seminal religious figures certainly seemed to know that there was a God who cared about mankind and yet they were expected to have faith in him. The Koran itself clearly presupposes that a man can possess knowledge (*'ilm*) while having faith (*iman*);[10] again, to turn to the Judaeo-Christian tradition, such men as Abraham, Moses and Jesus enjoyed such strikingly intimate relationships with God that one may say they had knowledge of the divine while simultaneously being faithful. Finally, to turn the religious coin and record a point that Penelhum does not clearly note, the whole scriptural emphasis on the perversity of rejection presupposes the compatibility of faith and knowledge. The perversity of rejection (*kufr*) can only be understood in terms of men's refusal to have faith in or believe in what they secretly know. The Old Testament, the Gospels and the Koran concur that men wilfully reject their creator. But this implies that men can disbelieve in what they know; knowledge does not entail faith although faith may entail, indeed encompass, knowledge. In other words, a man can meritoriously believe in God at the same time as he knows that God exists.

The religious opposition to an intellectually sophisticated approach to religious issues is, then, in part the outcome of a misunderstanding about the nature of the life of faith, and indeed of rejection. More specifically, not only can men of faith legitimately produce proofs and systematic theories in order to dispel the doubts and confusions of others, such as, for example, those who may not enjoy an intensely religious life, but they can also produce them in order to dispel their own occasional misgivings in the hour of crisis. For faith not only requires decision and commitment in the face of inconclusive evidence, it also requires decision and commitment in the face of conclusive evidence, in the face even of knowledge – as scripture itself teaches us.

VI

At this stage in the dialectic, the religionist is likely to shift his ground in the hope of knocking out his opponent in the second round – supposing that both parties survive the opening scuffle. Even granted that the rational philosophical study of religious faith is religiously permissible, it will be said, it is none the less to be discouraged for various religious reasons. The Koran is addressed, he may urge, to believers, at least in the first instance. ('O you who believe' is a frequent form of address in the sacred volume.) God is concerned to elicit a faithful response, not to make theologians or philosophers of us. The aim of revelation is not to provide us with the truth for truth's sake: the hope is that by knowing the truth we may be liberated from bondage to illusory divinities and attain success (*falah*).[11]

The religionists know not what they do. This objection is the outcome of confusing one correct observation with two incorrect inferences. It is true of course that the ultimate aim of the religious life is to find favour in the eyes of our creator. In that sense, the purpose of revelation is not primarily to satisfy the intellect but rather to show us the way to Heaven; a believer's motives in seeking to learn Allah's purposes from the teaching of the Koran should primarily be practical and devotional rather than academic and controversial. But it does not follow from this correct claim that there is no room for reasoned speculation in the religious life. Nor does it follow that the sole purpose of sacred literature is to preach to the converted.

Let me take these last two points in turn and explore them very briefly. There is clearly both a place and a need for reflection, including detached reflection, about one's religious beliefs and allegiances. In the occasional cool hour, one needs to ascertain, as far as it is humanly possible, the objective validity of one's faithful convictions. Most of us can and should take off the religious cloak, if only occasionally, and if only to mend it for renewed service. This must surely be the right thing to do given that we wish to live with intellectual integrity in an age of religious and ideological pluralism. How otherwise can we choose convictions (if indeed one ever chooses to believe) that are, all things considered, the truest to our complex experience of life and culture? Remember that unlike some of the seminal figures of the theistic traditions, hardly any modern believer lives in the heat of an active religiosity day and night. For us, it is both possible and necessary to alternate in the roles of participant and critical spectator.

The Koran is certainly not, to pick up the second point, just a sermon for the faithful. It is true that many of its verses are addressed to or report the actual and normative deportment of believers; it is also the case that all of it was originally vouchsafed to one particular believer, Muhammad. But none of this could imply that it is the exclusive property of the Muslim Club; the document of revelation is surely, in principle, the property of all mankind. The author of the Koran has no hesitations about exposing the religious document and its credentials to the scrutiny of the idolaters, the rejectors, the hesitants, the Jews, the Christians and indeed yet others. Is it too unnatural an extension to encompass the mild gaze of the believing thinker temporarily setting aside his religious commitments and putting on the sceptical cloak in the interests of objective study?

The religionist could reply that the Koran (K:56:79) itself warns us that 'none save the purified shall touch' the revealed Word of God. What are we to make of this? This verse has been variously interpreted; and it is not clear what it means. It could mean that the heavenly version of the Koran is inaccessible to those who are impure or it could refer to the Koran in earthly currency being out of the reach of rejectors. The only plausible interpretation is that a committed believer should place himself in a state of ritual physical purity before perusing the sacred text, i.e. he should perform the necessary ablutions. Such a requirement obviously cannot extend to those who disbelieve the Scripture's inspiration and claims. Any other interpretation is deeply problematic. Muslims could argue that the Koran should be inaccessible to non-Muslims, thereby erecting an unnecessarily high barricade of religious exclusivism.[12] They could argue that rejectors are somehow 'impure'; and it is a short step from here to suggest that those whose orthodoxy is suspect or dubious are also impure even though they claim to be believers. These speculations introduce intolerable complications. It is easy enough to accuse one another of impurity in doctrine or conduct. In fact, the religionists regularly accuse the thinkers. A thinker's potential for original kinds of perversity is, however, not always greater than the orthodox potential for familiar kinds of obstinacy. Both perversity and obstinacy nourish sinful attitudes, albeit in different ways. And there is no koranic authority for the view that God prefers the sins of the orthodox to those of the heretics.

VII

The patient religionist – who decides to stay for the evening – may feel that we have failed to get to the heart of the matter. Islam is not, he may retort, some kind of spectator sport: one has to be a Muslim, a submitter to God's will in heart and mind, in order to have any real idea about the whole thing. Submission to God's will (i.e. Islam) must include intellectual submission; one must believe in a total manner. And can the rejector, or for that matter the detached scholar, really understand the quality of total submission, itself rooted in genuine intellectual humility, that the Muslim faith demands? It is impossible, it will be said, to have a purely theoretical interest in Islam,[13] for either one genuinely understands it and then rejects it out of perversity (since to understand all is here to embrace all) or else one simply fails to understand it. And how can the outsider or the thinker who suspends his commitment to Islam even comprehend the faith and its scripture as momentous realities that secrete an immediate normative significance for all of us in this life?

Søren Kierkegaard has familiarised us with this kind of objection. I have elsewhere argued at length against his claim that all purely intellectual approaches to matters of moment are shallow or misguided.[14] Suffice it simply to assert here that men can fully understand a faith they none the less refuse to embrace. The proof that they can do so is, to put it naïvely, that they do in fact do it: some critics of Islam have had a profound knowledge of the faith, explored its impulse and yet sincerely, it would seem, decided to reject it.

Naturally, one needs some imaginative sympathy with the religious ideal if one is to avoid serious misunderstanding, even a complete failure of understanding. (In this context, a failure of imagination is tied up with a failure of comprehension.) Sympathy with any religious ideal – though preferably a monotheistic one – usually suffices. Certainly, it need not be a specifically Muslim one. However, if someone has no sympathy with the religious vision in any of its many manifestations or has never played or been tempted to play the religious language-game (or even any that remotely resemble it), then it is indeed somewhat doubtful that he would make a perceptive student of religion. (Think here of how most of us in the western world find it difficult even to grasp let alone accept the views of some remote tribes such as the Ik or the Yanomamo.)

Most of the western sceptics and secularists have a participant's understanding of religious belief and practice. They were brought up in religious – Jewish or Christian – homes; some were even raised in a strikingly pious milieu. It is, however, fair to add that the thread which ties these sceptics to their religious origins has become increasingly thin in recent years. It is, in general, important not only to have played the religious language-game and to have had sympathy with it at one time or another but also to exercise that sympathy actively when studying religion. Unfortunately, many in the intelligentsia in western societies have in practice failed to exercise such sympathy.[15]

Religion is indeed no spectator sport: no believer is neutral in his relationship to the struggle between good and evil. He must take sides. The antipathy to detachment is inspired by the correct observation that to recognise the availability of religious knowledge is also partly to recognise the importance of pursuing it, indeed implementing it through a course of practical religious devotion. One cannot fully grasp the truth about the nature of religious belief without also realising that it characteristically inspires specifically religious responses to reality. The religionist is mistaken however in concluding that a man must be a religious believer in order to understand what religious belief is. Understanding may be a precondition of faith; faith is certainly not a precondition of understanding.

VIII

What, then, is the role of independent reason in the interpretation of scriptural claims? What is the true office of reason in theology? The Koran itself implies a very optimistic assessment of the potential of human intellect (*'aql*); men are constantly invited to think and ponder in order that they may believe. But, in the final analysis, faith has decisive priority over reason: faith defines the offices, power and the limits of reason in matters theological. It may fairly be said that the predominant view among Muslim theologians today as in the past is the view called 'fideism' in Christian thought: an intellect unenlightened by God's grace cannot judge faith while an intellect enlightened by God's grace can only judge faith favourably. To put it less cryptically, fideism is the theological doctrine according to which faith does not stand in need of rational justification; faith is indeed, in religious domains, the arbiter of reason and its pretensions. While Islam has not produced any extreme versions of revelationist fideism *à la* Søren Kierkegaard or Karl Barth, the fideist outlook is easily discernible in the writings of many modern Muslim writers and, of course, in the works of the great al-Ghazzali.

Fideism in Muslim religious thought is in its impulse, if not in its ultimate character, essentially identical with fideism in Christian circles. The only significant difference here is due to the fact that Muslims reject the view that the human reasoning faculty has been irreparably damaged by the Fall of man.[16] Within orthodox Islam, therefore, one cannot find any extreme version of fideism – of the kind popular among evangelical Christians who celebrate paradox or uphold a kind of self-congratulatory irrationalism in religious matters. The Muslim view may indeed be said to be similar to the Roman Catholic view of St Augustine which later, through St Thomas, dominated Christian thought in the Middle Ages.

The primacy of faith is as much a feature of orthodox Islamic thought as of orthodox Christian thought. The Koran does frequently invite men to ponder the signs of Allah in nature, society and the self. But the reality of Allah himself is fully accessible only to faith – a faith that is itself a gift of grace. After all, Allah is in the first instance the subject of faith and loving obedience, not of rational inquiry or purely discursive thought. Unaided human reason is inferior in status to the gift of faith. Indeed, reason is useful only in so far as it finds a use in the larger service of faith.[17]

Ever since Muslims first encountered Greek philosophy, it has always been difficult to ease the necessary tension between the rational Hellenic element and the dogmatic Islamic one in the total religious synthesis. There has always been a friction between the demands of a rational thought that cannot in principle endure a curtailment in its autonomy by a supra-rational authority, on the one hand, and the demands of a dogmatic orthodoxy which sees itself as ultimately authoritative. For the orthodox believer, faith has always been a gift of grace to be accepted on the authority of no less an authority than Allah himself: *credere Deum Deo* (I believe in God on God's own authority) is the slogan.

IX

The problem of the role of independent reason in the interpretation of religious claims brings us sharply to a central issue. The basic disquiet here is clearly about the delicacy of combining a faithful fealty to Islamic convictions with an endorsement of free inquiry about their epistemological status. After all, can a Muslim, under the tuition of his scripture, see the issue of the truth of Islam as an open one?

This question is indeed important. For it does seem difficult to deny the fundamental and irreducible tension involved in the making of two such disparate commitments: one to the primacy of faith, the other to the primacy of reason. One way to effect an admittedly temporary armistice between faith and reason is to draw a distinction between the philosophy of religion, on the one hand, and theology proper, on the other. Now, the philosophy of religion is in effect the rational examination of theological issues without reference to the authority of any revealed dictum; theology, however, integrally relies on a supra-natural authority. Or, to put it another way, the philosophy of religion treats all types of religion and religious faith as its domain, not presupposing the privileged position of any type, but aiming at discovering what religious truths, if any, are implied by the psychology, sociology and history of religion. Theology, however, simply starts with the faith of some particular religion, the Jewish or Christian, for example, and expounds that faith while accepting the central tenets of the religion in question as revealed or otherwise authoritatively grounded truths.

If we accept the legitimacy of this distinction, then the believing philosopher of religion will, in his philosophical capacity, seek exemption from the normal religious strictures on any criticism of the allegedly revealed bases of faith. The theologian may, however, work and think securely within the ambit of faith. Institutionally, the faithful philosopher of religion may conscientiously teach the normal western university syllabus while his theologically inclined co-religionist would most appropriately teach in a seminary or *madrasah* set up by the religious authorities.

The Koran itself does not outlaw free inquiry. But it would be self-indulgent to read into its verses any celebration of free inquiry in the modern sense of the term. There are no specifically Islamic reasons for encouraging a Muslim to undertake any unduly critical study of his basic religious convictions. Within the Islamic tradition there are no theological resources which could be recruited in the service of free reflection. Indeed, philosophy has always been and remains a dirty word in the *madrasah*. Orthodox Muslims, like orthodox Jews and orthodox Christians, see no great value in free inquiry in matters theological. After all, what is the point of free inquiry if one already has the truth?

X

What are the basic presuppositions of a philosophy of Islam? What would be the *minimal* assumptions of any potentially objective study of Islam – a study in an analytical critical idiom? There are, I believe, at least *three* basic assumptions, each controversial, which any philosophy of religion (including a philosophy of the Muslim religion) must necessarily make.

Firstly, one needs to assume that religious belief is not *sui generis*: it can legitimately be subsumed under a sub-section of belief in general in the same way as historical or political or moral belief. Secondly, it has to be assumed that even if religious belief is indeed a special gift of grace, it is at another level simultaneously a purely human conviction whose content is subject to ordinary appraisal and scrutiny. Thus, even if it is true that authentic revelation is the only source of true religious ideas – that, in effect, the purely human quest for religious truth is necessarily doomed to failure – the thinker may still reasonably assess the truth and plausibility of revealed claims once these have appeared on the mortal plane. And thirdly, I take it that the actual existence of God is not a necessary condition of the very possibility of entertaining belief in God or belief that there is a God. Some religionists have, mistakenly, thought that the very fact that men actually believe in God implies that the human mind is an arena for the direct causal activities of God, Gabriel or the Holy Spirit.

These are all controversial assumptions. They are not, I trust, unjustifiable or implausible and I shall take their truth more or less for granted here.[18] Certainly, we cannot get our project off the ground unless we are prepared to accept, if only provisionally, the truth of these assumptions.

The religionist may rightly argue that, in making these assumptions, I have begged the question against an important theological position – the position one might call 'Islamic neo-orthodoxy' or simply 'Islamic orthodoxy'. This cannot be denied. But if the philosopher cannot keep all the balls in the air, neither can the religionist. No method, whether religious or philosophical, is fully presuppositionless.

The least controversial method is the one nourished by the minimum number of controversial assumptions. But questions are bound to be begged. (Is the trick merely to beg them *persuasively*?)[19]

In disputes of this kind, it is customary for both parties to contend that the burden of proof is on the opponent. While these arguments from location of onus are not compelling, they do, if successfully made, indicate a direction of inquiry. In this secular age, it may fairly be maintained that the burden of 'proof' (or at least of plausibility) is on the believer's shoulders: he must, in the face of secular reservation, justify his faith in the language of reason. If in the past men often instinctively sought to subsume the world, their world, under the aegis of revelation, to fit the rebellious mundane facts into the theological blue-print, today they naturally seek to interpret revealed dicta through the primacy of the purely human and rational.

In saying this I touch on a delicate issue. The characteristic and dominant mood of early and medieval thought in Islam, Judaism and Christianity was informed by a fierce conviction about the priority of supernatural insight. With the advent of modernity, the sceptical bent of mind has become prevalent, inspiring a mood of doubt and rejection, a mood that is not merely a passing or ephemeral component but rather a central and characteristic one in the contemporary religious imagination.

The right temper of the inquiring mind in matters theological is, I believe, to be identified neither with the mood of an unquestioningly submissive religiosity so characteristic of traditional Muslim piety which sees in rejection nothing but an exemplary embodiment of the will to perversity; nor with the aggressively militant irreligion of humanists who see in religion nothing but an expression of some infantile distortion of the purely human consciousness of this world. It is naturally difficult to describe the precise quality of this temper which is informed by at least these two radically opposed moods and which seeks to strike a middle path that combines the virtues of both with the vices of neither.

In the attempt to maintain a mood conditioned by these two opposed tendencies, I tend throughout this work towards the sceptical rather than the dogmatic. For this I offer no elaborate apology. It seems to me that only a pronounced scepticism can serve to redress a previous imbalance in Islamic thought; and, in doing so, bring about, to defy al-Ghazzali's ambitions, a revival of the philosophical sciences.

XI

The concern with temper has conveniently brought us to the last turn of the labyrinth. The religionists are adamant that human reason cannot properly be in the service of raising doubts about religious doctrines or be employed for any other potentially subversive purpose. Reason, like all other faculties, should properly be recruited in the service of faith; destructive criticism of faithful conviction is religiously unacceptable.

We have here a fundamental difference in temper, a conflict of basic loyalties: a religious mentality views scepticism and suspended commitment as being at root foreign to genuine faith while the sceptical secularised mentality vigorously seeks exemption from the dogmatic pressures of revealed conviction. Unfortunately, it cannot be denied that these are genuinely opposed moods which cannot be fully reconciled without a retreat from integrity. Philosophy, as an autonomous branch of learning, can, at best, only indirectly serve religious ends. In the first instance, it has to be in what it takes to be the service of disinterested truth, whether that be religious or secular. Since the philosopher cannot conscientiously assume that he, as a philosopher, will always arrive at conclusions favourable to his religious convictions, he must part ways with the religionist. Philosophy can only be an apology for truth. And there is no guarantee that religious conviction must always coincide with independently discovered truth. Indeed, there is no guarantee that the adoption of free inquiry will lead to the espousal of an orthodox religious stance, that the free religious quest will serve to amass evidence in favour of faith rather than rejection.

These worries are not merely academic. They arise in a practical form when men are faced with a conflict of loyalties. Faith and reason are indeed both implacable masters; and pleasing them both is not always possible. The devout hope is that they will not conflict; faith may well be mightier *than* reason but it is surely mightiest *with* reason. But where they clash, the philosopher, no less than the believer, cannot hesitate about which loyalty comes first.

3

'Poetry from Heaven'

I

The wandering desert tribes living in the Hejaz had long produced some of Arabia's finest poets. The Arabs, experts in the art of rhetoric, saw beauty of speech as one of the nobler virtues worth cultivation. Having a poet in the family was thought a matter for great pride. It had been therefore the age-long custom of the aristocratic households settled in the cities to send their children to sojourn with the nomadic Bedouins in the desert so that each new generation could, while living close to Nature and her ways, learn the mother tongue in its pure and undefiled form.

The advent of the Muslim scripture in the early seventh century marks *grosso modo* the end of the heyday of a whole genre of Arabian poetry. The Koran frequently eulogises its own supremacy of literary taste, reserving some mordant polemic for the poets. Both during the Prophet's own life-time and ever since, the sacred scripture of Islam has been widely admired – often seen as excelling in eloquence and charm all the poetry of its day. Muhammad had brought, if the expression be allowed, 'poetry from Heaven'.

The Koran plays a capital role in Islam, rendering the Muslim faith an intellectual religion *par excellence*. No assessment of Islam could hope to attain adequacy without an account of its scripture. In this chapter, therefore, I begin with some remarks about the received theological account of the nature of the Koran in Muslim conviction; remarks intended mainly for the benefit of readers unfamiliar with the Muslim scripture. This naturally leads me on to the whole complex of issues concerning its supposed authorship, its alleged authority and the Koran's claim that its own unrivalled literary genius is a basis of the argument for heavenly provenance. I explore these issues against the background of the so-called 'argument from stylistic merit'. I identify and distinguish another argument, often blended with this traditional contention, and dub it 'the argument from dramatic impact'. The theme of impact contains the germ of our modern worries – as we wax more philosophical in the remainder of the chapter. The central issue here is that of the correct extent of the intended relevance of the Koran, the question of making it relevant to modern man – of seeking a contemporary dramatic impact. This issue itself blends with a tangle of worries induced by the current scepticism about allegedly revealed knowledge. I conclude with some comments about the task of a 'critical koranic scholarship' – to be undertaken by a secularised Muslim sensibility – and the theological puzzles that such an enterprise may bring in its train.

II

The Koran has been, somewhat inappropriately, called 'the Christ of Islam'. Though Muslims do not, of course, worship the Koran (hence the inaccuracy of the slogan), the sacred scripture of Islam is, for believers, not merely a document about Muhammad's mission in pagan Arabia or even, more broadly, this mission in the larger context of previous sacred history. Rather, it is itself the revealed reality that points towards its revealer, Allah, who is the speaker through the sacred book. Thus, unlike Christianity and Buddhism, Islam – like Judaism and Sikhism – sees the messenger as merely the definitive vehicle of revealed insight.[1] The character of the Muslim understanding of revelation may be said to be kerygmatic; the written revelation in a sacred language constitutes the fulcrum around which the faith is organised. The faithful must go by the book.

The Koran is, in faithful Muslim conviction, simply what the Prophet said it was. And he himself was sincerely convinced that the sacred volume was an undeserved gift of grace miraculously 'descending' on an unlettered and grateful servant of Allah, a view that has up to this day been held without question by virtually all self-confessed members of *al-umma al-Muhammadiyya*. Orthodox opinion has, from the earliest times, rigidly maintained that the illiterate prophet faithfully conveyed to his amanuensis the heavenly words that came to him, through Gabriel, taking scrupulous care not to confuse the inspired utterances with his own ordinary speech.[2] The oral revelations preserved in the Koran are in fact, it is held, portions of a celestial speech whose original is inscribed on a guarded tablet in Heaven (K:85:22).[3] The contranatural descent of parts of this supernatural language marks a pivotal event in mortal history (K:97) completing Allah's gracious self-disclosure to men. The Koran in the original Arabic, safeguarded in Muslim memory and devotion, is therefore the literal[4] and immutable word of Allah, infallibly dictated to his messenger and constituting the final and conclusive expression of the divine will in relationship to mankind.

Unlike his illustrious Israelite predecessors, Muhammad claimed few miracles – a paucity destined to be ephemeral given the later legendary additions inspired by a reverent imagination heated by religious enthusiasm. He seems, however, to have firmly believed that the Arabic Koran was an 'intellectual' miracle of reason and speech which, it would appear, given its finality, excelled the earlier 'sensual' miracles of his prophetic predecessors.[5] What precisely was the special miracle of Muhammad? The Koran is held by Muslims, for the quality and purity of its diction, to be an inimitably miraculous literary production (*mujizah*). The dogma of the sacred text's utter matchlessness is actually among the articles of faith; attempts at imitation are punishable under religious law. (Muslims certainly take books and literary criticism seriously!) The scripture itself confidently challenges all the poets of Arabia to band together along with the *jinn* (elemental agencies held, by the contemporary Arabs, to be responsible for poetic inspiration) to produce something akin to the sacred volume (K:17:88). The challenge is subsequently reduced to merely the production of 'a chapter like it' (K:2:23) that echoes, however faintly, something of its sublime charm.

To the religiously inclined Arabs, the fact that an untutored compatriot had brought forth a work of supreme literary genius, quite apart from the powerful message itself, was a matter for amazement.[6] This amazement in turn gave way to the considered conviction, hardening almost immediately afterwards into a dogma, that the unapproachable excellence of the koranic diction necessitated nothing less than a divine author. The natural step from belief in the Koran's supernatural origin to the conviction about its status as an ultimate revealed authority hardly needs comment.

III

We need now to outline the related problems of the authorship of the Koran and the nature of Muhammad's experience of inspiration – problems that will conveniently lead us into deeper waters. One prefatory remark is in order. There cannot of course, for the committed Muslim, be two opinions about the authorship of the Islamic scripture. (Nor, incidentally, is this an open question for those who reject Islam.) In order therefore to avoid begging any important dogmatic questions at the very outset – questions begged with painful regularity both by Muslim controversialists and their opponents[7] – I shall here use the expression 'the author of the Koran' as an indefinite description which may be taken to refer, in accordance with the reader's own convictions, either to God or to Muhammad. I shall assume that these two possibilities are mutually exclusive: the Koran is not some amalgam of the divine and the human.[8]

As I noted earlier, Muhammad himself from first to last declined the privilege of authorship. The Koran was for him a verbatim report; he continued to insist throughout his life that he was merely the passive recipient[9] of the sacred sequences that Allah, via Gabriel, revealed piecemeal (K:17:106) in order to intimate his righteous will to Muhammad and hence to mankind – all in accordance with the exigences of event and occasion. Subsequent orthodoxy has maintained Muhammad's own view in the strictest possible sense. Thus, it is considered blasphemous to attribute authorship to the Prophet even as a kind of literary convention. We know for example that Milton, like many of the classical writers, conventionally attributes a work like *Paradise Lost* to the Muse while simultaneously appropriating the privilege of authorship. Muhammad, however, felt obliged to give all the credit to Allah.

The sceptics in the Arabian community of course gave all the credit to Muhammad and his allies. They suspected, as we know from the evidence of the sacred text itself, several human and indeed some supernatural (usually evil) agencies as being responsible (either singly or in community with their misguided compatriot) for the composition of the literary material. We cannot fully appreciate the place of the Koran in Islam without having a flavour of the lively disputes about its authorship – disputes that receive significant attention in the sacred volume itself. Since detail is inappropriate here, one example of a hostile attempt to explain the incidence of the Koran will suffice; it will give us a rough picture of the contemporaneous intellectual culture. One of the more famous of the many attempts, it receives a laconic mention in *surah* 16 (v.103). In their search for a human author of the Koran, the rejectors' suspicions settled on a Persian, identified by some commentators as a Christian slave who may have been among the early converts to Islam. But, as the author of the Koran remarks with withering contempt, the disbelievers had not found their man: the Persian in question had, in the Koran's enigmatic phrase, 'speech barbarous'[10] while the sacred volume boasts 'speech clear, Arabic'.

It is perhaps worth noting in this context a fact to which we return in the later and fuller discussions about revealed claims. Given their mental fashion, the Meccans were not particularly averse to the notion that some supernatural agency, possibly a demon, was inspiring their deluded compatriot. Thus, few of his contemporaries would have seen Muhammad as a finished master of the written word merely pretending to bring verses from a supernatural source. Most were merely opposed to Muhammad's claim to inspiration by the supreme being, Allah, whose sovereignty seemed to them so dignified and transcendent that any contact with ordinary mortals was thought incongruous. Indeed, the rich and proud Qureish sincerely wondered why Allah should choose to favour Muhammad of all people, an orphan and an upstart through a judicious marriage. Why didn't the supreme being choose some established poet[11] or someone from among the Meccan magnates? *Surah* 43, v.31 catches the sentiment: 'And they say: If only this Koran had been revealed to some great man of the two towns.'[12]

IV

We are now in a position to address some of our more central concerns. Did the Koran indeed originate in Heaven? Or is it all the product of one man's febrile solitude in the desert? What is the truth of the matter? Orthodoxy has no doubts about the answers and is deeply offended by the fact that there are people who do. Let us then examine the traditional arguments proffered in favour of the authenticity of Muhammad's mission and, in doing so, venture into the philosophical end of the pool.

This is a delicate task, and not merely for the usual narrowly intellectual reasons. The traditional arguments, if that is the right term for them, have rarely been formulated outside the original context of religious devotion, although the Koran itself advances them for consideration by rejectors and believers alike. Now, the believers who are convinced of the Koran's heavenly origin can quite naturally extol its literary virtues. But, to pose a potentially blasphemous question, can one, leaving aside *a priori* religious convictions, indeed infer God as the author of a book merely from an impartial examination of its literary qualities?

Things are seriously complicated from the start by the presence of a significant ambiguity in the Muslim conception of the status of the Koran. While all Muslims regard the Koran as divinely inspired, some would vehemently deny that it is a work of art. In this tendency they are supported by the Prophet's own apparently firm refusal (obscurely echoed in the enigmatic Koran, K:36:69–70) to see the sacred volume as a literary production, as higher poetry.[13] (This is the reason, incidentally, for my use of the disowning quotation marks in the title of this chapter.) The traditional emphasis falls squarely on the Koran as a document with the extremely serious purpose of warning the heedless Arabians, urging them to works of piety and threatening them with the penalties of wilful rejection (K:15:4; 16:44; 38:8; 41:41; etc.). If there be force and eloquence in the appeal to a wayward humanity, so much the better; but the notion of any conscious artistry is, it would seem, anathema. Thus, in the *surah* which takes its name from a reference to the poets (K:26:224–6), the author of the Koran sharply distinguishes in ethical terms – much to the detriment of the poets – the prophetic from the poetic vocation.

The orthodox instinct behind this distribution of emphasis is sound and well-directed: the artistic merits of a sacred text cannot be a primary consideration. But then it is not at all clear what the argument is. Is the scripture's literary excellence alone, as opposed to its content, meant to convince the sceptic of its heavenly provenance? Or should one consider both the content as well as the literary fabric in which it is wrapped? What precisely is the orthodox contention?

We can get our bearings here by asking: is the Koran a work of art? Surely it is. Presumably the religious concern here, understandably enough, is to deny that the Muslim scripture is a literary achievement in the same sense as Shakespeare's *Macbeth* or Goethe's *Faust*. Any suggestion that it is a work of imaginative literature, within the compass of undeniably human scholarship, is obviously unacceptable to the Muslim. The worry of course is that the various forms of literary art, imaginative prose and poetry included, are merely modes of eloquently expressing our own human, all too human, attitudes or our own personal and communal fantasies about this world or perhaps another world. This is true of much artistic endeavour; but whatever one may say of the possibility of a human author of the Koran, it is clearly not *merely* a literary work or *merely* a literary achievement albeit of the first rank. If it were, it could scarcely provide a comprehensive vision that retains the allegiance of millions. The truth is, I trust, that like all sacred literature, the Koran is indeed a work of art in the sense that it is informed by a characteristic quality of conviction and an artistic temper that recruits the appropriate linguistic equipment for its expression, but it is a temper that remains subordinate to the ethical imperatives of the prophetic office.

Assuming, then, for the sake of argument, that the Koran is indeed a work of art, albeit one in which art is tactfully subdued in the service of a very sober truth, and assuming also, for the sake of a case, that the issue of its authorship is an open one, let us examine the cluster of traditional claims about its alleged beauty and linguistic inimitability. Is the Koran indeed inimitably beautiful? How can we decide? Now, there is, as it happens, very little to compare with the Koran, even if we lay aside the orthodox inhibitions about any serious search for rivals. The reason for this lack of rivals is actually a very interesting one. Hostile scholarship has rightly recorded that after the military success of Islam all pre-Islamic poetry was systematically destroyed – presumably because of the implied threat of rivalry. (Two famous poet-ideologues, Nadir ibn al-Harith and Ka'b bin al-Ashraf, were executed by the early Muslims partly because of their claim to have produced works equal to the Koran in literary merit.) Beyond that, however, it has indeed long been the well-nigh unanimous verdict of critical Arabist opinion, including hostile opinion, that the Arabic Koran has, throughout the fourteen centuries of its existence, remained the crowning achievement of a rich and varied Arabian literature. It is generally agreed that no translation, no matter how successful in conveying the sense, even the learned nuances of its vocabulary, could hope to register the sheer range of its emotional effect, the unsettling impact of its sustained eloquence, let alone the imposing charm of its Arabian cadences.[14] Indeed, the koranic diction is still seen as providing the standard of the Arabic tongue even by those who reject belief in its pretensions to supernatural origin.

These remarks serve to bring us more directly to the issue, or rather to a cluster of issues of unequal and unclear import. I shall now formulate and examine several related contentions. Certainly no one has claimed that the Koran's (allegedly) sacred character derives from its choice of theme. A work which speaks of God or of other sublime matters does not thereby become a sacred text – *Paradise Lost* is not scripture – and conversely, a *bona fide* scripture would not lose its sacred character merely on account of its concern with profane or immoral or mundane matters, such as the Devil or sodomy or the laws of concubinage. The claims actually made (as opposed to merely the choice of subject-matter) have a crucial bearing on the judgement about the moral and epistemological character of a work.

Grace of expression is perhaps a more promising candidate for an appropriate criterion here. The Koran in the original (classical) Arabic is indeed distinguished by a grace of expression usually associated with the lapidary style characteristic of all sacred literature in the Hebrew-Christian tradition. This is a relatively uncontroversial judgement: disbelieving Arabists generally concur with their believing colleagues that the sacred volume is beautifully written.

Unfortunately, however, such a criterion is so obviously suspect on many grounds. For one thing, someone could sincerely refuse to acknowledge the charm of the koranic diction (though that may itself arguably be due to an undeveloped aesthetic sensibility). For another, and more importantly, someone could reasonably contend that works by countless authors, known to be uncontroversially human, either equal or even excel the experienced beauty of the Muslim scripture. These objections gesture towards a third, namely, the clear inadequacy of a consideration so inherently subjective to provide an adequate basis for a claim to divine inspiration. For surely one might, with as much plausibility, argue that the allegedly revealed literature of all faiths is reasonably seen as supernatural in origin by those who admire the grace and dignity of the style of those writings.[15] Indeed, one could even say, warming up to this thesis, that some works thought to be of purely human production may in fact be in part or wholly inspired by God, given the remarkable beauty of their style. (Couldn't Shakespeare, Milton, Jalal al-Din Rumi and Dr Muhammad Iqbal plausibly claim divine inspiration for some of their better works?)

We may try another criterion: 'correctness' of diction combined with a superiority of design. To Muslims, the Koran supplies the ultimate standard of linguistic propriety and hence cannot itself be judged against any further or higher standard of literary taste. But are the Koran's diction and style 'correct' when judged by some independent criterion? Certainly many critics have argued that the Koran has, to put it minimally, glaring peculiarities of style and discrepancies in design. The author of the sacred text seems to make all the standard mistakes – mistakes a beginner would be taught to avoid. Thus, for example, there are no prefatory explanations, the endings and beginnings of chapters are often abrupt, and the transitions from one theme to another are frequently awkward. Indeed, to continue the list, many narratives begin in *medias res* and presuppose much background knowledge; the scripture is notoriously repetitive, betraying a conspicuous lack of overall structure and design. There are all in all many loose ends and enigmas here to keep Arabists busy for a long time.[16]

There is, one supposes, a species of artlessness for which apologies could be offered. Indifference to craftsmanship, bordering on a denial of accepted technique, is characteristic of spontaneous and impassioned records: conscious artistry implies a measure of insincerity of mood. The Koran is certainly a work of deeply serious passion.[17] This is very noticeably true in the case of the short Meccan *surahs*, revealed early on in Muhammad's prophetic career but found at the end of the Koran in its final arrangement. Here the existing Arabic language is recognisably strained by the effort of containment as the massive burden of religious experience weighs down on it. The later and longer Medinan *surahs*, dealing with the detail and caveat of law and ritual rather than the immediacy and imminence of sin and nemesis, are less passionate though still honest in tone and direct in mood.[18]

As for repetition, the Koran is, on its own showing, addressed to a heedless (*ghafil*) humanity; it aims to jolt men out of their sinful complacency, urge them to recollect and remember their faithful heritage (K:38:1; 36:11; 41:41; repeated often). As for lack of structure, perhaps vigour is destroyed by any rigid environment of language and design. All in all, one might say that the Koran is a *soi-disant* literary production that preserves a remarkable consistency of theme while secreting its own artistic standards. To be sure, the author uses an outrageous method: agitate, then educate. And yet if the suitability of a method is properly to be assessed by its success in attaining avowed aims, the Koran's method is perfect.

The argument from literary perfection, then, seems rather an elusive one; it is difficult to state it in any convincing form. Features such as choice of theme, grace of expression, correctness of diction or superiority of design do not either singly or in combination serve to render the content true or authoritative. The stock philosophical reaction here, itself both predictable and justified, best states the sceptic's case: even if the Koran is indeed full of disturbingly beautiful verses written in an impeccable style, this fact (if it be a fact) does not guarantee the truth of the claims being made. The epistemological status of a piece of writing is unaffected by our perception – in this case, a specifically Muslim, or more accurately Arab, perception – of its charm and beauty. Beauty is not enough; we need truth as well.

It is worth noting briefly in this context a fact sometimes overlooked in modern discussions of classical perceptions of beauty. Modern thought, no doubt rightly, sternly distinguishes the beautiful both from the good and from the true. The beautiful could be false or illusory just as the false could be beautiful. Ancient thought, however, typically did not differentiate between the true, the good and the beautiful: whatever had one of these qualities was thought to be graced with the remaining two as well. Both in Greek and in early Islamic thought – the latter itself being in its sophisticated form usually of Greek origin – we have many examples of metaphysicians and theologians who believed in the unity of value, truth and beauty. (The best instance here is Plato's thought.) Allah is described in Muslim tradition as good, 'the Truth' (al-Haqq) and, in some of Muhammad's traditions (hadith), as beautiful.[19]

The philosopher does not deny the importance, in matters of ultimate commitment, of the aesthetic appeal of a doctrine. For while truth may indeed be sovereignly independent of beauty and human emotion, our access to it is certainly complicated by the passionate side of our nature – as David Hume, in his own way, so clearly saw. In the end, however, the appeal of a doctrine is one thing, its truth another.

There is, as it stands, something aridly intellectual in this standard philosophical reaction. Surely, the religionist may argue, religion and its associated art should liberate emotion and embellish the world of sound and sight. (Think here of the almost sensuous impressions of Islamic calligraphy or of the striking colourfulness of Roman Catholic ritual and liturgy.)[20] Surely, the argument may run, some kind of beauty attached to truth is needed if one is to win allegiance for a vision, since we are not merely rational or even truth-seeking beings but rather intelligent beings with complex non-rational emotions and passions. The beauty of a vision is not irrelevant to the question of plausibility or of demand on our allegiance. Would we adhere to truths we found aesthetically unappealing or simply ugly? Truth may not be enough.

But beauty is certainly not enough. The philosophical objection remains in the field. The appeal to the peculiarly musical charm of the koranic resonances, admittedly at once both ennobling and disturbing to Muslim ears, cannot bear the whole burden of the normal demand for probative evidence in support of the (alleged) truth of the vision they evoke and represent.

V

Both the believing reader and the disbelieving critic may be forgiven for feeling dissatisfied with the discussion of the preceding section. Somehow, it will be rightly felt, we remained in the shallow end of the pool. After all, men do not live or die for the sake of the beauty of a book. There must be something else, such as its power to transform those whom it touches. The fact is, of course, that concealed behind the argument from the majesty of the sacred diction is a related argument from one experienced effect of it – 'the argument from dramatic impact', as I shall call it. It is time now to formulate and examine this contention.

The Koran is an incalculably influential document. It can boast the unique privilege of having directly inspired a major world civilisation based upon a religiously sanctioned respect for literacy and scholarship. The Koran still supplies the main literary support for the civilisation of the Arabs in some traditional lands, being often the only book that is taught. And we can easily see why the sacred volume has such widespread influence. It is written with a humility that makes it, for all its enigmas and learned nuances, accessible – perhaps necessary – to all of us who are willing to read and think. But while it is not pretentious in any literary sense, it pretends to great things in respect of content. The reader or listener of the Koran becomes instantly engaged with a tremendous theme which dwarfs the mere beauty that conscious artistry brings. He finds himself in the grip of a reality that is at least as elemental and as intense as the human vocation.

The Koran has an aura of passionate conviction that cannot fully be appreciated without visiting a Muslim, preferably Arab, land in Ramadan, the month in which the sacred volume is traditionally held to have 'descended' and which is in consequence marked by intensified devotion. When the Koran is chanted in public gatherings in one of the more ornate styles favoured by distinguished Arab reciters, the believing audience listens to it with a dedicated sobriety that must be the envy of less deeply held faiths. The converted Englishman Marmaduke Pickthall – the first English translator of the Koran who was himself a Muslim – was perhaps not merely indulging in a new-found religious enthusiasm when he described the Muslim scripture as 'that inimitable symphony, the very sounds of which move men to tears and ecstasy'.[21]

It would indeed be difficult to exaggerate the Koran's most dramatic impact upon its original audience. This was a remarkably devout generation whose pious exclamations must have shattered the deep silence of the sanctuary on many a Ramadan evening. The impact of the sacred writ was so powerful and the fear of the Deity thus occasioned so profound that men would collapse, faint, come close to death, and at least one man actually perished while savouring its fatal charms. What did these men experience while listening to this wild melody from the desert? It must surely have been an ecstasy, an *ekstasis* in the original and literal sense: one stood beside oneself, or as the French say, outside oneself, in the larger attempt to forge an authentic if elusive link with the transcendent reality of a supremely righteous Will.

Faith does indeed move mountains. But, as the philosopher reminds the religionist, *every* faith moves mountains. ('Faith moves mountains' is an English as well as an Arabic proverb.) Many different, indeed incompatible doctrines are capable of radically influencing men's lives. Belief in Allah, like belief in the Buddha, the Christ, and indeed in ideals centred around various secular realities (such as reason, love and power) are *all* known to have powerful effects. Thus, Christianity offers, according to its devotees, a saving truth that has had a dramatic impact upon the lives of so many who were obviously among the greatest of our species; the Marxist holds out a similar claim, and so on. Indeed no religion or secular ideology could hope to win assent and allegiance unless it had the capacity to evoke a deep sense of its own moment in the listener. But, of course, the persuasive ardour of conviction – any conviction – is not a guarantee of its truth. The powerful, even hypnotic, effect of the koranic rhythm does not conclusively support the truth of its claims.

It is important to be clear about the issue here. The question is *not* about the possibility of believing, even passionately believing, a proposition even when it is in fact false; rather the issue is about the epistemological merits of thinking that the peculiarly powerful effects of belief in a given proposition are sufficient or necessary or even relevant evidence of its truth. And when we put the matter this way, we see clearly the weakness of the traditional religious position. Dramatic impact is no guarantee of truth. (Is the truth of a claim related to its power to alter our outlook on the world? Does truth also move mountains?) It is no secret that men are as likely to be emotionally influenced by falsehood as by truth for there is, as it happens, no inherent tendency in their psychological constitution that makes them solely or even particularly susceptible to truth. An emotionally appealing view may be false though we adhere to it just as an emotionally unappealing view may be true though we reject it.

Islam is of course a major world religion. In terms of extent of influence, quality of the allegiance given to its doctrines by Muslims and the intensity of their commitment, it can hold up its head in the best ideological company. Large sections of mankind find fulfilment in living according to its dictates; it satisfies deep human needs and certainly stirs men to some kinds of moral greatness. But one cannot, in any straightforward way, move from these relatively uncontroversial judgements to the much more controversial inference that Islamic doctrines expounded in the Koran provide us with the ultimate and comprehensive truth about the human condition.

VI

The argument from impact fails but the concern with impact stays. Indeed the attempt to achieve relevance, to achieve a contemporary dramatic impact, is perennial. Only its exact nature and the details concerning the manner of achieving it differ from age to age. For the original audience of the Koran, the worry about impact was, given the nature of the Koran, by and large a theatrical one.[22] Our task today is more fundamental. We need to make the Koran relevant – intellectually

relevant – to modern man by somehow bridging the conceptual disparity between current secular scientific thought and the outlook secreted
by the original locale of the Muslim scripture. This is, needless to
emphasise, a not inconsiderable task.

It is axiomatic that the Koran is a work the content of which is suited
pre-eminently to the Arabian outlook of the early seventh century.
Muslim divines have, in casting their religious net much wider, implicitly
held the view, somewhat unclearly it would appear, that Muhammad's
Arabia provided a blue-print for every conceivable kind of human
community: perverse, sincere, cynical, trusting, fanatical, kind, cruel,
clever, stupid, indeed every kind of man existed in it. God therefore
chose that society, it is said, to be the recipient of his final revelation – a
revelation intended for the benefit of all mankind. Thus, every narrowly
historical reference is also thought to have a general import transcending
the original context in which it was revealed.

The Arabian impress of Islam cannot, however, so easily be erased.
For one thing, the Koran itself not only concedes its Arab character, it
repeatedly insists on it (K:12:2; 20:112; 39:28; 41:3; 42:7; 43:3; etc.).
The message is not simply in the form of a lecture (qur'an) but rather
a lecture in Arabic addressed, naturally enough, to Arabs (K:41:44).
No secret is made, either within the Koran or the wider Islamic tradition
derived from it, of the fact that the Arabs aspired to become a scriptured
society (K:36:6; 42:7; 43:5) like their Jewish cousins whom Allah had
already favoured. There is, within the scripture itself, no apparent
misgiving that such a distribution of emphasis may jeopardise its wider
appeal. Indeed, one of the arguments for the scripture's heavenly provenance is, as we saw earlier, precisely that it contains within the parameters of its content the climax of the literary genius of the Arabic
tongue. Small wonder, then, that some engagé Jewish and Christian
writers have, within the polemical context of inter-religious exchange,
seen Islam as merely a specifically Arabian form of Hebrew monotheism, or, to put it in the form of a slogan, 'Judaism for the Arabs'.

At another level, the very fact that the language of the scripture is
Arabic, quite apart from any implied or explicit emphasis on this feature, would, it is fair to urge, significantly restrict its range of relevance.
Arabic is a human language with a whole tradition sustaining an associated metaphysic. An influential school of recent thought, taking its
inspiration from that mercurial genius Ludwig Wittgenstein, has contended that language, far from being the mere servant of thought, as
many believe, is in fact its master. Language, this powerful contention
has run, determines in large part, perhaps wholly, our view of an
allegedly independent reality. Now, even if we reject this view as
extravagant (and it is not clear that we can) we cannot deny that,
through choice of language, the Araberthum – the Arab idea, one might
say – is closely tied to the religion of the Arabian Prophet. At any rate,

the stamp of the Arabic language on Islam – itself an Arabic word – cannot simply be ignored.

While one cannot deny the Arab origins of early Islam, or even the Arab ambience, through its scripture, of all Islam in all ages, history and geography together offer the best refutation of the claim that Islam is the religion of the Arab Club. For if by that is meant that Islam is in fact the religion solely of Arabs, it is clearly untrue. Indeed, only 10 per cent of all Muslims today are Arabs. And, historically, the imperial community of the early Arab conquerors was comprised of members of many races and tongues. In the days of Islam's triumphant monopoly, the Arabs saw their religious good fortune as worth sharing with others; in general, non-Arabs were not hindered from embracing the latest Abrahamic faith. Certainly, no Arab scholar of any distinction has claimed that the Koran was revealed for the exclusive benefit of the Arabs.

Even so, however, to change the emphasis somewhat, the conceptual issue stays. If we are to make the Koran relevant to people fatefully placed in different cultures and eras, nurtured in different linguistic environments, entertaining a different metaphysic of man and Nature, we must at once recognise the conceptual disparity that exists among the denizens of different ages, a disparity partly represented and partly nourished by differences in the linguistic apparatus of different societies. The exegetes may well be right in claiming that the variety in the moral attitudes of human nature in seventh-century Arabia is representative of mankind in general. It is one of the recurring themes of the sacred volume that none of the contemporaneous perversities regnant in the Prophet's Arabia can claim the accolade of novelty: all the many ways of sin are time-honoured. That indictment may arguably encompass us too. But it is obviously untrue that the metaphysical outlook of the first custodians of the Islamic creed, displayed in part in the Arabic language, is representative of all possible or actual world-outlooks among human beings throughout history. Whatever we may finally say about the Arabian colouring of the Muslim faith and the scripture that dominates it, we surely should not take too grand a liberty with the recalcitrant facts.

And the facts are as simple as they are troubling. To take just one salient example, the koranic *Lebenswelt* is sharply contradicted by the currently dominant scientific picture of the world as a self-contained matrix of patterned empirical sequences intelligible to us in terms of a theory of natural causality. The monotheistic world-view contains a pattern of thought in which a supernatural world is represented as acting within, interpenetrating so to speak, the natural realm. Apart from Allah's activities – which include the prevention of the lowest heaven, our sky, from collapsing on sinful mankind on the ground and the sending down of the rain to quicken the dead earth – the empirical world is regularly visited by supernatural agencies. These visitors from a non-spatio-temporal realm interfere not only with phenomena in Nature, they influence human individuals too. Gabriel visited Muhammad at Mount Hira; some of the angels fought on the Muslim side in the decisive Battle of Badr. The Prophet and his companions regularly conducted exorcisms to cast out unwanted guests – demons and certain kinds of misbehaved spirits held to be responsible for disease or mischief. In fine, the koranic cosmology, like the biblical one, presupposes regular commerce between the natural and the contra-natural realms.

The Koran often refers to non-human agencies. Apart from Allah himself and the angels, there are also the elemental beings created from fire – the *jinn* – who are invisible denizens of our world. These beings, familiar to westerners from the fairy-tales of Arabia, figure prominently in the scripture, being perhaps most notable for possessing the poets and inspiring inferior poetry. From the eponymous *surah* (K:72), we gather that these spirits are also avid listeners to Allah's latest message, have the free will to accept or reject faith, and are, like men, destined for similar hopes and fears beyond the grave. The *jinn* are an integral part of the koranic outlook. Indeed, the sacred volume is addressed to them as well as to men.[23]

The modern scientific outlook of course rejects the notion of a world populated with spirits and other entities without a specific spatio-temporal location. Even when recalcitrant events occur in the external world, the scientist insists on looking for causal explanations couched in terms of purely natural factors. Indeed, to turn to the human sciences, the human personality is generally thought to have mysterious inner motivations but these are understood in terms of the behaviour of secular entities postulated by analytical psychological theories rather than in terms of visitations from some contra-natural realm.

VII

The koranic world-outlook may, without begging any questions against it, be termed 'pre-scientific'. Fortunately, contemporary Islam is not deficient in scholars who wish to render their scripture relevant, even acceptable, to modern scientific man. Unfortunately, however, nearly all of these attempts are so completely misguided as to be worse than useless. There is much optimism in the Muslim camp, with some writers even claiming to have rendered the Koran fully acceptable, in terms of its scientific content, to western scientific humanity for whom the tide of religious faith is at its lowest ebb. I hope to show soon that it is not mere cynicism to say that had these writers not mentioned this achievement in the preface to their endeavour, it would have taken considerable ingenuity to discover it in the text.

Let us begin by examining the general pattern of these attempts. The characteristic (and surprisingly popular) technique for making the scripture relevant to modern science-influenced readers is to impose a variety of obviously tortured and self-indulgent interpretations on the ambiguous parts of the sacred text. The original koranic lexicon becomes clotted as preferred contemporaneous meanings both religious and secular compete with classical significances.

Such a tendency in exegesis would perhaps be acceptable were it not for the fact that the modern significances, in the hands of some writers, sometimes dwarf the original import of the sacred passages. Ambiguities in words and phrases, potentially ambiguous events, obscure remarks that need a reading, and laconic hints are all, in the hands of a religiously motivated if self-indulgent ingenuity, recruited in the service of many diverse views that are totally removed from the Koran's original context of incidence or indeed its original intent. Thus, for example, the Koran has, in different apologetic hands, become variously a work of natural science, a journal of socio-political thought, a surprisingly detailed commentary on modern secular culture – not to mention more esoteric interpretations.[24]

To be sure, the Koran lends itself superlatively to interpretative treatment, given its own studied ambiguities both in words and incidents. Actors in the Arabia of its incidence are rarely identified clearly: only two men in the Prophet's entourage, it would appear, are singled out by name for special comment.[25] Many important figures in sacred history are referred to by means of titles or indefinite descriptions.[26] Events are usually alluded to in a general and didactic rather than a severely particular fashion. The text is remarkably elastic; the vocabulary typically conceals both latent and patent meanings with some words, as is usual in scripture, displaying striking fecundity.[27] By and large, the Koran can absorb a large number of significances, primarily religious, without any undue torture or distortion.

The sacred text, however, visibly buckles under the pressure of modern secular interpretations. Let me take just one example here. The view that the Koran is a work of science has recently gained much popularity among Muslims. Maurice Bucaille has argued that the Muslim scripture is not only compatible with our modern findings in astronomy, it actually anticipates, in astonishing detail, some of the recent scholarship in experimental physiology and biology. Bucaille is in good company. Aisha Abd-ar-Rahman at-Tarjumana has contended that the essentials of modern nuclear physics are to be discerned within the covers of the sacred volume; and S.A. Wadud goes further than any of these writers in arguing that the Koran is a rich manual of scientific information – leaving the distinct impression on the reader's mind that the Muslim scripture is primarily a scientific work with only an incidental interest in religious matters.[28]

We need not here go into the details of the attempt to attain a prescience of the latest findings of natural science. Suffice it to say that the arguments, if indeed that is the appropriate term for them, carry conviction only with devotees. While the Muslim reader may celebrate the hitherto undiscovered scientific potential of his Holy Book, the critic thinks the religionists have completely missed the boat: the entire attempt is nothing but a remarkably ingenuous and facile handling of scripture in the service of unconvincing apologetic ends.

The intent is indeed apologetic. The age-old desire to declare religion victorious – to remain in the field – here re-emerges in the form of the koranic appropriation of science at a time when the scientific establishment has admittedly scored an elephantine victory over religious orthodoxy. There could be, it is said, no conceivable purely human explanation for the presence of verses expounding, albeit enigmatically, scientific learning in a work produced well before the advent of the age of science.[29]

Muslims are, of course, not alone in holding such views about their scripture; nor is the tendency a disreputable one for any reasons to be adduced *a priori*. If indeed an allegedly revealed work did unequivocally provide scientific knowledge in a pre-scientific age, that circumstance would certainly suggest the possibility of a superhuman author. In fact, my own view is that if a scripture produced in a pre-scientific era even managed to attain a broad and rough compatibility, through studied ambiguity, with the general picture secreted by secular scientific learning, that would already constitute evidence *inter alia* in favour of its claim to heavenly origin. But, unfortunately, revelation is rarely lucid – itself a theologically puzzling feature of God's intellectual dealings with men. Thus, the Koran can sustain different, even incompatible interpretations: one apologist may extract one piece of scientific learning from a given passage, another may extract a different, even rival, scientific claim.

Predictably, the criterion in question here is in practice rarely applied consistently. If the koranic claims tally with scientific views, it is cause for celebration in the religious camp; if not, it is declared either that the beliefs currently prevalent in the scientific community are, conveniently enough for Muslims, erroneous or else that secular scientific truths are irrelevant to judgements about the truth of revealed claims. These kinds of reactions betray confused if not dishonest attitudes. In general, if the cap fits, the religionists claim it for themselves; if not, they discard it. This way of employing a criterion cannot be recommended; the appeal to the scientific criterion should be principled and consistent, not *ad hoc* and desultory.

The religionists fail to employ the criterion consistently – and this is understandable enough. For to accept a consistent application of the criterion is, as the religionists themselves vaguely sense in some moods, in effect to impose a very exacting demand upon revelation. Is the Koran's authority, then, dependent upon its being able to achieve conformity with current scientific scholarship?

There is also in fact one deeper reason, in the same vein but not often noted, for abjuring the tendency to recruit science for scriptural ends. Shall we believers celebrate now that the modern scientist allows us to accept the word of God as authentic? Should the religious establishment borrow all its credentials from whichever side happens to be winning? Or should our slogan in this secular scientific age be what it used to be: *credere Deum Deo* (I believe in God on God's own authority)?

There is potential for misunderstanding this entire discussion about the relationship between science and revealed monotheism. The notion that the Koran is itself an enigmatic manual of science is to be sternly differentiated from the distinct, related and correct view that koranic monotheism facilitated the modern achievement of autonomy for Nature – an autonomy presupposed by secular science. It is indeed a justified boast that Islam gave a major impetus to the development of modern science; monotheism is the natural habitat for natural science. (After all, polytheistic India is rich in spiritual traditions but not in scientific ones.)

It is important, however, to see precisely how the Muslim faith patronises the nascent scientific establishment of the Arabs and the peoples they conquered. The Koran condemns, in no uncertain language, both pagan polytheism and its associated techniques. Thus, magic is castigated as a misguided method, inspired by false religion, to compensate for men's genuine ignorance of the ways of Nature; sorcery is seen essentially as a pseudo-technique that fails to recruit the normal processes of manipulation and knowledge which serve to build a reliable technology. Paganism cannot, it is argued, achieve satisfactory knowledge of a world which, on its own confession, is the battleground of capricious rivalries between opposed sacred forces – a circumstance that frustrates any rational intelligibility of the created order.[30] The monotheistic message liberates men, the argument continues, from the unpredictable whimsicalities of the pagan order by placing the world under a single dominion. Both the unification of the experienced cosmos and the consequent sense of regularity upon which science could rest derive, for the Muslim, from an awareness of the unique sovereignty operative within Nature: the dominion of Allah (K:21:67). Men can thus, as worshippers and inquirers, rationally seek to understand systematically, an order under intelligent suzerainty – and indeed develop a science of Nature and her secrets, perhaps as a preface to a morally constrained exploitation that would in turn yield fruit in a reliable technology.

VIII

I have just briefly examined one attempt, misguided in my view, to 'update' Islam for the needs of the secular age. While this attempt can safely be dismissed as facile and unconvincing, the underlying concern behind modernist exegesis is admirable. The aim is to recruit koranic dicta successfully in the service of modern needs. Religion, it is rightly thought, can only flourish in relationship to the current intellectual milieu that lends structure to the daily lives of ordinary believers. The worry, again rightly, is that unless traditional religious beliefs are brought into a relevant relationship with current intellectual trends, religion will be compartmentalised and the religious understanding isolated from the mainstream of contemporary thought. And the creation of a religious ghetto is often a preface to the effective elimination of religion, quite apart from the fact that such a circumstance encourages believers to indulge in certain kinds of 'doublethink'.

The exact form which modernist exegesis assumes is, unfortunately, open to devastating criticism. The emphasis on the secular scientific resources of the Koran loses all focus of its rich resources as a *religious* document. Modernist interpretation is rightly concerned to render the Koran relevant to us, to find within its pages a cure if not a panacea for our modern aches; but its results cannot be acceptable if they fail to appropriate the primary *religious* significance of the sacred volume – a significance to be determined in part by its role in the early community of Islam and in part by the religious needs of the secular age. It is worth emphasising that the Muslim scripture is the record of a religious mission *par excellence*. It was delivered, in the first instance, in essential part, as an indictment of Arabian paganism. That was the original intent of the revelation. It would be nothing less than laughable to suggest that the Koran was motivated by a desire to supply scientific learning, and that enigmatically, to a generation placed one and a half millennia later in the stream of history.

It is a truism to say that the Koran is first and foremost a theological document. This is so with all sacred literature but it is particularly the case with a Muslim scripture that is famed for its indifference to or omission of secular details. The Koran often declines to supply non-religious information and indeed explicitly relegates it to a peripheral status. Its concern is primarily religious and it discourages debate over religiously irrelevant details. Thus, for example, *surah* 18, in relating the controversy over the number of men who slept in the Cave,[31] voices a characteristic protest against seeking knowledge of what is beyond the bounds of legitimate curiosity:

> They will say, 'Three; and their dog was the fourth of them'. They will say, 'Five; and their dog was the sixth of them' guessing at the Unseen. They will say, 'Seven; and their dog was the eighth of them'. Say: 'My Lord knows very well their number, and none knows them, except a few'. So do not dispute with them, except in outward disputation, and ask not any of them for a pronouncement on them.[32]

Even when it comes to its specifically religious mission, the Koran puts a stereotypical monotheism into the mouths of all prophets, caring little for the extra-religious differences in the locale of the different personalities: David and Solomon declare more or less what lesser Arabian messengers such as Hud and Salih declare and all declare roughly what Muhammad is now commanded to declare. The Koran contains, unlike the Bible, very little purely secular history. Wherever the Koran can avoid giving secular or historical details, it usually does so.[33] However, it does supply complete secular and historical details where such a provision would serve a religious end – to remove or resolve a religious controversy – or where such details are explicitly demanded by rejectors seeking confirmation of the authenticity of Muhammad's mission.[34]

If we are to explain the lasting persuasiveness of the message vouchsafed to Muhammad, we must examine its *religious* resources. The Koran is, in effect, intended to be a supernatural comment on human nature in its normative relationship to a supreme moral Will. It is a guide for social and personal criticism in the larger attempt to realise, through restraint or cultivation of appropriate proclivities, a kind of moral excellence that inherently seeks the mercy and forgiveness of God as its crowning finale. In saying this I touch on possibly the deepest of our many concerns in these pages. The conscious wish to surrender every circumstance of chance and biography, no matter how inherently profane or impious, to the total sovereignty of a supremely righteous personality, supplies at once an integral part of the definition of Islam and the self-definition of the Muslim believer. The tools for cultivating the attitude of surrender (*islam*) are gratitude and repentance in deep and mutual alliance. Hence, of course, the Koran's oft-repeated emphasis on the need for rendering thanks to the creator. A man understands an event in Nature; it provides him with knowledge and, in alliance with technique, the technology for dominion. But the specifically religious import of the observed phenomenon is focused in the act of gratitude born of reverent self-incrimination. The koranic message is not simply 'Understand Nature' but rather 'Understand Nature in order that you may give thanks to her creator'. Science is therefore a means to an end – the religious end. We can now see clearly why the attempt to decode the Muslim scripture – in order to find significances that interest contemporary scientific minds – is religiously suspect.

The Koran was, if nothing more, a critical comment on Muhammad's Arabia. The modern task (for the Muslim) is to show that it is potentially also a relevantly critical comment on modernity and the culture it has bred. This is certainly a delicate task. An authentic revelation must have a perennial quality even though it enters history at a specific juncture and a given location. It must be able to speak to the special condition of one particular generation while simultaneously retaining the potential to communicate with the common, or human, condition of all. Part of our condition today is of course the secular one, which is inextricably tied up with the experience of modern scientific man in the West. The Muslim theologian must render the Koran relevant to modern secular scientific man, but must do so without merely prostituting the scripture in the interests of a topical obsession with science.

The traditional Muslim view is, as we saw earlier, that the miracle (*'Ijaz*) of the Koran is rooted in its literary excellence; and some recent scholars seem to have seen hints of the miraculous in the Koran's allegedly decisive prescience of secular scientific learning. My own view is that the miracle of the Koran, if indeed it is a miracle, is to be discerned primarily in its religious and spiritual capacities and resources. How is it that one short book may plausibly be interpreted as offering the religious pabulum to nourish all the many moods and colour the many shades of an authentic species of religiosity? How is it that one volume could offer a penetrating diagnosis of our perversities, old and new, individual and social, religious and profane? How is it that one book can constitute a universal plea to rigorous self-examination? And if indeed a work with so momentous a message can simultaneously recruit the most profound powers of style and language in order to achieve a dramatic impact upon a wayward humanity, then the believer and the rejector can concur that we have here at least an extraordinary if not miraculous achievement.

IX

Let us temporarily shunt our train of thought on to a related rail before returning presently to the problem of achieving a contemporary dramatic impact upon modern man. I need now to touch briefly on a theme that will concern us at length elsewhere in this work. There is today widespread scepticism about allegedly revealed knowledge. Belief in the very possibility of such knowledge seems markedly odd and unjustified to the modern mind, given its secular proclivities. Can the religionist, then, offer arguments to satisfy the sceptical bent of mind and, in doing so, pave the way to a contemporary achievement of a dramatic impact of the word of God?

Scepticism about revealed knowledge is both natural and justified. In view of the sheer variety of claims to revealed insight, how is one to recognise a *bona fide* revelation and distinguish it from teaching that is falsely claimed to have that status? Thus, for example, in Muhammad's own day there arose some prophets – even one prophetess – whom Islam condemned as false. Yet how is one to decide? Has God indeed spoken to any one? If so, to whom and when? Or is it all a product of the tortured imagination of the *homo religiosus*?

I remarked earlier in this chapter that Muhammad's detractors rejected his claim to heavenly inspiration. Their various reasons for scepticism receive mention in the Koran. Since the Arabs of the time believed in an other-worldly realm of gods, demons (*jinn*), angels and so on, they tended to take seriously the possibility that some demon, possibly the Devil himself, had got the better of the Arabian iconoclast. Indeed, the potentially damaging incident of 'the satanic verses' (K:53:19–23), recorded in detail by a scrupulously honest Muslim tradition, had demonstrated the possibility that the Devil could interfere with Muhammad's reception of the revealed text. This incident gave much satisfaction to the rejectors: if Satan could occasionally interject verses, as the Muslims themselves admitted, why not always?[35] As for the text's undeniable charm, many of the disbelievers argued that it was produced easily enough if one knew a little sorcery, an art much in vogue at the time and, ironically, one from whose destructive effects the Koran is thought to provide protection and deliverance (K:113:4). At any rate, the rejectors were convinced that Muhammad had not attained any privileged access to Allah's views giving, at times, very curious grounds for their doubts. *Surah* 25 (v.32) records possibly the most insubstantial of the many objections to the truth of the Prophet's claims: if the Koran were truly from Allah, it was said, it would descend all at once rather than be revealed piecemeal!

To this and related charges, the author of the Koran offers good *ad hominem* responses. Within the Koran there is indeed a great awareness of the variety of assumptions made by different kinds of rejectors. Thus, sensing that the Arab idolaters were sceptical about Allah's wish to reform them, the Muslim scripture appeals to the Jews and Christians to accept the new faith. The Jews were at the time (as some of them still are) expecting a prophet or prophet-like figure. The appearance of Muhammad served to heighten their expectations and there followed a number of influential conversions to the new religion; but, by and large, the rabbis argued that the idea that Yahweh would choose a prophetic envoy from among the Gentiles was wholly incredible if not blasphemous. The Christian communities saw Islam, as they still do, as simply an inferior Christian heresy. The Koran responded to Jewish and Christian reservations by claiming that if the Koran had come from a source other than God, it would have had much inconsistency in it (K:4:82) whereas, in fact, the argument continued, it is fully consistent both in itself and also wholly compatible with the earlier scriptures vouchsafed to the Jews and Christians (K:12:111; 10:37). To this, the Jews and Christians replied that the Koran was incompatible with parts of the Torah and the Gospel. The Muslim scripture in turn accused the Jews and Christians of having distorted or wilfully misinterpreted the revelations sent to them.

The majority of these already scriptured folk, 'the People of the Book', as the Koran calls them, rejected Muhammad's claim to prophethood. Perhaps if the Jews and Christians had accepted Islam, the Arab idolaters would have followed suit. As it happened, the latter remained firmly sceptical. They conceded the Koran's claim to compatibility with the earlier scriptures vouchsafed to Moses and Jesus but drew the original conclusion that the world had been fooled by three confidence tricksters in succession: Allah had not spoken to the Jews, the Christians or the Muslims.

We need not detain ourselves with details of the many exchanges between Muhammad and his detractors. Some of these will concern us again in chapter 9 when we deal with Islam's rivalry with Christianity and Judaism. There is, however, one important controversy between the Prophet and the pagan Arabs that is worth examining in some detail here for it points clearly to one radical difference between the character of an ancient scepticism, reared on the kinds of objections we have noted, on the one hand, and the character of much modern scepticism, based on a much deeper reservation about the religious outlook and being in consequence of a different vintage altogether. The Meccans had freely awarded Muhammad the title 'the trustworthy one' (al-Amin) on account of his exemplary character and integrity displayed even before the call at Mount Hira. When he declared the uniqueness of Allah and claimed to be the recipient of heavenly messages, the Meccans were sceptical of his pretensions but, in general, remained reluctant to accuse him of being an impostor deliberately seeking selfish ends. After all, Muhammad's honesty was, on their own confession, proverbial; he had certainly established himself as a sober and trustworthy citizen. (The disbelievers never hesitated to deposit their valuables at his house!) The Meccans were in two minds: either their compatriot was as honest concerning the revelations from Allah as he was concerning all mundane matters or else he was dishonest about the former while being honest about the latter.

This dichotomy is, of course, as we today so readily notice, a false one – or at least misleading since it omits an important third possibility. Even honest and great men can be mistaken – sincerely mistaken. It is true that part of one's greatness consists in the ability to safeguard against the insidious power of a false self-image; but it is equally true that greatness of character is not always a bulwark against the powerful illusions that self-deception creates. The problem, then, is not whether or not Muhammad was consciously a liar or deliberately insincere. It is of course extremely unlikely that he was insincere, whatever one may say of his claim to prophethood. (The view that Muhammad was sincere but misguided is certainly possible; that he was insincere and misguided is a polemical accusation rather than an impartial historical judgement.)

But beyond that we must fear to tread. Do the verses of the Koran contain the ultimate truth about the human condition? Or are they merely the product of a Semitic solitude reared in the open desert? The fact is of course that our modern verdict about the validity of claims to revealed insight finds a complex basis in *inter alia* moral considerations about the message and the messenger and, more importantly, in very intricate considerations about the possibilities of self-delusion, the possibility of alternative secular scientific explanations, and so on. To put it minimally, the issue, as we today perceive it, is radically complex.

The Koran and the Prophet were no strangers to scepticism and rejection. But it is the character of these tendencies that has suffered change since the days of early Islam. Again, admittedly, some of the criteria used by the Meccan sceptics are very similar to those we might use: we too would wish to examine the moral credentials of the man and his faith. And yet even such a criterion (or, more accurately, its application) is likely to find a very different status in our considerations. Suppose we say, as the Meccans would also have said, that prophets should be exceptionally virtuous men. If the old religious appeal to the moral excellence of God's spokesmen is *epistemologically* beside the point – good men can be mistaken – it is also, in our day and age, even morally of questionable force and indeed questionable assistance. Even if we leave aside the possibility that God's ways can encompass moral choices beyond our understanding and assume simply that God, as a righteous being, reveals himself only to virtuous men, it is not at all clear any longer what moral criteria should be employed today in order to identify such men. Given our cultural and moral distance from the cultures to which the seminal religious figures of the monotheistic religious complex belonged, we cannot confidently declare that, say, Abraham, Solomon, David, Jesus or Muhammad were morally good men. Should we use modern moral standards (say, those prevalent among conscientious liberal intellectuals) or ancient ones prevalent in the prophet's own culture or an amalgam of both? After all, in terms of our current moral sensibilities – the 'our' here ranging over educated and hence secularised theists – it is not clear that Abraham, Moses, Saul or Muhammad had morally attractive personalities.[36] What would we today think, for example, of a man who thought he dreamed that God wanted him to sacrifice his son and who actually took it seriously?[37]

Let me put an end to these perhaps unduly sceptical reflections; these issues will return to trouble us again later. In bringing this section to a close, I make one general observation. The Koran was of course addressed, in the first instance, to a group of people unaccustomed to modern secular proclivities and their underlying sceptical bent. The sacred volume sets out to provide, in its own words, 'guidance to the godfearing' (K:2:2). It does not claim to be a work of academic philosophy and it would therefore be silly to seek within its pages any philosophical arguments that would satisfy or even seriously interest the modern sceptic. This circumstance underlines the pressing need for a sophisticated apologetic that is fully aware of and conversant with modern scepticism about theistic claims. If the Muslim writers should fail to develop an adequate response to the current sceptical challenges, they cannot reasonably hope to see the Koran making a dramatic impact upon a modern secularised audience.

X

The Koran eulogises itself as the perfect manual of education (K:30:58; 39:27). It claims to be offering clear guidance (K:12:1; 28:2; 27:1; 26:2), indeed 'an explanation of all things' (K:17:12; 18:54). The sacred author insists that the Koran is literature at once comprehensive in its scope and distinguished by its freedom from confusion, inconsistency and error (K:4:82; 41:42, etc.). It sets forth with unparalleled clarity all that men need to know in order to attain ultimate felicity. Like the Holy Ghost of John 14:26,[38] Allah's teachings are said to cover the entire terrain of human concerns. But, laments the sacred author, men wrongly seek knowledge of matters beyond the limits of reasonable concern (K:5:101–2).[39] Many a *surah* voices the protest that human beings are unnecessarily contentious, perversely resisting surrender even when faced with conclusive arguments (K:16:4; 18:54; 36:77).

The Koran claims to contain within its covers 'an explanation of all things'. Some religionists have insisted that this should be taken to mean *all* things, not merely religious affairs. Hence, of course, the concern with reading contemporary scientific significances into the verses of the Koran. I hope that I have shown in the previous sections that this reading is incorrect. The only reasonable interpretation is that the scripture is claiming to be *religiously* all-sufficient,[40] and, in what follows, I shall assume that this latter interpretation is intended by the author of the Koran.

We are now in a position to examine the Koran's claim to religious all-sufficiency. In order to do so, let us explore the reaction of a modern non-Muslim reader who comes to the scripture for the first time. It is likely that he would be repelled by the very tone of the revelation. The scripture of Islam is, like all sacred writing in the Hebrew tradition of revelation, essentially an aristocratic genre of literature. The writer asserts; he does not argue. The Koran's own posture is, in general, not conducive to any human contribution to understanding or assessment: Allah reveals, Allah explains (K:75:16–19). Men listen, in reverent silence and obedience. This is, of course, in a sense, perfectly natural. As is always the case in sacred literature, but very particularly in the case of the Koran, the author's superior profundity is never in doubt. The reader is likely to be struck by the audacious tone of the opening verses of many *surahs* (K:2:2; 10:1; 11:1; 32:2; 39:1; 40:2). The magisterial tone, found also incidentally in some secular writings,[41] is clearly unsuited to any kind of sustained and open exchange about controversial issues of moment.

To turn to the content of the Koran, a modern disbelieving reader may be surprised to note the presence of areas of silence – silence even on religiously significant and obviously important issues. To take a few famous omissions, the scripture does not prescribe circumcision or the five daily prayers[42] – both universally accepted practices among Muslims. More importantly, it seems to be totally unconcerned with many issues, theological as well as broadly human, that intensely worry us. The scripture has almost nothing to say about issues such as free will and predestination; and it says little to alleviate the mystery of the widespread rejection of God in all ages. Such matters are often relegated into the province of the *ghayb* (mystery) of Allah's doings. And yet these are not the kinds of matters that excite merely academic or narrowly intellectual controversy. They have severely perplexed the religious mentality and continue to do so. But the Koran's only answer here seems to be in the form of the oft-repeated refrain, 'Allah does whatsoever he wills', a statement that provides a centrally important clue to the Muslim understanding of the ultimate style of the divine art.

To make things worse, the Koran is preoccupied with some issues that a modern sceptical sensibility would find unimportant or trivial. Thus, for example, one might say that several incidents, quite narrowly particular in character, concerning the Prophet's domestic life, could well have been excluded from the sacred text without undue loss.[43] But, in any case, where relevant themes are discussed, what we have are merely bits and pieces – itself a feature distasteful to us moderns who prefer pedantic precision and scrupulous detail to enigmatic claims issued piecemeal, and moreover wrapped in a laconic style.

Suppose, for the sake of argument, that we lay aside these kinds of objections and make do with what we have. Suppose we accept the minimal demand that revealed claims should cohere with other revealed claims and with the basic canons of reason and experience. Does the scripture of Islam by and large make claims that would be acceptable to those who made such assumptions?

This is a large question and it will, in a sense, concern us throughout this book. To focus the issue provisionally, let us take three related statements found in the Koran, the first and third common to the monotheistic tradition as a whole, the second peculiar to Islam. I shall merely outline each claim and then examine it briefly here although some of the issues raised will receive extensive treatment later on in the book.

1 Primitive man was a monotheist.
2 All communities have been warned by an ethnic messenger about the consequences of faith and rejection.
3 All human beings naturally believe in one God even though many refuse to avow it.

(1) The Koran seems to hold that the original conviction of mankind, of all mankind, in the early stages of the world's existence, was pure monotheism. Now, while this view may well be true, we today cannot uncritically take it to be so. That primitive man worshipped one supreme deity is directly contradicted by the secular understanding of

the evolution of religion.[44] The claim that the human religious consciousness passed successively through animist and polytheist forms to
arrive gradually at a refined version of monotheism has, it may fairly
be said, been carefully formulated, examined, and shown to have evidence in its favour. The rival scriptural view of a pristine Adamic
monotheism slowly degenerating into polytheism and animism and
punctuated by occasional irruptions of the primordial monotheism has
not, in general, received the benefit of reasoned historical support. Few
Muslims at any rate have attempted to lift this view beyond the level
of dogmatic assumption.[45] And an assumption it remains. After all, to
distil undefiled Semitic monotheism out of the dark and colourful mix-
ture of ancient cultic superstitions is, to put it minimally, to take a few
liberties with the anthropological data.

(2) The Koran claims distinctively that although Allah particularly
favoured certain communities, such as the Children of Israel, revealed
guidance has been vouchsafed to every community at one time or
another (K:13:7; 35:24). The sacred volume offers us many glimpses
of the manner in which various communities had received the heavenly
despatches. Unfortunately, however, the Koran's choice of messengers
whose careers are to be discussed is, as it happens, representative rather
than comprehensive, hence making it difficult to know, using the
koranic material alone, whether or not the claim about the universality
of guidance could be made to bear a strict interpretation. Thus, while
the scripture discusses in relative detail the careers of the Israelite predecessors of the Arabian Prophet – Jacob, David, Solomon, Jesus and so
on – we cannot obtain much information about messengers who allegedly arose among communities other than those settled in the Near
East. Did Allah inspire anyone in China or India or indeed the Americas
– in any age before the coming of Muhammad in seventh-century
Arabia? To be sure, the Koran does provide us with additional details
about the prophetic careers of some minor Arabian figures, such as
Hud, Salih and shuʿaib, who were sent to warn small wayward tribes
flourishing in pre-Islamic Arabia. Many groups – Jews, Christians,
Sabians, Hanifs, Magians and the Arab idolaters – receive mention.
Indeed there are enigmatic hints that a prophet may have appeared
among the Africans (K:31:12ff.).[46] But that still leaves on our hands
large tracts of the inhabited world: the Far East, the Americas and parts
of Europe – although Europe may be said to have been covered, if
inadequately, by the Christian dispensation. At any rate, if we patiently
sift the (empirical) evidence by discipline of scientific method, it does
not seem to issue forth in a verdict favourable to the traditional Islamic
position. Unfortunately, most Muslim writers remain content to *assert*
the koranic claim about the universality of revealed guidance and education; few, if any, have even sensed the need to endow this claim with
the additional virtue of reasoned support. In these circumstances, the

critic is entitled to reject the koranic view on the ground that it does violence to reason and probability.

(3) Consider briefly the influential religious claim that all human beings naturally believe in one God, a subject that will concern us at length in the coming chapters.[47] To put the issue in specifically Islamic terms, man is naturally inclined to worship his unique creator, Allah: man is *homo islamicus*. Now, this is a claim which is at least controversial if not unempirical, perhaps even false. Even if it is true that all human beings secretly or tacitly acknowledge the existence of God – denying it merely out of perversity or pride – to deduce such a conclusion from the observed evidence alone would be a clear instance of an inference at least unstable if not unreasonable. If we actually examine, without any religious preconceptions, the hurly-burly of history, it is difficult to resist the conclusion that a plurality of pieties has found favour in the eyes of different peoples and that any conviction about the monolithic religiosity of our species is at least unempirical. The existence and nature of God have been keenly disputed throughout history; there is an enormous range of convictions here. Are we not forcing an artificial unity upon the empirical data in claiming that there is a unique form of religious faith – a somewhat stereotypical theism – that cuts across all the vagaries of the religious record? Isn't such a forced unity being conscripted in the service of the *a priori* (and hence unevidenced) dogma of the essential religiosity of human nature? And what indeed are we to make, especially in our day and age, of those individuals and societies that apparently lack religious sentiments altogether? There is after all an increasingly large number of people who do not seem to believe in a supreme transcendent being (or in a plurality of such beings) or in the possibility of a future life in which the errors in the moral government of this world are eventually rectified. There are sizeable communities of 'godless' folk, to use rather loaded terminology, whom the religious theoretician cannot simply ignore. Does the evidence in favour of the traditional religious position not weigh as a feather in the scale beside the apparently more weighty evidence in favour of the opposite opinion?

All in all, then, those who uphold the biblical-koranic theory of the origins and prevalence of monotheistic religion are hard put to reconcile their theology with our recent findings in archaeology and anthropology. If one approaches the issues with a monotheistic bias, one naturally tends to interpret the empirical information as favouring the religious contention; the secular opponents interpret it as favouring their secular interpretation. The evidence itself conclusively supports neither view. The religionist, however, cannot take too much comfort from this fact. For his task in this secular age is to demonstrate (or at least strongly indicate) the superiority of the religious contention and to do so while partly respecting the constraints of reason and secular science.

In looking at all these issues, we should bear in mind the important truism that the Koran was addressed, in the first instance, to a group of people whose mood and temperament as well as dogma and perspective differed radically from that prevalent today in modern industrial societies. The Koran's original audience was composed of people naturally innocent not only of modern scepticism but also of the secular proclivities associated with the rise of critical history and all its rigorous canons of authenticity. Moreover, we are today less willing to tolerate hyperbole or exaggeration. It could be that the notions of 'historical accuracy' and of 'value-free fact' are anachronistic for most pre-Renaissance thought. Today there is a great concern that the facts, including historical facts, be suitably isolated from sentiment and ideal. There has certainly been a paradigm shift in our outlook. We must bear these considerations in mind when trying to achieve a contemporary dramatic impact on secularised audiences.

XI

'It is better to profane the Torah than to forget it.'[48] This judicious rabbinical maxim can best serve to introduce the problem of the contemporary need for a textual criticism of the Muslim scripture – a 'critical koranic scholarship' – in the larger attempt to make it relevant to modern man.

Muslims are notable for having refused to develop any such discipline, for remaining resolutely opposed to the proposal for its need or topical relevance. The reasons for this reluctance are not far to seek. The Koran as the literal word of Allah is, the religionists predictably claim, beyond human appraisal, whether favourable or unfavourable. It is not subject to the jurisdiction of a limited human reason. Revelation judges men; men do not judge revelation. If modern man is sinful enough, it will be said, to declare the Koran irrelevant to his aches and pains, so much the worse for him. The idea of a critical koranic scholarship is blasphemous. It is better to forget the Koran than to profane it.

The religious worries are both genuine and understandable. But the attempt to immunise the Koran against current sceptical scrutiny carries with it one signal danger. Islam is interesting primarily because it is at root relevant to our mortal condition: because it can, it is felt, ease the burden of this condition. It is *worthwhile*, one thinks, to examine our perversities and virtues in the light it casts; otherwise, many indeed are the benefits of the unexamined life. If the Koran is irrelevant, we are at liberty to ignore it.

Unfortunately, these remarks are too much in the nature of a reasoned contention to carry conviction with the older generation of Muslim intellectuals. But fortunately, subtlety is unnecessary here. The Koran is palpably becoming a dead relic from a dead past. It is fast becoming an irrelevance to our daily lives, to the mental travail of ordinary existence. All that remains today of this potentially powerful document that has shaped the intellectual traditions of a major world civilisation, are the parrot-like recitation in the seminary (*madrasah*), the routinely thoughtless appropriation of its verses by a misguided enthusiasm, and the self-indulgent interpretation of its claims by politicians and modernists who seek ever and anon within its pages a justification for their own ephemeral and illicit slogans.

It is indeed difficult to find in the voluminous literature on the Koran, both devotional and critical, any that deals seriously, engages patiently, with the important but neglected problems I am here posing. It will be impossible for the reader to appreciate the nature of our task in these pages unless he or she recognises the large measure of novelty in my proposals. I say this not in order to claim any undue originality – if others before me have had these ideas, I lay no claim to them as mine – but merely in order to alert the reader to the sheer size of our task. It is indeed a project which has been shelved for too long; it is high time all Muslims were on this case. What I offer here are merely the rude beginnings of a long and arduous project. Our journey to Mecca is, I hope, not any the less worthy of its destination for being paved with intellectual perils.

Someone might say that while professing Muslims have refused to develop a critical koranic scholarship, surely western scholars of Islam have succeeded in doing so. This is a popular mistake. The writings of western critics are, in general, profoundly unsatisfactory. Most of these writers have been and remain committed Jewish and Christian religionists, deeply convinced that Islam is an inferior and unoriginal religious rival. Shooting from the same bow, they often assume, without argument, that Muhammad was an insincere impostor who copied, rather badly it would seem, a Bible that fell into his hands – perhaps during his trading journeys to Syria – and added a few legends of purely Arabian origin in order to enrich his account. The next step, predictably enough, is to detect discrepancies and anachronisms[49] in the Koran, by using the Judaeo-Christian scriptures as axiomatic. Such a procedure is of course not incompatible with religious zeal; but it is, unfortunately, incompatible with an acceptance of the canons of free impartial inquiry. It begs the question, and does so a little too obviously. Can one indeed use the Bible as a criterion for detecting error or truth in a work that claims to be a rival interpretation of the nature of the same alleged reality, without effectively begging *en masse* every significant question at stake?

Islam's rivalry with the other monotheisms will preoccupy us later. For the moment, let me try to clear the ground for the development of a critical koranic scholarship within broadly faithful parameters. Firstly, the application of modern historical scholarship to the Koran is, the religious veto apart, a relatively simple task. The Muslim scripture, unlike the Hebrew Bible and the New Testament, is not the hetero-geneous work of many hands over centuries in different locales and varied languages. It is rather a unified canon, revealed in less than a quarter of a century, addressed to one man in two geographical locations in the same country and written in one language – the language of the recipient and the first audience. The period between its oral revelation and its canonical formulation is extremely brief. Apart from occasional variant readings that do not significantly alter the sense, the content is fixed and defined. Moreover, the text has retained a perfect purity, as Muslims rightly boast.[50] A unique version enjoys universal currency today as in the past.

Secondly, Muslims should have no illusions about the dangers of developing a textual criticism of the sacred volume. There will be headaches; though, to be sure, not as many as the Bible inspires. But the central perplexities are a plague on all our houses. The main reason for undertaking the task is to render the Koran relevant to modern man. Concealed in this circumstance is a paradoxical potentiality: the Koran may indeed win the allegiance of the secularised mind or else the scripture could become a major source of theological puzzles that may eventually alienate even some of those committed to the faith.

It is a painful circumstance – but there we have it. There will be perplexities, not least the difficulty of justifying the puzzlement itself. For if God has instructed men clearly and decisively, whence the per-plexity? Should we be puzzled? Are we religiously obliged – that is, as Muslims – to quell any puzzlement we may sincerely experience? If so, how is a believer to maintain his intellectual integrity? Could there be an enclave of legitimate doubt and hesitation within the sanctuary of faith and commitment? I do not know the answers to these questions. In some moods I think that perhaps, just perhaps, the theological queries persist in the sinful finite mind despite their effective resolution in the sacred volume, much as a man's sense of personal guilt may, irration-ally, outlive his knowledge of self-exoneration. But more of this else-where.

A final remark before we begin a detailed exploration of some of these issues. It is undeniable that contemporary sensibilities reared on a predominantly sceptical diet are becoming increasingly unresponsive to religious imperatives. Any constructive engagement between Islam and modernity must involve the rejector: the rejector must reserve the right to examine critically the contents of the Koran. At the same time, Muslims themselves should study their scripture with as much detachment and objectivity as possible. It will be the task of the Muslim theologian to deal with the religious puzzles that are thrown up in the process. It is in general a safe rule that if the scripture is authentic, it should be able to withstand in some measure the tests of sceptical secularity. If it is false, one is at least spared the error of mistaking falsehood for ultimate truth.

XII

The discussion in the preceding section has put us in a position to see more clearly the nature of our task. There are, broadly speaking, two kinds of related but distinct worries that render the divine message inaccessible to modern audiences. There are, firstly, *intrinsic* problems: arguably false or unempirical claims within the revealed text, morally unacceptable imperatives, and so on. Secondly, there are *extrinsic* difficulties arising out of the fact that scripture was presented to a generation largely ignorant of rational scientific thought and method.

I have already outlined both kinds of worries. It is time now to examine some of their implications. In order to do that, I shall explore the Christian response to these difficulties since no Muslim writer has, to my knowledge, even recognised them let alone sought to resolve them. Since most of the issues are relevant both to Christian and Muslim thought, I need to rehearse, with appropriate changes, some of the challenges and arguments originally formulated in the context of an attack I recently launched against a group of Christian writers.[51]

Let me outline the Christian stance since it provides an instructive instance of the difficulties inherent in all attempts, whether Christian, Muslim or Jewish, to secure an authentic enclave for scripture in the post-Enlightenment world. A totally fundamentalist attitude towards scripture – an attitude marked by misological tendencies – was dominant in western Christian thought until fairly recent times. Although it was the European Enlightenment that first unleashed the forces of destructive criticism, it was the nineteenth century that supplied the secular last straw. After Darwin, Nietzsche and Marx, the forces of tradition have been in constant retreat.

It is important to note the relative novelty of the controversy over the epistemological status of the problematic parts of the Bible. Even as recently as the close of the cataclysmic nineteenth century, almost everyone in the clergy settled for a straight duel between the God of St Paul and the English scientist Darwin. Unfortunately, as quite a few in the clergy would now admit, Darwin seems to have won. Some Christians conceded that their faith had suffered a heavy blow from the Darwin affair. Others argued that the victory was in fact empty, perhaps even a blessing in disguise: not only had secular critique failed to damage the religious core of the biblical revelation, it had in fact inadvertently done a service to Christians by alerting them to the distinction between the false non-religious husk and the concomitant true religious kernel.

Fundamentalist and neo-orthodox Christian thinkers – Karl Barth immediately comes to mind – continue to insist on scripture as a corpus of factually inerrant propositions about history, man, Nature and divinity. The Bible, we are told, has an intrinsic authority independent of the verdict of secular rational thought. A growing number of Christian writers, however, touched by modernity, reject the ancient view that the Bible is the infallibly dictated word of God that must be accepted root and branch. The advance of rational thought and the spectacular increase in the scope and authority of the sciences of man and Nature have, many secularised Christians concede, together served to expose as embarrassingly fantastic, if not utterly false, some of the extra-religious accoutrements of the faith. We can, it is said, no longer accept traditional ideas concerning revelation, inspiration and, more generally, the whole thrust of literalist exegesis.[52] 'The "light" in the Enlightenment was,' as one distinguished Christian missiologist puts it, 'real light.'[53]

All secularised Christians agree that the light was real enough. But, we are told, the traditional understanding of the epistemological status of the scriptural record is defective. Thus, Richard Swinburne, a typical member of the club of 'sophisticated' Christians, has carefully argued that the account of creation in Genesis (to take an example that encompasses both Christian and Muslim concerns)[54] is not intended to convey factual scientific information. It is rather meant to teach a basic religious truth about the dependence of all things on the creative activity of an infinitely wise and powerful Mind or Spirit. The attempt to extract historico-scientific information here, contends Swinburne, by imposing a strictly literal interpretation, betrays a misconstrual of the resources of a primarily religious document.[55]

Swinburne continues, predictably enough, that religious teaching, in order to be intelligible, needs to be embodied in the received historical and scientific presuppositions prevalent in a prophet's culture and era. It is therefore important for us to know the context of revelation – that is, a pre-scientific culture predating the rise of critical history – in order to arrive at a valid assessment of its contents. We today must distinguish between the religious import of sacred literature and the possibly false cultural trappings once needed to convey the message to an ignorant people. Swinburne's proposal is that we simply excise the false, culturally conditioned, elements while retaining the eternal religious truth.[56]

Things are not that easy, however, for the sophisticated religious believer. If he endorses the autonomy of secular reason, he not only finds it difficult to resist the obvious concession that some statements in the Bible or the Koran are unempirical or false,[57] he is also obliged to admit, I would argue, that conservative confidence in the authenticity of the *religious* core of revelation cannot remain intact. Can we indeed conserve the religious authority of scripture once we reject its factual claims as untrue or obsolete? Can we distil a residue of religious truth? After all, if a book can be fallible in its claims about secular and historical matters, there is no reason *a priori* why it should be none the less infallible in its pronouncements on religious doctrine. Nor can one, I should contend, distinguish in any unquestion-begging way (despite

Swinburne and the sophisticated Christians), between the religious message presumed to be true and the culturally specific incarnation presumed to be false.[58]

These are important worries. I have much sympathy with the claim that scripture is primarily religious in import. Indeed I have argued against the view that the Koran is an enigmatic manual of secular scientific learning. The Koran is indeed a religious document addressed to people living in a particular environment. However, it is one thing for an allegedly revealed text to be culture-laden, it is another for it to be error-laden. A book, any book – even a revealed book – cannot be culture-free. But that need not entail that it cannot be error-free.

One response to the problem of arguably false claims in scripture is simply that revealed insight cannot be brought within the purview of a purely human understanding and its mundane logic. Revelation supersedes our rational strictures, even our logic; it is not subject to potentially blasphemous human criticisms. Such a response is of course perfectly justified if one accepts the religious assumptions that nourish it; and it is likely to be the standard response of those orthodox and neo-orthodox writers, whether Christian, Muslim or Jewish, who remain untouched by or indifferent to secularity and hostile sceptical probing.[59]

A more plausible response, often made by Christian thinkers influenced by contemporary scepticism, is that God is primarily concerned with the spiritual efficacy of his message, not with its factual accuracy. It is indeed true that the power of scripture does not lie in its factual dimension; but it does not follow from this alone that we should accept every manner of factual untruth in a putative revelation. Of course, we may even accept the occasional pious fraud. But the sceptic is perfectly entitled to question even that impulse. For if the aim of God's revelation is to show us the way to Heaven rather than satisfy our idle curiosity, why not remain silent on matters unrelated to the purely religious dimension of human life and destiny? Or, indeed more plausibly, why not attain prescience of secular scholarship by a studied ambiguity in the non-religious claims made in scripture? Thus, for example, revelation either need not commit itself to any precise cosmological details or else do so only vaguely, so that a subsequent science would have no occasion to discredit its contents. Surely, 'The world was created in six periods' (with 'period' signifying an indefinite duration) is true if uninformative, whereas, 'The world was created in six days' would now appear to be outrageously false if precise.

In an attempt to account for some of the scandals to the rejectors' intellect, St Augustine and others in the patristic tradition held the fascinating view, officially promulgated by Pius XII in his encyclical *Divino Afflante*, that God had deliberately inserted puzzling features into the Bible. The presence of apparent errors and discrepancies was intentional; forced to study the word of God with greater care, men would attain a measure of intellectual humility as they would collide with the bounds of their limited understanding.

This kind of reasoning is clearly appealing to all theists. And there is something to be said for it. We certainly should not dismiss it on the sole ground that it is apologetic. (Aren't we all apologists for one thing or another – if only for the truth?) Indeed, the proposal is not *ad hoc*. Scripture itself tells us that God tries both our hearts and our minds.[60] The presence of errors deliberately woven by God into the fabric of the revealed text could, then, be in effect an intellectual trial to test the mettle of the children of the Lord.

The problem with this suggestion is that it begs the question against the rejector, or at least does so too straightforwardly. Being apologetic is one thing; being naïvely so is another. To be sure, once we accept a book as the infallible word of God, the presence of occasional errors need be nothing more than minor worries internal to the faith. The religionists can safely be trusted to find one reason or another for their presence, by looking, for example, into the vast repertoire of God's mysterious ways. The rejector of course will not be impressed by such a strategy. He will see it as nothing but an over-developed and deplorable tendency to take refuge in the convenient *exit in mysterium* – a manoeuvre particularly worth discouraging today since sceptics discern evasion in it.

There is, in any case, one powerful consideration that spells disaster for the theist. It may be argued that God has deliberately contaminated scripture since if it were perfectly error-free it would necessitate a faithful response. This, however, is not the case. Men are, on scripture's own showing, perverse sinners who reject the truth even when they recognise and indeed secretly acknowledge it; rejection is merely one of the privileges of sinful perversity. It is certainly possible to reject the truth or, more narrowly, scriptural truth. But if even the availability of a perfectly error-free scripture would not necessarily compel faith – sin and perversity being the true causes of our rejection – why doesn't God send a wholly true written revelation?

The presence of what seem to be errors or discrepancies in an allegedly revealed text poses a theological problem. It puts all our worries on a new level of seriousness. For it *is* religiously puzzling that God does not wish to correct some culturally prevalent errors and instead accommodates his message to them. Or is this simply a part of the *ghayb* (mystery) of his doings?

The concession that scripture contains false or implausible claims has been staunchly resisted by Muslim apologists and, until relatively recently, by most Christian apologists too. We can now perhaps see clearly the many excellent reasons why Christian thinkers of the nineteenth century were reluctant to say calmly with Swinburne that part of Genesis is 'evidently a piece of poetry'.[61] It was seen – and rightly so in my view – as a singularly damaging concession.[62] The great controversies that raged between the ancient Church and the nascent scientific establishment were not all sound and fury signifying nothing. Those Christians were *not*, their modern secularised co-religionists to the contrary notwithstanding, sincere but misguided. They were sincere and properly guided: they showed a sound intuition in opposing Darwinist and neo-Darwinist thought. Whatever may be said about the details of their unconvincing polemic, and for all the obvious flaws in their arguments, they certainly took the right side in the battle.

It is an amusing irony that modern sophisticated Christians manage to patronise at one stroke both the Christian apologists and their secular critics of the previous century. The apologists, we are told, had misdirected their hostility; the secularists had failed to keep the target clearly in focus. One party had missed the mark; the other should not have joined the battle at all. But the truth of the matter is of course too clearly the other way. Swinburne and his secularised friends are completely mistaken in thinking that Christians (or indeed Jews and Muslims, for that matter) can read Darwin or Marx without undue alarm. The truly revolutionary ideas of these secular thinkers are indeed cause for alarm in the religious camp. Thus, for instance, the notion that men had evolved from a neighbouring (and rather unflattering) lineage in the animal kingdom was rightly thought to be damaging to Christian faith. The apologists saw clearly enough that the secularists had been out to discredit the entire older allegedly revealed view of the natural and historical order and of man's place in it. Men were no longer to see the world under the aegis of an allegedly superior dictum emanating from Heaven. St Thomas's vision was on the gallows.

Let me say a little more about this. A significant concern of post-Enlightenment Christian thought, reared on an awareness of the findings of radical historical criticism and secular thought, has taken the form of an attempt to distinguish between the alleged quintessence of Christian religious belief and its supposedly incidental (historically and culturally specific) features. This distinction between the true religious message and its false socio-cultural expression trades on a controversial if not suspect construal of the nature and scope of religion. Unlike science and history, religion claims to be all-inclusive; the former deal respectively with whatever is subject to lawful regularity and whatever is significant in the human past while the latter deals, in some important sense, with everything. The distinction presupposes for its tenability that the cultural embodiment of a religion can be exclusively secular (i.e. extra-religious). But to presuppose this is to beg the question about the comprehensiveness of religion. This may appear like a quibble to readers reared in the West but the distinction between 'the things of God' and 'the things of Caesar' is actually occidocentric: it is not a feature of every faith. In fact, it is, even in the case of Christianity, applicable only to a distinctively modern conception of that religion, dating from the Enlightenment which marks the beginning of the tradition of modernity.

Someone may fairly contend that the distinction between the sacred and the secular *ought* to be drawn even if Islam and pre-Enlightenment Christianity do not draw it. The major worry, however, is over how precisely one should delineate the ever-dwindling estate of the sacred and the ever-growing domain of the secular. How much, then, of revelation is indeed religiously necessary and how much is extra-religious and hence, in an important way, dispensable? The problem here is that as more and more of the traditional claims in scripture are exposed as false or embarrassingly fantastic, sophisticated Christian thinkers disown the suspect parts of their revelation without offering any systematic account – a body of theory – which would serve to mitigate the arbitrariness of this procedure. While scripture need not be viewed as a collection of rigidly unrejectable data of equal significance, one should not jettison *ad hoc* whatever is found offensive to current secular sensibilities. If today we disown what we take to be factually erroneous, perhaps tomorrow we will reject apparent moral anachronisms – such as scriptural claims about the relatively low status of women or the impropriety of 'deviant' sexual behaviour, not to speak of the occasional questionable doctrine about the nature or activity of the Deity. We surely need a principled account of the limits of this sacrifice at the altar of secularism; we need grounds rather than motives for establishing a coincidence between the essence of a faith and just exactly those scandals to the intellect which today's worldly folk will tolerate.

These are significant worries; they have ramifications beyond the scope of our present discussion.[63] Although we shall return later to some of the issues raised here, one final remark will serve to close this penultimate section. 'Fundamentalist' handling of scripture is often derided as a religious cul-de-sac. The term 'fundamentalism' deserves comment – a comment that is, incidentally, not simply a matter of words, for it arises from far too serious a substantive concern to be merely terminological. I understand 'fundamentalism' to be the position that scripture contains a basic source of wholly correct guidance. Such a view need not be the sole prerogative of orthodoxy, neo-orthodoxy or of what is normally called, somewhat pejoratively, fundamentalism. A theological modernist can also be a fundamentalist in my sense of the term; the usual contrast between modernism and fundamentalism in matters of scriptural interpretation may well be wrongly drawn.

The idea that revelation is an 'all or nothing' affair is extremely unfashionable among educated believers. But it conceals, as I hope to have shown, perhaps the only defensible attitude towards what one takes to be the word of God. For if the non-religious elements in scripture be dispensable, false or fallible, why not the religious ones? Once again, can we indeed accept the authoritative integrity of a partly fallible scripture? It is sad but true that distinctions between religious truth and secular error are rarely so neat and obliging as to coincide exactly with the wishes of contemporary Christian apology.

XIII

We are not yet at the bottom of this barrel. I need to return briefly now to the central theme running through this chapter, indeed this entire book, namely, the problem of ensuring that the Koran makes a dramatic impact upon contemporary audiences. The problem is complex. Can the Koran indeed influence the heart of a civilisation that is in the midst of an arguably sterile materialistic phase? Can we even make the Crescent interesting and relevant to a culture in which the Cross at any rate is increasingly the despair of a certain kind of rationalism itself reared on a diet of scepticism and mental independence?

The modern historicist temper sees revelation in terms of cultural conditions and social pressures rather than in terms of eternal verities and principles vouchsafed, indeed imposed, from outside. To be sure, the Koran, like all sacred literature – like all critical writing – partly transcends its environment: it is more critical than representative of its own age and surroundings. The sacred Book of Islam consists largely of an indictment of the pre-Islamic 'ways of ignorance' (al-jahilliyyah). But, in an important sense, it is necessarily tied to its socio-historical location. And this circumstance creates serious difficulties for the modern Muslim interpreter of the sacred text. How much of the original world-view of the first recipients of the koranic message do we today need to entertain in order to believe that the scripture is still a revealed authority with the *de jure* right to direct modern lives? If the occasion of the Koran's revelation be specific, why should its verses enjoy a normative universality that embraces all places and eras?

Unfortunately things are not made any easier by existing Muslim attitudes and loyalties or by the tightness of the classical straitjacket of koranic exegesis. Many modern Muslims believe that the theologians and exegetes of the early centuries of Islam were authorities empowered to interpret the Koran – once and for all. Who gave them the authority to speak with authority? The answer is, predictably enough, Allah himself. Thus, for many Muslims, both the Koran and its interpretation are the perfected gifts of God's grace. Indeed, the sacred volume lays down its own rule of interpretation (K:3:7) – a rule which has itself been interpreted by some purists as being in effect an authoritative veto on human interpretation *per se*.[64] Men should not be presumptuous enough to interpret the word of God! Read it, we are told, as it is. Of course, the koranic rule about interpretation is itself open to interpretation – is indeed the subject of intense controversy.

We cannot pursue that particular dispute here. Two remarks will serve to bring this chapter to a close. Firstly, the Koran may safely be interpreted to consist of the authentic proclamation of certain basic (alleged) truths and injunctions partly inaccessible to the unaided human reason. But while revelation necessarily, at least in part, transcends human reason on account of its genesis, it need not — once it has appeared — offend against rational strictures through inconsistency or internal contradiction. It is one thing for an alleged revelation to surpass reason; it is another for it to contradict the deliverances of rational thought. Where revelation contradicts rational claims, we have a theological puzzle on our hands. The Muslim theologian should attempt to identify and, if possible, resolve these puzzles. In the final analysis, of course, the theologian may have to concede that these perplexities are a part of the *ghayb* (mystery) of God's doings, a concession which could excite the charge of evasion.[65]

Secondly, we can no longer *assume* that a document originally addressed to seventh-century Arabs is relevant to all human beings irrespective of their historical and cultural location. After all, why should the rules of the early Muslim Club apply to all of humanity, including modern man? Is it even credible that God has communicated his will once and for all in terms of the thought-patterns prevalent in the early seventh century in Arabia? The onus of proof here is surely on the Muslim rather than on the rejector. To be sure, the Koran is among the great and curiously impressive masterpieces of the world's literature — there is never any shortage of those hoping to deride it, extol it or account for it — but only Muslims see it as also the eternal and incontrovertible word of a merciful creator. To the rest of mankind, it is simply a collection of systematic polemic against errant monotheists, appeals for social justice, condemnation of paganism, promises and threats about a world yet to come, and a fervent denunciation of a communal and personal wrongdoing that is denied the last word. To discern in all of this a transcendent wisdom and a panacea for all the varied ailments that afflict our common humanity is indeed a task, a large task, a specifically Muslim task, to be undertaken with courage, frankness and integrity as the turbulent twentieth century draws to a close.

The Silence of Allah

In the *surah* which takes its title from a reference to the table used at the Last Supper,[1] there is an intriguing passage (K:5:101) inviting men to ask Allah any questions they please while the Koran is still being revealed. The discouraging hint is immediately added that a previous generation had accepted the invitation and had then been vexed by the answers from Heaven. So, it is perhaps best, one thinks, not to ask questions that may return an unpleasant answer.[2]

The complete descent of the Arabic Koran in the early seventh century marks, for Muslims, the end of the age of revelation. In the Koran, Allah has spoken clearly, decisively and for the last time; he will not speak again as revealer and warner.[3] And it will be an evil day when he does speak again – as judge and punisher.

We live, according to Muslim thinkers, in the age of realisation. The religious evolution of our species is complete: man has come of age. He should therefore discover and reflect upon the signs of Allah in Nature, history and the self, without seeking any reliance on a dramatic divine self-disclosure in the old style.

In this short chapter I explore contemporary scepticism about the alleged presence of divine forces in or behind Nature, setting the exploration against the larger implied context of the modern radical rejection of God. The complex problem of rejection along with the theological puzzles it generates will together continue to be on our agenda in this and several subsequent chapters.

I

There is a familiar religious sentiment behind Joseph Addison's stirring poem about the impressive harmony of Nature promulgating

> . . . to every land
> The works of an almighty hand.

This religious idea is also extremely popular in Islamic thought, particularly in Sufi and mystical poetry. Thus, Muhammad Iqbal in his celebrated *Payam-i-Mashriq* (*Message from the East*) speaks for a whole school of devotional thought when he proclaims:

> The mountains, the sea, the setting of the sun
> There I saw Allah without his veil.[4]

There is, according to orthodox thinkers in the Mosaic traditions, ample and entirely convincing evidence within the external world for the existence and activity of a supreme creative being. It is not that there is enough concealed evidence that would convince, say, the scientist who professionally probes Nature's mysteries but rather, it is claimed, the existence and power of the Creator are manifest – to all and sundry. Though God himself and his intentions are admittedly hidden and irreducibly mysterious, the heavens daily declare his glory.

The Koran constantly emphasises the religious significance of the created natural order. Indeed, it contains ten times as many verses about the signs (*ayat*; *ayah*, singular) of God than it does about religious law – a particularly surprising circumstance in view of Islam's justified reputation as a law-centred faith. Allah reveals himself through Nature. The divine portents are not typically in the form of miraculous interventions: Nature's routine sequence of events discloses to the heedful penitent the mercy and wisdom of Muhammad's subtle master. One can, as the deists would say, read Nature, the open Book of God. The metaphor is peculiarly apt: the same word, *ayah*, denotes both the verses of the Muslim scripture and the ordinary or extraordinary events transpiring in a natural environment under divine sovereignty.

A sign is enough for the wise – and Nature abounds with the signs of Allah. But only the heedful can detect them; one needs to discipline emotion in the hinterland of a religious obligation to interpret the natural world as the locus of the divine providence. It is a religious duty to acquaint oneself properly with Nature: men should learn to be arrested by the beauties of the created world while simultaneously cultivating the capacity to marvel at an underlying normative order in which power, mercy and justice are continuously sustained in a perfect equilibrium. Thus, in the moods of the seasons, the tempers of natural forces and the pregnant silence of the empty space, the truly vigilant student should be able to discern (decode, if you wish) not merely the material for science, technology and secular marvel but also, and more importantly, a powerful if subtly concealed testimony to the glories of an altogether blameless sovereignty.

Tragedy and triumph are both the fruits of perception. Men refuse, laments the sacred author, to bring a proper attentiveness – a reverent facility – to their perception of the events in external Nature (K:40:61; 63; 27:73; 10:60; etc.). Many are heedless (*ghafil*) and callous; others fall victim to the temptations of paganism, seduced by the temporary benefits of the illusory technique of magic. Few indeed recognise the ubiquitous presence of a merciful providence that counteracts their failings (K:34:13; 36:33–46). A wanton humanity that misreads, sometimes despises, the multiple tokens of Allah's goodness, becomes in time justly the victim of his wrath.

II

Do the heavens still declare the glory of Allah? The contemporary mind sees clearly enough the natural world but, in general, the spirit of God that somehow (allegedly) pervades the created order completely eludes it. Nor is this due to any lack of interest in Nature and her ways. Contemporary scientists have thoroughly probed the external world up to the very limits of the observable universe; and many a poet continues to marvel at Nature's charms, extolling an almost humbling gravity that is perhaps most poignantly experienced in the company of a lover. But there is in general though not always (there are countless notable exceptions)[5] a firm if familiar refusal to assign any theological significance to this knowledge and experience of Nature except in a purely metaphorical way. Must Nature elicit a specifically religious response from the heedful observer? Are our disbelieving scientists and poets then necessarily heedless (*ghafil*)?

The religiosity of Nature is no longer an experienced reality for the modern mind. For our forefathers, desirous of being reared in the lap of divine providence, the experience of the religious dimension of Nature became an integral part of their consciousness of the world. Intuitions of the divine saturated their experience of the external environment. Nor was such experience akin to some inferred religious demand or merely a decree waiting to be realised in practice. Rather, their intuition was similar to a sensation. The heavens declared the glory of God.

The religious character of Nature is of course significantly less palpable than its purely physical one. Thus, the human perception of the signs of God allegedly present within Nature is unlike the perception, say, of the odour of the trees on a sultry summer day or, to take one of Nature's subtler moods, the aspect of a deserted road on an autumn evening. Men can and often do think of these features as beautiful. Even this is a relatively uncontroversial judgement: most of us possess an aesthetic sensibility. But the claim about the religiosity of Nature somehow mysteriously secreted through its purely physical character – that remains controversial.

Many people, except those who have totally lost sympathy with the religious ideal, have felt a quasi-religious sense of sanctuary in some particularly beautiful spot in a secluded wilderness. For many of us this is an experience, not merely, so to speak, the inferred requirement of an abstract piety. But, as it happens, the religiosity of Nature can always be seen today as simply an optional addition to a purely secular or profane interpretation. It is important to be clear about the issue here.

It is not so much that a man must be able to prove to others that what he takes to be the glory of God is indeed the glory of God. That would be an unreasonable demand: there are few important truths that are capable of conclusive demonstration. Nor is it that one insists that the sacred must come within the purview of everyone's consciousness in order to be genuinely sacred. The problem simply is that for whatever we experience, there is, arguably, always an adequate secular explanation at hand. Unprejudiced observation often sincerely fails, it would appear, to detect the hand of God in Nature.

This brings us more directly to the problem of the ultimate character of the natural world. For the religious believer, it is both the focus of purely human interest as such while simultaneously concealing an invitation to discover an underlying order in which righteousness is applauded. The signs of God have a transcendent reference but are somehow mysteriously mediated through the ordinary natural environment. Men need to educate their potentially religious instincts in order to recognise these signs for what they are – in order to read them properly.

Now Nature is, like all ambiguous articles, necessarily subject to more than one interpretation and, consequently, open to potential misunderstanding and abuse. Thus, a man may study Nature and her sequences but do so out of purely theoretical secular interest. He may also, through the exploitation that technique renders possible, dominate her or partly alter her course or simply extract some benefit from her serviceability. And yet he may refuse to concern himself with Nature's potentially *religious* gravity and significance. From a religious point of view, such an explorer remains simply an explorer: he is not a worshipper.

The point is important and worth labouring. Let us take our cue – nothing more – from the admittedly questionable if popular metaphor of the veil. God veils himself in Nature in order to approach his creation with care and caution: he both hides himself and yet reveals himself, to say something that sounds strikingly Pascalian. But, as with the popular practice of the woman's veil, such an arrangement cannot, in the nature of the case, exclude the possibility of abuse, even of total misuse. The veil, originally intended for dignified seclusion and reverent invitation, is yet capable of deteriorating, in the hands of female adventurism, into an instrument of seductive provocation. Similarly with Nature: to understand and subdue her through crass exploitation and the irreligious supremacy of technical manipulation is precisely to misunderstand her, to fail to note her original and intended function.

Thus it is that the heavens declare the glory of Allah – but only to the heedful penitent. And yet how is it a *declaration*? If one needs to educate one's instincts, to place them under the tutelage of a specific order of piety, in order to recognise the signs of God for what they really are, this recognition, when achieved, cannot, by definition, be a part of the psychological foundations of common sense. For common sense alone does not seem to suggest that the external world is in fact a concealed testament of praise – the praise of a supremely righteous transcendent Will.

III

I need to digress briefly now in order to record a hackneyed strand of argument, still very popular in Muslim circles, before returning presently to the larger problem of the current failure to discern the signs of God in Nature.

I began this chapter by quoting two religious poems, one by Addison, the other by Iqbal. I could, however, also have cited the views of one of the sceptical protagonists in David Hume's seminal *Dialogues Concerning Natural Religion*: the created world as we have it today may well be the work of some 'infant deity' or of a deity 'ashamed of his lame performance'. Nature is, it may be argued, imperfect; her operations are a mixed blessing providing as they do material both for gratitude and trust as well as for rejection and cynicism.

Many modern thinkers have carefully argued that neither the existence nor the character of the natural world supports the conclusion that it is the medium of manifestation of a morally constrained supernatural power. It is a striking feature of revealed scripture that it principally bases the accumulation of evidence for God's existence and activity *not* on the fact that there is a world at all but rather on its assumption of a given actual character. This is particularly true of the Koran with its explicit and frequent appeal to the flawless harmony of Nature to which every obedient Muslim responds with admiration. God's world is perfect, created as it is, in the Koran's phrase, 'in accordance with the requirements of wisdom' (K:15:85; 16:3). Unfortunately, however, there has appeared now much sophisticated argument to show that the actual *character* of the world is particularly incompatible with the existence of a morally and metaphysically perfect creator. The natural order, it has been argued, is not in any obvious way dominated by a purposeful harmony that conceals the authorship of some benevolent intellect.

The contention is familiar; examples are unnecessary and we need not stop our tale to probe the issue in detail. It is, however, worth recording and commenting on one standard (and extremely popular) religious rejoinder. Surely, it may be said, it is 'impossible' to believe that Nature, in all her grandeur and detail, simply happens to exist, simply happens to be what she appears to be, namely, a reality devoid of any sustaining transcendent agency. The short and unsympathetic way with this is of course to retort that modern scientists have satisfactorily assigned to the concept of Nature complete autonomy and that, therefore, the residual problem of human incredulity in the face of the sheer beauty of the natural order is more or less an issue in the psychology of wonder.

This may appear to be a rather flippant suggestion. But the fact remains that wonder or amazement do not conclusively support any *logical* demand for explanation any more than the fact that one is hungry implies the availability of food. No argument can be based solely on an emotive claim; even if men's awe in the face of the cosmos psychologically demands a theistic explanation, it does not logically require it. Thus, the very existence of the natural world, surprising and remarkable as it is to most of us in one mood or another, cannot in itself entail the existence of a divine architect. In fine, then, neither the fact that there *is* a world at all nor the fact that it is what it actually is can conclusively support a theistic explanation.

IV

Classical theism made no distinction between laws of Nature and the normative signs of God. The divine ordinances were, no less than the lawful natural regularities, wrought into the fabric of the universe; indeed they were often thought to be identical with natural laws. The ultimate constitution of the world was thought, indeed experienced, to be simultaneously both factual and evaluative, natural and normative.

With the emergence of the fact–value distinction – unarguably among the most influential discoveries in the history of ideas[6] – and the concomitant triumph of the modern scientific outlook, religious values ceased to be experienced as immanent in the external environment. Indeed, in time men began to see the natural world as autonomous, as both morally and metaphysically neutral in character; the very idea of a sustaining agency behind Nature was slowly expunged, completing the destruction of the notion that divine forces operated within the empirical realm. So the elimination of purposes and goals allegedly inherent in Nature was the essential step towards the achievement of completely value-free autonomy for Nature. The world was itself, it was said, the ultimate reality.

Muslims have always thought that the world is full of miracles in the sense of indications and intimations of the infinite and mysterious even in the familiar finite phenomena of daily existence. Allah's activities are, it is believed, typically mediated through a sustaining providence rather than through miracles interpreted as divinely planned spectacular derogations of natural law that effectively weaken or discountenance hesitancy and perverse unbelief. It is this picture of a ubiquitous divine presence that is rejected by the scientific *Lebenswelt*.

In our secularised age the experience of the external world seems compatible with two rival and incompatible interpretations, sustaining as it does both naturalistic and theistic world-outlooks. Our current experience is often ambiguous. The alleged signs of God in Nature no longer compel recognition. Unlike his forefathers, modern man sees theism as over-determining (as opposed to simply determining) the shape of his experience since there is always, it is thought, an adequate secular explanation at hand.

These are not the halcyon days of faith. In the past it was thought that God would occasionally intervene in the world, launch an intrigue, reveal a mystery – effectively tangle the course of Nature and human lives. But the modern sky seems empty. This is certainly a distressing circumstance for the religionist; the retreat of the divine forces from the external world is damaging to the theistic outlook. After all, Nature's beauties alone could still conclusively outdo the technological marvels of modern science.

V

'Allah is shouting,' says the believer, 'but we turn a deaf ear.' We have here a characteristically orthodox claim that will serve to introduce the larger context of our discussion. The detailed examination of the koranic account of rejection and the current sceptical response to it will together occupy us in the next chapter.

Men, then, perversely refuse to hearken to the call of the minaret; though they see Allah's portents in Nature and elsewhere, they turn a blind eye. A forbearing and merciful Lord runs out of patience; and permanently if reluctantly debars some men from receiving the gift of grace.

What are we to make of this? It cannot be sufficiently emphasised that we today are living in the age of realisation, not revelation, as Muslim scholars themselves admit. The age is past in which the Lord of Creation looked down daily in anger or compassion on his wayward flock. God may still be somehow responsible for all that occurs – through the mechanism of a sustaining providence – but he does not appear to intervene regularly now in Nature and human community. God is silent today.

Muslims do concede that Allah no longer reveals himself in the old manner: the whole apparatus of prophethood and scripture has been abolished. But, and this is the significant point, this current silence on God's part is not seen as being in any way theologically problematic or puzzling. Rather, it is thought to be both natural and justified. The coming of the prophet Muhammad has set the seal on prophecy. Why should Allah speak again?

It seems to me, however, that in justifying the ways of the Almighty to the modern questioning mentality – to pursue Milton's ambition – the current silence of God takes a place at least as prominent as the more time-honoured problem of the calamity of natural and moral evil. The problem of evil has been and remains, in all civilised communities, among the most enduring sources of the rejection of a powerful yet just creator. My own view is that the religious perplexity about God's radical inaccessibility and essential elusiveness could, in the decades to come, become for modern sensibilities an even richer source of argumentative material in favour of a reluctant agnosticism if not an outright atheism.

We need to note these theological conundrums against the background supplied by an aggressively secular culture. The modern reservation about the truth of the religious metaphysic is deep and radical. Indeed, one may perhaps conveniently gauge the extent of this truth by noting that since the rise of logical positivism – a kind of Marxist materialism for philosophers – men have experienced difficulties not only in *accepting* the monotheistic outlook but, more fundamentally, in even *grasping* a particular version of it. Thus, the ancient worry about putting the cart before the horse in matters religious – the problem of the priority of faith over reason and the associated question of the rationality of religious conviction – has been recently replaced by the more basic worry about whether or not there is a horse to pull the cart. The question of the very coherence and intelligibility of transcendent theism heads the modern agenda.[7]

VI

The silence of God in this increasingly religionless age is certainly damaging to the faithful outlook. It does seem to open up the possibility of supplying impressively plausible cases for the atheistic stance. Indeed it creates a serious doubt about God's alleged miraculous activities even in the past. Is it not an arguably superior assumption that the different human claims about the miraculous are better explicable in terms of a cultural shift in our thinking rather than in terms of God's decision to introduce in recent years a basic alteration in his ways? Given the credulity and gullibility of early man, his ignorance of the moods of Nature – an ignorance poorly compensated by the pagan appeal to magic and its illusory technique – the atheist's suggestion is surely not altogether implausible.

The current silence of Allah could spell a crisis for Muslim faith. Nature is as revealing as it is ambiguous, hence of course the need for a revelation in a sacred language in the first place. The God of Islam seems to have retreated from Nature and community, the two matrices in which, according to religious believers, he typically used to reveal himself. To be sure, no one thinks that his arm is any shorter today. Yet it remains the case that his activities in recent history and the modern environment are difficult to discern in any satisfactorily uncontroversial fashion. Allah is no anaemic, idle god. If so, why is he silent today even in the face of widespread rejection and strident requests for self-disclosure?

Someone could object to such a proposal for conclusive self-disclosure on the grounds that faith requires ambiguity in our experience of Nature and life. If men knew there was a God, they could not have faith in him. This is a spurious worry. Faith (*iman*) can co-exist with knowledge (*'ilm*): since men are perverse, they can reject God even if they have knowledge of his existence. The Koran recognises this in the suggestion that unbelief (*kufr*) is really just culpable self-deception. The rejector conceals the truth in bad faith. The sinners, then, are under no obligation to believe what they know: to be able to reject the truth is merely one of the many privileges of sinful perversity.

Why, then, does God not reveal himself openly today? Is it not a *religious* demand that God reveal himself to us again in a manner at least as dramatic as that in the past? With the proliferation of belief-systems, both religious and secular, it is essential to know how to discern which, if any, is or are true or partly true. Since the religious life involves in significant part the entertainment of correct belief (as Islam and Roman Catholicism so pre-eminently insist) the prevalence of doubt and unbelief raises a serious religious problem. If the responsibility for faith or unfaith rests with each of us, perhaps we may reasonably expect God to disclose himself to mankind in every age and circumstance. Perhaps we today need a miracle, candidly performed, in order effectively to sort out our scandalously ambivalent current intellectual situation *vis-à-vis* faith and rejection.

How would believers react to these claims? Some will be unsympathetic: there are, and there should be, no such theological puzzles for the pious mind. Allah or the Holy Spirit or some other transcendent agency is still, it will be said, daily revealing his will to those whose hearts are pure. I see in this familiar orthodox reaction a kind of bloody-minded will to obscurantism. For the undeniable fact is that the extent of our isolation from God in this age is increasingly heavy on the heart of every reflective believer whether Jewish, Christian or Muslim. A man of faith could indeed legitimately see in our current circumstance, as the Rev. Kenneth Cragg does, 'the sheer generousness and diffidence' of a God who has allowed the denial of the divine to remain a human prerogative.[8] But it seems harder simply to deny the reality of our modern predicament. Obviously, the atheist cannot be expected to have any sympathy with Cragg's essentially religious interpretation of the current silence of God. But sympathy or no sympathy, the silence of God is a fact both undeniable and religiously disturbing.

Nor can we conscientiously avoid the implications here. Indeed it could be the case that, in the absence of a conclusive proof of God's reality, and given the current deadlock between faith and rejection as well as the age-old impasse between any one faith and its religious rivals, one justifiable modern attitude towards the will and purposes (if not the very existence) of a divine being is a reluctant agnosticism, itself rooted in intellectual integrity and sincere reservation. It is not the heedless alone who today need a new sign from Heaven.

Part 2

THE VIRTUES OF HERESY

Ah, love! Could thou and I
With Fate conspire
To grasp this sorry
Scheme of things entire,
Would we not shatter it
To bits – and remould it
Nearer to the heart's desire!

'Umar Khayyam

The Wisdom of the Fool

It is perhaps not only the foolish who today have said in their hearts 'There is no God' (*La ilah ha*). Many thoughtful human beings are finding it increasingly difficult to discern an order under benevolent supervision. Ever since modern science and its auxiliary technology together desecrated a traditional life lived close to Nature and her harmonies, an increasingly large number of people have, especially in western and western-influenced societies, been unable to locate the gracious providence that had once secured them against the indifferent caprices of history and destiny.[1] The modern fool has perhaps fallaciously but not unreasonably said in his heart, 'If God is nowhere to be found, then there is no God.'

In this chapter I shall begin with a detailed examination of the koranic account of rejection (*kufr*) and shall set it, in subsequent sections, in a dialectically fruitful tension with the current sceptical response. In doing so, I shall extract a theory about rejection and embrace which, while not exhaustive or satisfactorily nuanced, is, I hope, more sensitive to the crisis of secularity than is the standard received account. I shall then make some comments on the theological puzzles generated by the current silence of God, thereby picking up again the issues outlined at the end of the previous chapter.

I

Men's rejection of the sovereignty of Allah is one of the Koran's ruling preoccupations. Much of the Muslim scripture is, in effect, a document about the consequences of rejecting the momentous doctrine of the divine unity. God, warns incessantly the sacred author, is not a superfluity. Whatever their private opinions on the subject, men need Allah. In a world visibly labouring under the burden of a conclusive if deferred nemesis, it is merely a dangerously tragic delusion to fancy that one could sin with impunity, let alone prosper without the grace of God.

Rejection (*kufr*) is, according to the Koran, a deeply damaging form of deliberate perfidy to the higher believing aspect of human nature. Unbelief is a wilful rejection of a truth one secretly acknowledges. ('*Kufr*' literally means to 'conceal or cover up the truth'.) Out of hubris and perversity, men prefer their own self-destructive folly to the wisdom of a merciful God and thereby place themselves outside the ambit of his grace. Their intellectual self-deceit alone leads them to concoct specious defences of an admittedly indefensible posture – a posture that itself thrives on culpable prevarication. In rejecting God, men betray a woeful ignorance of their own religious best interests. Rejection totally ruins a man – for it ruins him for ever. Its calamitous consequences extend beyond death into all eternity.

The Koran's overall portrait of the rejector (*kafir*) is unflattering. There is no saving grace here: the disbeliever is a totally ignorant, perverse, hard-hearted, presumptuous, disobedient and, above all, ungrateful human being. He is accused of being worse than an animal on account of his refusal to ponder the signs of God (K:8:55). The rejector is, says the sacred author, in a particularly intriguing phrase, a 'stranger to truth' (K:16:22). Naturally, the disbeliever is not fit company for the believer whose life displays such qualities of character as gratitude (*shukr*) – a quality the Koran opposes to the ingratitude (*kufr*) of the rejector.

II

Knowing what rejection is or implies is one thing, explaining it is another. And for the purpose of explaining unbelief, the Koran, like all sacred literature in the Hebrew tradition, is of limited assistance and relevance. In the Koran itself, no less than in the Old Testament and the Gospels, unbelief appears as a well-nigh incomprehensible phenomenon: at best a most radical kind of stupidity, at worst madness. The *kafir* is stupid: he ought to know better. At the least, he is in 'manifest error' (*dalal-im-mobeen*).

The Koran discusses in some detail the many moods of rejection – the varieties of the disbelieving posture found both in the Prophet's Arabia and in previous sacred history. Rejection never seems to be due to incredulity or plain ignorance. It is due, variously, to heedlessness, indifference and unconcern, a complacency itself rooted in an unduly optimistic assessment of human potential, sinful rebellion and obstinacy, perversity and spiritual myopia. It exhibits itself, variously, as a casual neglect of Allah's ordinances, as lapse and hypocrisy punctuated by occasional belief, a deliberate and obdurate negligence of the divine, and indeed, in many cases – as for example in the case of the Qureish and of Pharaoh – as a militant refusal to acknowledge realities harmful to vested profane interests.

Rejection is deeply puzzling to the faithful temper. In the Judaeo–

Christian tradition, disbelief is explained in part as being the result of a hardening of hearts by divine arbitrium. Within the Islamic tradition, rejection is thought so incomprehensibly asinine (K:2:130; 2:171) that a similarly crude machinery of setting seals on hearts and covers on eyes and ears by divine fiat (K:2:7) is seen as constituting a more credible explanation than the religiously puzzling possibility that men can somehow sincerely prefer to remain aloof from the gift of grace. To be sure, God only hardens the hearts of those who wilfully reject him; after repeated rejection, Allah permanently debars a man from receiving his grace (K:7:100–1; 10:74).

The Koran's standard explanation for rejection is in terms of the normal human proclivity to heedlessness (*ghaflah*), a cause that is mentioned often and in an astonishingly large variety of contexts. The charge is that men are forgetful of a truth they (secretly) acknowledge in their more reflective moods. The Koran's constant appeal to reason and sentiment (through parable and edifying narrative) would suggest that *ghaflah* is a complex compound of a self-imposed limit of imagination in alliance with an obstinately fierce resistance of will. Beyond that, unbelief, as man's radical resistance to the will of Allah, is merely condemned, the unbelievers vigorously excoriated for the refusal to acknowledge their creaturely dependence. Unfortunately these bitter diatribes against the hubristic rejection of Allah's sovereignty are of little explanatory value.

Our search for explanation could lead us to look at the Koran's relatively detailed discussion of the phenomenon of hypocrisy in the religious life (K:8:49; 9:66–8; 9:72ff.; 63:1–8) – a phenomenon that is, in the Koran, intimately associated with ordinary unbelief. As it happens, the discussion here is in a primarily political (as opposed to heart-searching or meditative) context; the main concern is to eradicate the social menace of duplicity in the midst of a faithful community still struggling in its infancy. The treatment of the issue is naturally legalistic and, in our modern eyes, perhaps somewhat perfunctory and unsympathetic. But one important relevant point emerges. The Koran draws no sharp distinction between hypocrisy (*nifaq*) and rejection (*kufr*). This ambiguity is no doubt deliberate; and it seems to imply that both these culpable attitudes have a common origin in the human personality, are species of a single ailment. This ailment is the human proclivity to recruit perversity in the service of self-deception. Men are treacherous towards their own better or higher nature, hence rejection. Placed in a social context, we have a betrayal of the believing society, hence hypocrisy. The suggestion would appear to be that unbelief is itself a species of hypocrisy – towards oneself.

Neither unbelief nor hypocrisy is identified, in the Koran, with straightforward impiety or sinful disobedience. After all, believers, even seminal religious figures, also sin and disobey God.[2] What then is the crucial causative difference between faith and rejection? Several *surahs* make cryptic references to an actual disease (*marad*), presumably spiritual, which flourishes in the sinful hearts of hypocrites and rejectors alike (K:8:49; 33:12) and which is increased by Allah as a recompense for the hard-hearted perversity of man (K:2:10).

Beyond this, we have little to go on. The Koran is not primarily concerned to offer theoretical explanations for rejection. Rather its concern is with faith, the demands of faith, and the many difficulties in sustaining it in the face of Satan's enmity to man. It may fairly and, I believe reverently, be said that the koranic material is, by itself, clearly deficient for the purpose of developing any adequate theory of modern rejection – a theory about the causes of *kufr* in its varied forms.

III

If a theology of rejection should begin within the compass of revealed scripture, it cannot end there. The Koran's encounter with rejection is limited in extent and variety; consequently its discussions are lacking in scope. It is not so much that the author of the sacred volume uses too wide a mesh to catch the details that would concern his *original* readers; it's simply that *our* experience of rejection is much richer today.

Before I begin to deal with the problem of the modern rejection of God, one extremely important point, which has significant ramifications, needs to be made at the outset. There is a danger that the author of the Koran and the modern sceptic are talking at cross-purposes. The Torah, the Gospels and the Muslim scripture all famously presuppose that the question of the reality of God is a primarily practical rather than speculative (or theoretical) one. The issue of God's metaphysical existence is touched on at best indirectly through the issue of his uniqueness. Worship, not intellectual assent, is the focus of religious faith. Thus, the Koran, like all monotheistic sacred literature, makes the question of the reality or unreality of Allah a matter exclusively for practical resolution, for practical acknowledgment or denial – never for purely theoretical interest or for purely intellectual certitude. Presumably, the notion of a theoretical atheism that disputes the very existence of a transcendent being (or indeed, in the latest fashion, the very coherence of such a concept) was not a live issue in the age of revelation – much as the issue of the objective existence of other minds or the external world has never been a live issue for the overwhelming majority of people in all ages and cultures.

The existence of God, then, and *a fortiori* the coherence of the very notion of God, were thought too obvious to stand in need of elaborate proof. The modern folly of speculative atheism was, if you wish, thought to be unthinkably mad. The real question, as the Prophet and his contemporaries saw it, was whether or not one could maintain a conformity between the creaturely human will and the divine will for man

– with the attendant fear that men were somehow inevitably doomed to lapse into a damnably casual relation to Allah and his ordinances by failing to live up to the admittedly exacting demands of koranic piety. *Kufr*, then, was not metaphysical disbelief in the reality of a divine being but rather a practical neglect that informed one's daily life.

The point here is important if elementary. And it is not always clearly noted. 'Nothing,' writes Sartre, 'can save a man from himself, not even a valid proof of the existence of God.'[3] Sartre's observation is not without a point but it is beside the point. A valid argument could save no one – from anything. (Even a sound argument wouldn't save a man, though this is a technical quibble.) The important point here is that the emphasis in which faith is seen as being more than an intellectual aptitude is itself a characteristically *religious* one. Sartre's claim is true but misleading; if proofs alone were powerful enough to save, one would hardly need active piety, let alone the grace of God.

IV

We are now in a position to begin a detailed investigation into the problem of the modern rejection of the divine.

In the advanced industrial societies of the contemporary world, many observers have noted a marked scepticism about the reality of a divine purpose for human existence. Such scepticism is, *prima facie* at least, both intellectually well grounded and morally worthy in its character. It is, to all appearances, sincere in its refusal to locate a gracious providence behind the dark saga of humanity and the ambiguous mercies of Nature. Certainly, modern atheism challenges the complacent spokesman for theism who claims that the cosmic order conceals powerful testimony to a providential project.

In the past most men instinctively believed in an inherently religious purpose within human life and Nature. Religions crystallised and institutionalised this instinct. Founders of faiths certainly showed men a purpose if not a reason for living. With a sufficiently absorbing purpose, thought the disillusioned man, one can always put up with yet another season of torment. After all, the worry has always been: 'Why should I live?' And to this it was sufficient to answer that no one needs to die merely for want of a purpose. It was often recognised that the religious purpose was one which reason alone could never establish. But, fortunately, a defeat for rationality is one thing; a defeat for teleology another.

The religious goal for life, however, has become increasingly irrelevant for many people in modern societies. Nor has it become so without consideration and reflection. Indeed, there has often been an extraordinary amount of thinking behind such rejection of a God-given purpose. And at the end of such reflection, there has rarely been the exultation of a triumphant emancipation but rather a kind of reluctant despair that recognises the sordidness of life without celestial foundation.[4]

The burden of life must somehow be borne, without succumbing to illusion and the comforts it brings. This is always the hope – both the devout and the secular hope. The modern rejector often reasons that given our knowledge of the social and individual causality of human lives, the sophisticated body of theory about the grounds and motives for the acceptance of traditional theistic faith, the current chaos in the human world, the irreducibly ambiguous aspects of a Nature that sustains religious as well as profane interpretations, and the deadlock between faith and rejection – the case for theism, he reasons, is bleak. Accordingly he opts for rejection.

Now, given the nature and context of contemporary denial, the orthodox religious claim that atheism is *always* insincere is, it would seem, to put it minimally, questionable. Certainly, the claim that unbelief is always insincere is not well-evidenced. No one has shown, with any degree of plausibility, that a man cannot sincerely reject God for sound theoretical and moral reasons.

Let me pursue this a little. The claim that all men believe in the existence of God, that the knowledge of God is a part of our natural endowment as human beings, is in need of elaborate justification, especially in our secularised age. The Islamic tradition has emphasised the centrality of this conviction but few Muslims have *argued* for it. Many a Muslim writer will quote, with routine conviction, the koranic passage (K:7:172) according to which the postulate of Allah's unity is inscribed in human nature.[5] Since all of us have already professed the monotheistic faith, the Koran is, as it describes itself – among its many honourable titles – just a *reminder* to a heedless humanity. Thus, men have been reminded of the eternal covenant between Allah and the descendants of Adam. Consistently with these claims the Koran implies that no one radically lacks the potential for acquiring the faculty appropriate to belief,[6] although many men do, of course, deliberately suppress the will to acquire it. Small wonder then that the rejector is charged with moral blame.

These are important claims, the truth of which cannot be taken for granted, least of all today. Is belief in God indeed natural? Is it intrinsic to human nature? Are men born believers – then sometimes perverted into disbelief? Or are they indeed born atheists – and later perverted into theism? Belief in the divine seems natural to some people and yet, to others, it seems strange, strangely difficult, even rather unnatural. Take, as an extreme case, the scepticism of an Ivan Karamazov in Dostoyevsky's *The Brothers Karamazov*. Here is a man who earnestly wants to be, indeed humanly needs to be, religious but simply cannot bring himself round to being so. He fails, sincerely fails, to discern a beneficent supernatural force behind the human condition. Or take, as a less extreme case, the milder, less dramatic yet none the less genuine scepticism of some of Thomas Hardy's characters, especially Angel Clare in *Tess of the D'Urbervilles*. Nor will it do to say that these are fictional characters. To be sure, they are, but their counterparts in real life and experience are easily found. Whatever we may finally say here, belief does not seem equally natural to all of us; and yet I would argue that the truth of the traditional religious claim would imply that religious conviction is *roughly* equally natural to all human beings in all contexts of existence.

This is not the place to develop an empirical sociology of faithful conviction. But one or two brief, admittedly desultory, remarks are worth making now if only to give a flavour of the full dish. Belief in God is certainly related to temperament and has some interesting connections with human traits such as intelligence – although it is generally independent of circumstance. Thus, an easy life need not lead to faith any more than a difficult one leads to rejection. Religious conviction is not explicable in terms of excess or lack of intelligence but paradigm cases of both faith and rejection involve men of exceptional intelligence. Thus, many great saints have been great thinkers: Anselm, Aquinas, Augustine, al-Ghazzali and Maimonides immediately spring to mind. And many profound thinkers have been consciously and emphatically inclined towards rejection: Nietzsche, Marx and Bakunin would head the list.

Although religious belief is said to be natural – with the implied assumption that atheism is unnatural – presumably such belief remains a matter of responsible choice. Men should consciously choose to believe rather than disbelieve. And yet the notion that belief is related to choice or volition is itself *prima facie* odd. Can one really choose to believe in something – a proposition or an entity? Can one choose to disbelieve in God if such belief arises naturally in the human mind? There are of course recognised techniques for inducing belief in God, such as deliberately living in environments of great religious fervour (in deference to the maxim 'Faith is caught not taught'), cultivating habits of intended devotion ('O God, if you exist, quell my sincere doubts') and so on. But if faith is natural to us, why is it so hard to come by, so difficult to sustain? Is it indeed a matter of choice, a deliberate and responsible choice?

One final remark: it is often said by religionists that rejection is due to self-deception. Men deliberately – if you wish, *choose* to – ignore or suppress the religious truth. But is this indeed true? Is rejection due to self-deception? Are even extremely perceptive students of human nature – men like Nietzsche and Sartre – simply deluded about their self-image? And if rejection is due to self-deception, is such self-deception necessarily immoral? Presumably, self-deception, as the cognitive component of sin, is held to be culpable because it is thought to be, after due effort, avoidable. But it could be the case that self-deception is actually rooted in weakness of will or even some quirk of temperament rather than active perversity. If so, it is more problematic to say that self-deception is avoidable and hence immoral. Now the failure to believe in God is itself a moral failure to live up to a religious demand. If so, it must be a matter of guilty (and hence responsible) choice. The traditional religious explanation for the failure to make the correct choice is, of course, that men fall victim to self-deception. I am suggesting that this claim is questionable on a variety of grounds.

V

'Faint not,' exhorts *surah* 4 (v.105), 'in seeking the heathen; if you are suffering, they are also suffering as you are suffering; but you can hope from God for that for which they cannot hope.' There is no hope for those who reject the signs of Allah: their deeds are as insubstantial as the ashes which the wind on a tempestuous day scatters forth in all directions (K:14:18). God has rendered vain all their works though these may appear beautiful in their own eyes. Their deeds, says *surah* 24 (v.39) are like a mirage in a spacious plain which appears as water to the thirsty man, yet when he comes to it, he finds it is nothing. Instead, there he finds God – and tastes the bitter draught of nemesis.

A harsh verdict, no doubt; and one that will serve to carry us forward into our theme. Perhaps it is suited to its age for, to be sure, those who lived in an environment as religiously charged as seventh-century Arabia may well have been hard put to reject the prophetic message. When the Almighty's hand could almost be seen in history, rejection was arguably unreasonable and sinfully presumptuous. The sacred author could legitimately lament a generation who saw and yet still sought to bite the very hand that fed them. It is for this reason that *surah* 111 voices a fierce condemnation of the disbelieving Abu Lahab – the only opponent of the Prophet who is singled out by name for special censure in the sacred text. A forbearing God in alliance with a patient and long-suffering Muhammad try to obtain salvation for this man; yet he himself leaves no stone unturned in his efforts to destroy his benefactor. This kind of rejector's heart may indeed be said to be 'uncircumcised' (K:2:88); his reward unsurprisingly is Hell – 'an evil journey's end' (K:4:97).

Modern rejection cannot uncritically be classed in the same category. It is today, often enough, based on honest doubt and sincere disbelief themselves inspired by complex worries about the very coherence of the theistic picture, its plausibility in an age of reason and religious pluralism, and its moral potential. Surely such sincere reservation can be neither a sin nor a crime. It *is* theologically puzzling that sincere unfaith can exist at all. But it does seem to exist. And we see that once we ask: '*Why* hath the fool said in his heart . . . ?' It is wrong for the religionist to content himself with a perfunctory analysis of the complexity of rejection. It is, it seems to me, entirely impossible to take the full measure of the seriousness of rejection and impossible to retrieve atheistic humanism, unless one revises the older image of the rejector and of the rejecting society. Abu Lahab should have been hard put to reject Islam when he could almost see the hand of the Almighty. But is that true of our modern rejectors?, Who, then, is the fool who hath said in his heart . . . ? Is it indeed, say, Bertrand Russell or Karl Marx or Nietzsche?

There is, within the koranic world, an uncompromising opposition between faith and rejection. The whole of the Muslim scripture throbs with the tempo of this fateful choice. The community of faith, as a group set apart and dedicated to the service of God, is emphatically distinguished and separated from the disbelieving society. The subsequent Islamic tradition has rigidly maintained the integrity of the same political division between the household of faith and the household of rejection. Once the former becomes effectively co-extensive with the whole world (or at least the whole of the civilised world), the distinction will disappear. But until that time comes, the world of rejection is of concern to Islam only as a place to be subdued or at least segregated from the believing society. After all, the pious Muslim thinks, what fellowship (to borrow a Christian phrase inspired by the same impulse) hath darkness with light?

But darkness hath fellowship with light – because of the failings of our common humanity, the bond of common origin and common limitation. It is a truism that the rejector is also a human being living and dying in the same world and within essentially the same metaphysical parameters. The rejector's humanity cannot be denied on pain of rendering this entire dispute pointless. For his humanity is the *raison d'être* for our attempt to rescue him from the clutches of rejection.

This is an important point with important implications. The believer must see the rejector as a fellow human being who deserves care and respect. To be sure, God has every right to see the *kafir* (or indeed anyone else) as a misguided fool worthy only of condescension and disdain. But such a privilege cannot extend to the believer who is himself often no less a moral failure than his fellow rejector. The believer must today think of a way, a characteristically modern way, of taking rejection seriously. Now, the Koran takes rejection very seriously, after its own fashion. The threat of the fiery furnace alternating with the occasional gentler plea may indeed have constituted the appropriate strategy for dealing with rejection in the age of revelation. Certainly, the author of the Koran is never condescending; and Allah takes the question of human rejection seriously enough to have made a Hell for those who don't.

And yet a modern Muslim cannot take all his cues from the koranic attitude to rejection. We must develop a characteristically modern way of handling denial. And the first step towards doing that is to see the sinful and rejecting society for what it really is – an attempt often obscured if not wholly frustrated by an unforgiving, narrow-hearted, almost pharisaic morality. The world of rejection is a world composed of individual sinners, individual failures, individual workers, individual criminals, individual prostitutes, individual thinkers, individual men, individual women – each cutting out his or her own path to a dusty and inevitable death. Too often there is a tendency to see the rejecting community as if it, like the larger world of which it is a part, were some elusive realm, somehow irreducibly evil, given over to a conscious and deliberate desire for wrongdoing, without the saving grace that even unintended virtue brings in its train.

VI

'It is a characteristic feature of an irreligious age that it takes humanity more seriously than divinity: "Glory be to man" is its motto.' We can well imagine such an orthodox religious reaction to the contents of the preceding section. There is a whole specifically religious vocabulary for expressing one's rejection of any excessive concern with the human world at the expense of the supernatural. The orthodox religionist will piously distance himself from the current obsession with man – the purely human rational heritage, the autonomy of the secular intellect, and the whole of the kudos that now attaches to enlightened man. Contemporary man's excessive respect for the human and the natural, it will be said, is the reason for his alienation from the divine. Modern man is an idolater: in making himself a god, he naturally cannot tolerate another.[7]

To be sure, it is said that our idolatry (*shirk*) in the contemporary mood is different from the ancient varieties: it is subtler. The modern pagan does not lose sight of Allah's sovereignty in a whirl of false divinities carved out of wood and stone.[8] Rather he loses it in the proud secular sense of his own self-sufficiency as a human being in possession of supremacy over Nature and destiny – without any help from Heaven. What are the mechanics of this new idolatry? Men, the apologists claim, can suppress but not destroy their knowledge of God. This, we are told, is evidenced by their desire both to reject God and yet to invent a substitute deity to take his place. In this way, men allow purely human realities to exhaust an allegiance properly owed to the divine ruler alone. Now, the void created by dethroning God is filled with a variety of realities, all human, the subtlety of the replacement varying considerably. 'Wine, women, and song' (in Johann Strauss's memorable phrase) are enough to ruin the majority of mankind. For others, notably the Sufis and mystics in other religious traditions, it is the egocentric predicament that is the ultimate locus of inveterate idolatry; the idolatry of the self-centred sinner persists as long as God is second in the queue. Between these extremes are all the varied deceptions of our condition: the perversity of a jingoism that can boast 'My country, right or wrong, Left or Right', the desire for wealth and the privileges it brings in its train, the error of trusting in the deliverances of human reason and the efficacy of secular education and technique, the illusory and transient charms of a romantic love that culminates in the heavy burden of marriage and progeny, the misplaced trust in political power as providing panaceas for social ills, and all the many temptations that plague the labours of the righteous will.[9]

The religionists conclude, however, that the reality of God and the associated divine imprint on human nature cannot be removed. False absolutes can at best temporarily attempt to usurp it. But, at the end of the chapter, 'God is greater' (*Allah-u-akbar*), in the words of Islam's battle-cry.

The charge that modern man is idolatrous is one that is frequently made by Muslim and Christian writers.[10] That it is made by Muslims is unsurprising; that it is also made by Christian writers touched by modernity is *prima facie* rather odd.[11] For surely this accusation is rendered problematic by our currently failing attempt to rehabilitate the transcendent categories of reflection into the fabric of a modern intellectual culture that is self-consciously naturalistic in its dominant assumptions. At any rate, as I shall now show, the accusation of *shirk* cannot be *straightforwardly* levelled against an increasingly secularised contemporary mankind.

Although the theme of idolatry is of common relevance to all of us within the Judaeo-Christian-Islamic religious complex, I shall here generally restrict my attention to the subject of idolatry in Islamic thought. What I say about it also applies, however, *mutatis mutandis* to Christian and Hebrew concerns.

The term *shirk*, often translated idolatry for want of a better expression, means 'to associate the true unique divinity – Allah – with one or more false ones' thereby compromising Allah's uniqueness. Strictly speaking, therefore, an idolater (*mushrik*) is an associationist, not a polytheist, although typically he is both. But a person who believed in a plurality of false gods without also believing in the one genuine God would not, in Islam, be classed as an idolater. Thus, for example, it is controversial whether or not a modern Hindu polytheist is a *mushrik*. (Is the Arabian paganism condemned by the Koran essentially equivalent to Hinduism?) To get over this fence, of course, we have the basic religious assumption that all men instinctively believe in Allah which implies that it is impossible to be human and yet believe solely in a plurality of false deities. At any rate, the Jews and Christians could sometimes uncontroversially be accused of idolatry. The Christians are taken to task for 'associating' Christ with Allah – although Christians legitimately dispute this interpretation of their creed. The Jews are rarely accused of doctrinal errors: they are, like Muslims, strict monotheists, but one isolated passage (K:9:30) implies that they commit *shirk* in 'associating' Uzair (Ezra) with Allah.

The point to note here is that the Koran is on safe ground in accusing certain groups of committing idolatry since the outlook and background that make that charge a meaningful one are largely available: the Arab pagans knew about Allah and the Jews and Christians were monotheists if, according to Islam, errant ones. But such presuppositions are not, in any uncontroversial fashion, available in the case of non-theistic faiths and, to take up our present concern, in the case of western atheistic humanism. I take it that in order to commit the sin or crime of *shirk*, a man must consciously or otherwise believe in both the true God, at least in some moods, and also believe in one or more divinities that he, by religious persuasion, could be made to recognise as being, in a significant sense, illusory. This admittedly (and in fact appropriately) vague definition captures, I would argue, the original religious significance of the term. The question on our agenda is simple: can one meaningfully accuse the modern rejector of idolatry (*shirk*) given that a necessary condition for committing this one 'unforgivable sin', as the Koran has it (K:4:48), is belief, no matter how casual or intermittent, in the existence of God.

In order to see clearly the issues here, consider the nature of the koranic *Lebenswelt*. The sacred scripture of Islam presupposes the existence of a realm of supernatural beings, with Allah as the true divinity. Muhammad's mission is to show his Meccan detractors that Allah tolerates no partners in his divinity. Hence the iconoclastic refrain from cover to cover: 'There is no god but God'. Presupposed by this claim is the fact, hardly in need of elaborate demonstration, that the original recipients of the message were, like many ancient peoples, pagans in the proper sense of the word. They were deeply religious in outlook and wished to placate and worship some supernatural (or at any rate superhuman) being or beings. As it happens, according to the Islamic verdict, they made the wrong choice. The Koran is concerned to alter their loyalties, indeed their priorities in the matter of allegiance. Allah alone deserves human worship.

It is important to note that the pagan Arabs believed in the existence of Allah; the Koran does not invent the name 'Allah' but merely expatiates on the supreme being's utter uniqueness and majesty. The central concern of scripture is to advise men in detail against the dangers of entertaining an irreverent attitude towards the supernatural. The attempt to argue for the very existence of the supernatural world is seen as unnecessary. Thus, for example, the idolater – particularly in the role of magician – deliberately develops a profane relationship with the supernatural, manipulating the sacred for profane ends and thereby earning the wrath of God. The prophetic figure, be it Moses or Muhammad, is shown as providing the model for a truly reverent relationship with the sacred forces.[12]

To demonstrate the existence of God, indeed the very coherence of such a concept, is today no superfluous task. To modern man, whether rightly or wrongly, the very notion of a world populated with gods is foreign if not entirely suspect. His total outlook – which prescribes a specific course for his loyalties – differs from that of ancient man. How disheartening an irony that the first part of the Muslim creed is today very much accepted: 'there is no god'. But its revolutionary continuation ('. . . but God') would today presuppose not so much a dethronement of a few false divinities, as it did in the past, but rather an acceptance of a concept which conscious atheists have for at least a century been vehemently denouncing as empty.

Explicit and total atheism as the denial of the existence of all supernatural realities is a relatively recent phenomenon. The tradition of radical rejection was forged mainly in the West during the late eighteenth and nineteenth centuries. The whole notion of a supernatural realm populated with angels, gods, demons and so on, was declared a figment of the religious imagination. To the extent that this new radical denial of the transcendent can be justified, the accusation of *shirk* becomes to the same extent difficult to sustain. For surely, to accuse atheists of committing *shirk* when they consciously and proudly wish to place themselves outside the very parameters of religion requires an elaborate justification. The religionist cannot, in this secular age, accuse rejectors of idolatry without due recognition of the fact that he is making assumptions characteristic of earlier, more religious, epochs.

There are, I believe, minimal conditions for (successfully) committing the sin of idolatry; and the central one is potentially conscious belief in the true divinity. It follows that there is something *prima facie* odd about accusing someone of *shirk* when he refuses to believe that there is, or even could be, any supernatural reality such as God. An important presupposition is being rejected. Think here, for comparison, of how the totalitarian party, in George Orwell's political masterpiece *Nineteen Eighty-Four*, intends to remove the possibility of certain crimes being committed by eliminating the very outlook they presuppose. Thus, for example, the party hopes to prune language so that creatively variable associations and implications of fertile words are systematically removed; in this way, indulgence in private heretical thought is not so much made discoverable but rather, more radically, rendered impossible. Where genuinely free thought is impossible, deviations from orthodoxy are actually unthinkable: one cannot commit 'thoughtcrime' unless one can think. Is it even possible, then, for modern man to commit the sin of idolatry?

I have argued that, in the past, the *un*believer was really just a *mis*believer who devoted himself to what he recognised, in many moods, to be unworthy of unconditional respect. At the same time, he ignored or devalued, whether wilfully or through *akrasia* (weakness of will), what he recognised, in some moods, to be worthy of allegiance. My contention is simply that the modern rejector cannot be taken uncritically to be in the same condition.

The Muslim apologist may deny this. He may say that contemporary rejection is of the same vintage as ancient paganism. Men need, he may insist, ultimate ideals, whether secular or religious, to retain their allegiance. Man is by nature, he may continue, a worshipper; if he does not worship the truth, he will certainly worship falsehood. When irreligious ideals seek to usurp the *de jure* sovereignty of Allah, they are the new gods that the creed condemns as illusory.

This line of reasoning is not unfamiliar. It has indeed long been a favourite *motif* of argumentative apologetics that the restless craving of human hearts and minds for one ideal or another is itself evidence of a universal basis for the desire for God. But this view is remarkably unconvincing, particularly today. For one thing, not every ideal is 'religious' in the standard or normal sense of the term. Some ideals are explicitly and consciously irreligious or even anti-religious: they have purely mundane referents. Indeed the religious ideal itself presupposes the possibility of espousing irreligious, even anti-religious, ideals; if no ideal could be authentically irreligious, the contrast between the sacred and the profane – a contrast essential to religious faith – could neither be drawn nor, *a fortiori*, transcended. The idea, then, that any and every ultimate norm for human allegiance is essentially religious implies the impossibility or at least the trivialisation of a contrast fundamental to the religious outlook. In view of these considerations, we should be cautioned against labelling as religious certain purely humanistic or purely naturalistic belief-systems (such as Marxist humanism). It is impressively plausible to argue that we should reserve the term 'religious' for describing ideals that have or presuppose a transcendent reference.

We are not yet at the bottom of this pit. 'Have you considered the case of the one who took his own fancy,' asks *surah* 45 (v.23), 'to be his god (*'ilah*) . . . ?' The next verse offers a description of the pagan Arab conception of humanism: men live and die all within the parameters of this world and the ravages of time (*dahr*). We know from the evidence of the Koran itself that the ideas of resurrection and eternal life were received with sincere disbelief and scorn by the pagan contemporaries of the Prophet (K:75:3ff.) The religionist may not unreasonably wonder whether we have in all this something close enough to our modern paganism. Is it not possible to recruit the quoted koranic passage in the service of a distinction between the intentional (or manifest) idolatry (*shirk-e-jali*), so dominant in the past, on the one hand, and the unintentional (or concealed) idolatry (*shirk-e-khafi*), so dominant today, on the other?

The answer is, I would suggest, in the negative. Why? There are at least three reasons. Firstly, the passage could reasonably be interpreted to mean that men's conception of the true divinity (Allah) is fashioned in accordance with their own human, all too human fancy – not that human fancies are themselves elevated to the status of divinity. Secondly, even if we adopt the interpretation that human fancies become gods, we must recognise that such a reading is unusual and the resulting emphasis incidental. Thirdly, and most importantly, the idolatrous attitude implicit here amounts to an intentional (as opposed to accidental) preference for irreligion. We see that clearly when we note that *shirk* is often discussed in the larger context of Allah's oft-repeated warnings about Satan's enmity to man, the dangers of befriending or seeking guidance from diabolic sources (K:36:60). This is an extremely significant point that must be in the forefront of our minds when discussing modern idolatry. The Koran presupposes the existence not only of Allah but also of Allah's supreme opponent, the Devil, who is an active agent in human history (K:12:5; 12:42; 18:63).

The third point needs explanation. And the explanation is best given by citing an example from western Christian thought although the lesson is for all theists. Goethe's epic *Faust* records the legendary pact between Dr Faust and Mephistopheles. Faust sells his soul to the Devil in exchange for knowledge, a bargain expressly condemned by Christ: 'What does it profit a man to gain the whole world and to lose his soul?' This is a paradigmatic case of idolatry: an inferior reality is deliberately made to replace what one knows and admits to be superior. It were as though, to shift quickly to the Muslim outlook, a Muslim were to say expressly: Allah is not greater (*akbar*) than all else, thereby openly defying the ubiquitous sentiment of Muslim piety so aptly expressed in the short formula 'God is greater' (*Allah-u-akbar*). But such clear idolatry is a far cry indeed from the idolatry of the worldly or weak-willed man addicted to wine, women and song. To enthrone a lesser reality on the pedestal of allegiance is not necessarily tantamount to a deliberate decision to dethrone a higher one. Most of us at the church or the mosque or the synagogue are not like Faust who, in the manner of a modern satanist,[13] intentionally made an explicitly irreligious choice.[14]

I have argued that our modern alienation from God may well be different in character from the ancient alienation of the pagan. Idolatry is, in the first instance, a religious term; it is only by a massive, perhaps illegitimate, extension of meaning that we can appropriate it for purposes of accusation in the modern world. The whole notion of the misguided deification of the natural and human world – a notion presupposed by the religious concept of idolatry – needs to be reassessed.

While we can no longer employ the concept of idolatry in its fully traditional role, we cannot and should not abandon it altogether. It is a powerful concept which is as central to the religious lexicon as, say, power is to the political one. Within Islam the centrality of the concept of *shirk* is entirely undeniable. The iconoclastic conscience feeds on it; the creed cannot be formulated without presupposing the integrity of this concept. The concern with *shirk* is at root an ideological concern *par excellence* (if 'ideological' be understood without its usual pejorative connotations); the creed of Islam is in effect a warning against placing a disproportionate trust in the efficacy of profane forces. To say, with emphasis and understanding, that 'There is no god but God' is to impose an operative veto on oneself from attributing any ultimate reality or power to those ideals that enslave individuals and societies.

The reinterpretation and proper use of the concept of *shirk* are central, difficult and important tasks for the Muslim writers. The importance of *shirk* is clear once we note that it is the only recognisable form of rejection in the koranic world and, in consequence, provides the only substantial link with the modern debate on faith and unfaith, a debate that centrally involves that characteristically modern notion of speculative atheism. The task is delicate and difficult for we must formulate the notion of *shirk* in conscious awareness of the fact that the outlook it once presupposed is now largely unavailable. The notion of idolatry has lost its original iconoclastic impulse and dwindled at best into a merely metaphorical usage. To be sure, modern secular culture is irreligious but we are not pagans in the old sense of the word. It remains to be seen whether or not we can preserve the essentially religious role of the concept of *shirk* as a tool of revolutionary accusation.[15]

VII

'Not equal are the inhabitants of the Fire,' says *surah* 59 (v.20), 'to those of the Garden.' No, indeed; they are not equal. (How quaint an understatement!) To sympathise with the rejector, to seek to understand the causes of modern rejection, to note its precise character – none of this is tantamount to mitigating the radical difference between faith and unfaith, still less to overlooking the total wrongheadedness of disbelief. In the final analysis, rejection is, for the religious believer, the ultimate error, the ultimate sin. That is undeniable. But, and this is my point here, given our modern understanding of the nature and causes of rejection, including a deeper appreciation of hubris and secular pride, we should be gentle (though not condescending) in our treatment of atheism.

'Be not like those who forget Allah and whom he has caused to forget their own souls' (K:59:19). So reads one of the milder pleas for men to ponder the consequences of rejection. The mood and impulse here are patiently edificatory, moderate, mellow, conciliatory, tender, long-suffering. It is a far cry indeed from the predominantly harsh tone of many a *surah* which describes the case of those in the midst of the luxuries of Paradise and then suddenly asks rhetorically if their state is equivalent to the state of those in the depths of Gehenna drinking, unforgettably, boiling water that tears their bowels asunder. It is this latter attitude towards rejection that is today so out of place. To be sure, it may well have been the appropriate attitude in an age and in a world 'charged with the grandeur of God', to put it in Gerard Manley Hopkins's famous idiom. But our world is hardly like that. Our rejectors do not have the stiff-hearted, almost starched perversity of an Abu Lahab. It is enough for us to say today that the rejectors will not prosper; there is no need to turn the dagger in the wound. Alienation from God is a sufficient punishment: atheism is its own reward.

The polemical tendency is always to see the rejecting opponent not as a man with principles to which he is deeply committed but rather as an insincere human being, an abstract foe of a sacred cause. That bitter and unfruitful invective litters the faith-rejection debate is hardly surprising. It is true of course that there is scriptural precedent for polemic: God himself engages in it. But God is God, almighty and wise; we are merely men among other men, all equally fallible and finite.

VIII

The task is and has always been to bear the burden of the human condition, without succumbing to the temptation to illusion. Both faith and rejection are arguably, in different ways, attempts to emancipate us from the chains of illusory realities. The worry is which of them, if either, actually achieves that end.

This has always been a deep and complex issue. Apart from the age-old impasse between one faith (such as Islam) and its religious rivals (such as Christianity or Judaism), there is now, in this secularised age, a further stalemate between theistic faith and atheistic humanism. One cannot, it seems, claim that one belief-system is superior to another without begging the question against the opponent or at least without appealing to a highly controversial standard of rational plausibility. The philosophical arsenal alone cannot ensure victory for any given party; and there seems to be no higher tribunal for settling fundamental controversies. Is it all then a matter of philosophical preference? How do we settle the clash between various religious and ideological options?

The problem of incompatibility of opinion is highly characteristic of modern intellectual culture. And the differences between various camps are deep, perhaps intractable. It is important for us to understand the nature of our modern epistemological predicament and we can begin to do that by noting that faith is, according to the faithful, no subject for the faithless writer. The rejector retorts that rejection is not the theologian's business. And yet both parties are centrally concerned to interpret the truth-claims of the rival. More generally, protagonists of a given cognitive system Y attempt to render void the claims of Z, a rival belief-pattern. Apparent counter-evidence may be transformed into neutral data or even positive evidence; in this way, adverse critical comment is neutralised by a device internal to a system so that the implied threat of counter-evidence is rendered ineffective. Now, in the case of religious belief-systems, there are internal devices that can be used to neutralise both irreligion – to use a rather loaded term – and every other religious rival. Thus, for example, a Muslim has specifically religious warrant for accusing atheists of sinful perversity and, say, attributing to satanic influence some of the theological opinions held by people of rival faiths. The atheist can in turn accuse the Muslim believer of wishful thinking; and people of other faiths, particularly Jews and Christians, will no doubt suggest that the Devil has no qualms about extending his influence to Muslim belief and practice.

The problem of course is that it is effectively impossible, once each party to the dispute adopts such an outlook, to remain genuinely alive to the critical pressure of recalcitrant facts which normally constitute counter-evidence in intellectual controversy. Men in the grip of a vision – any vision – are always keen to expose all opposition as baseless if not sinister. We have the familiar attempts at ideologically motivated reversals of the significance of apparent counter-evidence. Unfortunately, such attempts can, in effect, amount to a betrayal of truth, reflect an ideological posture in the pejorative sense of 'ideological', since one is actually seeking an assurance that no question ever returns an unsettling response. The overall result of this total circumstance is seen in the bitter and fierce deadlocks which now obtain between various rival ideologies that all make a claim upon the allegiance of modern man.

To be sure, the problem of impasse has always plagued us throughout our intellectual history. What makes it a particularly pressing concern today is that the current stalemate is, in this age of widespread rejection and scepticism, asymmetrically damaging. Let me explain. Atheists beg the relevant questions no less often than their opponents but do so, if you like, more persuasively. Thus, while two can in principle play at these games, in practice the theist is more likely to lose. For there is a certain asymmetry in the presence of experienced ambiguity in the world. The very fact that the world is susceptible to both naturalistic and theistic interpretations puts faith, it might be argued, under great pressure – possibly reduces it to a kind of absurdity. It is no doubt, logically speaking, faulty reasoning to infer the non-existence or the inactivity of God merely from an examination of the apparently chronic ambiguity of our current experience. But isn't it, in practice, the only plausible inference? The atheist, not unreasonably, suspects a kind of absurdity in a religious conviction so accommodating that it readily conforms to every possible situation in the world of human experience. What kind of God is it, then, even supposing he exists, who is intimately concerned with us and yet is nowhere to be decisively found, eluding equally both the obstinate rejector and the conscientious seeker in the contemporary world?

God may have his reasons for the current silence; perhaps it is a strategic silence before the terror of the Last Day. Unfortunately such speculation carries no weight except with those addicted to the logic of mystery; the atheist will only see evasion in such a response. To the rejecting temper, it is easier to believe that there is no God at all rather than to make the existence of a mysteriously silent deity compatible with the disturbing reality of evil, the ambivalence of modern experience *vis-à-vis* faith and unfaith, or indeed the general chaos in the human world. Why does God tolerate sin and rejection on today's impressively large scale? Where is the deluge of destruction for our modern rejection?

Allowing men to reject God involves a divine decision that is, by assumption, part of an ultimately undiscoverable motive. Certainly, had Allah willed, he could have made mankind into a single community of faith (K:16:9); but, mysteriously, he has not willed this. The religionist has to offer a justification, necessarily partial, for this decision, especially in the face of a contemporary questioning that often borders on mockery. The religionist's task is difficult for one special reason: the question, 'Why is rejection permitted?' unlike the related question, 'How is faith to be explained?' is by definition a theological puzzle. It involves a perplexity about the decisions of a deity whose intentions are, by assumption, irreducibly mysterious. For the unbeliever, the issue of the extent of acceptance or rejection of faith in God is usually a complex one, no doubt very interesting, or, if his atheism is part of an organised socio-political effort, a matter for human concern. (How can so many intelligent and sincere people still believe in this pre-scientific legend of a God-governed cosmos?) But the religionist has on his hands a problem, probably intractable, the solution of which necessarily involves reference to the radically inaccessible motives and intentions of a *deus arcanus*.

The atheist naturally cannot be expected to have much sympathy with this kind of reasoning. In fact he is likely to have very different views about the alleged silence of God. He may think, not implausibly, that even if the intellectual economy in atheism be a risk, it is no longer a great risk. Perhaps, he may argue, it is a risk well worth taking. After all, hardly anyone is now overly impressed by Pascal's threatening choice between 'Eden or extinction' on the one hand, and 'damnation or extinction' on the other. The religious goal appears not only long-term but also illusory. Can we any longer be sure that there *are* any benefits and burdens beyond the grave? The modern rejector will no doubt contend that there is something fundamentally misguided about the popular apologetic disparagement of men's willingness to do so much to attain finite worldly goals while, irrationally, doing so little to attain an infinitely more important goal in the world yet to come. Indeed, he may continue, even religious believers today are often more

concerned to pursue short-term goals that carry a greater and more
secure prospect of success – goals centred around the wish to alleviate
the genuine anguish of life on this side of the grave – than to pursue
the traditional goal of the fully godly existence with all its remote,
uncertain and deferred threats and benefits.

IX

We have returned, then, via a circuitous route to the theme of the
previous chapter – namely, a cluster of concerns conveniently collected
under the cover of 'the silence of God'. Does God still speak to anyone
in this age? Has he spoken to anyone in the past? If so, to whom? Is
Islam the only true faith? How do we know? How should one address
the sceptic who says God does not exist at all?

It seems to me, to make a point that arises naturally out of previous
discussions, that there are today some specifically *religious* reasons for
expecting (requesting?) God to reveal himself again in a manner at least
as dramatic as that in the past. The familiar biblical-koranic claim that
only an evil and adulterous generation seeketh after a sign was plausible
enough in religiously charged milieux such as first-century Palestine or
seventh-century Arabia. Today, however, I would maintain, the demand
for a miracle is actually a reasonable religious demand; a miracle-
performing deity would not be merely pandering to a sinful human
desire for the spectacular. It could be that, in this secularised age, our
innate belief in God is overlaid with a surfeit of profane scepticism so
that we need a further revealed communication that could be seriously
considered by everyone, believer and rejector alike.

One should see this admittedly grandiose request against a much
larger religious background which can itself be most coveniently can-
vassed through *two* observations. Firstly, consider the sheer variety and
range of opinion about the nature and existence of the Deity. It ranges
from atheism, through agnosticism and indifference, to orthodox
theistic conviction; and such orthodox conviction is itself hardly
monolithic, covering as it does various fundamentally opposed attitudes
conveniently labelled as Muslim, Jewish, Christian and Sikh. The ethical
monotheistic faiths are internally divided by sectarian differences; and
these differences are sometimes quite substantive. And this range of
belief does not even include the whole world of rival patterns of piety:
non-theistic faiths such as Buddhism, Hinduism, animism and so on. I
need not extend this list in order to make my point. Has God indeed
made his intentions perfectly clear? What are we to believe about his
nature and existence? Or is our confusion both today as in the past due
simply to our sinful tendency to dispute the clearest of evidences?

The problem with religious claims is, of course, that there are no
uncontroversially accepted criteria which could effectively provide a

decision-procedure. Religious assertions, if that is the correct term here, are, it would seem, not publicly testable. Unsurprisingly, given the prevalence of keen controversy, both inter-religious and intra-religious, many sceptics have concluded that theological propositions are not factual, even putatively factual, in content. Consider the following propositions, factual, historical, evaluative and religious:

(a) 'Professor John Hick' is among the entries for the 1986 *Who's Who*.
(b) There are more poets than cars in rural India today.
(c) Johann Fichte was a Fascist.
(d) There have been two 'European', not 'World', wars in this century.
(e) Poets were ideologues in pre-Islamic Arabian societies.
(f) Ghalib is a greater poet than Iqbal.
(g) Christ is indeed the saviour of sinful Adam's progeny.
(h) Allah is the author of the Arabic Koran.

I have arranged these various kinds of propositions roughly in increasing order of susceptibility to reasonable dispute. Apart from (a), all the claims are, in some measure, controversial. There are, in all the cases, some recognised criteria for deciding the issue although the dispute may in practice remain intractable. But the last two propositions express well-nigh entirely untestable claims, involving as they do appeal to evidence that is itself exclusively based on highly controversial interpretations of already complex and keenly disputed historical and social data.

I deliberately omitted propositions about normative realities since claims such as 'Cruelty is morally wrong' or 'Beauty is the highest aesthetic value' are not always seen as factual in content. Religious propositions, however, are usually classed as factual although it is admitted on all accounts that they inspire deep disagreement. Indeed, theological propositions have been compared with aesthetic and moral ones: religious claims are characteristically so saturated with controversial assumptions that one might reasonably argue that 'religious knowledge' is at best a form of purely normative, perhaps emotive, rather than factual or historical, insight.

It is inappropriate for us to pursue this issue any further here.[16] Let me instead briefly record the second point – a point about the extent and nature of the divine engagement with mankind. God, particularly the God of Islam, does not merely permit men to find him, he commands them to seek him, to make every effort to live in accordance with his will, in fine, to seek to please him – all on pain of the terrible consequences of the failure to do so. The Koran frequently proclaims with clarity and emphasis the need to 'struggle' (*jehada*)[17] in the way of Allah (K:9:18–19; 9:23; 4:100; repeated often). Men should earnestly seek to recruit every faculty and circumstance in the service of the divine Lordship. This is a central obligation in the religious life. If so, isn't

God morally obliged to make clear to us, in every era, both his existence and the moral demands he wishes to make upon human nature?

Life is, on the religious outlook, a very serious business, though there is no harm in the occasional gaiety. Tragically, men do not always see it in this perspective. The Koran frequently insists on the moral serious-ness of the human vocation: Allah has not made the world either for his own, still less his creatures' amusement (K:21:16–17). And yet, laments the sacred author, men refuse to take heed, prefer heedlessness (*ghaflah*) though their reckoning has already drawn nigh (K:21:1–3). It is clear, then, that the choice between faith and rejection is momen-tous: its consequences extend into all eternity. If so, isn't it important for God to dispel the ambiguity of modern experience and clarify his will for mankind, especially in an age of widespread confusion and unclarity?

X

'If only the host had the guest's appetite, if only God thought like man. But he doesn't – and that makes all the difference.' Such may well be the orthodox Muslim response to my claims in the previous section. The pious believer will certainly be irritated by my demands. Who is man, after all, to dictate the terms on which God is to involve himself with mankind? To be sure, it will be proudly granted, the economy of God's (alleged) revelation, its scandalous silences, its casual attitude towards things that agitate so many thoughtful moderns, its painstaking concern with things that seem to us irrelevant – all this is indeed disturbing. It disturbs our standards of what is or is not truly significant in human experience and existence. It offends our intellectual and moral norms. But so it should. God, it will be said, judges us; we do not judge God. It is God, not man, who has the last word in the affair. *Allah-u-akbar* is the slogan.

The mystery of God's actions and intentions does, it will be conceded, leave us with a blank page to fill. But there we have it. Such is the ultimate style of the divine commerce with the human world. And, it will be said, it is at best idle and pointless, at worst unwise and sinful, to raise such fundamental questions the solutions of which transcend the limits of human understanding. The splendidly intelligible deity of the thinkers – a figment of the imagination fashioned after their own image – is not the Lord of Muhammad and the prophets. The correct attitude here, it may well be concluded, is to accept that Allah is Allah, far above the constraints and demands of profane philosophies. *Allah-u-akbar* is the slogan.

The error in the view that God should speak directly and clearly today is, the religionist may continue, warming up to his view, the misconception that God ever has. There has always been ambiguity in his dealings with men, even in the age of revelation. The faithful see him everywhere in this world and the next, to echo Jalal al-Din Rumi's famous line; and the rejectors do not see him at all. Such then is the God of faith speaking to whom he wills both today as in the past. If only man, including modern man, could triumph over his own perversity.

XI

We have heard this song before. My response is an indirect one scattered throughout this work. In bringing this chapter to a close, let me mention one neglected issue before offering some concluding reflections.

Apart from atheism, the religionists also have that little business of indifference on their hands. The fool hath said in his heart, 'I don't care whether or not there is a God.' Apathy and indifference are as characteristic of our age of secularity as heresy and enthusiasm were in the heyday of religious conviction.[18] Nor is indifference a phenomenon peculiarly western; it is discernible among the educated classes of Muslims too, albeit hardly ever openly discussed.

Indifference to religious faith is a large and neglected theme. Firstly, indifference is by its very nature inarticulate. Once a man has given up on the religious solutions to life's problems, he naturally no longer sees faith as a live option; he may refuse to discuss religious issues, refuse to tell us what precisely needs to be ironed out. In a way, then, indifference is an even more disturbing phenomenon than atheism. How can a religionist deal with an opponent who shows no interest in the issue? The only way to retrieve indifference is, I would argue, to encourage the man who has given up on faith to re-examine and honestly confront the problems and worries of the religious life. Once a man is prepared to tell us what agitates him in his thoughtful moods, once he is ready to wash his dirty linen in front of the religionists, there is room for optimism. It is perfectly possible, however, that apathy has taken root too deeply so that a man may keep his worries to himself and simply refuse to show interest in matters that he already has, at some stage, resolved to his own satisfaction. In such cases of advanced indifference, so to speak, there is nothing to be done. The religionist however may take comfort in the fact that such an indifferentist's plight is more a defeat for intellectual curiosity than for religious faith.

Secondly, indifference to established religion is one thing, indifference to God another. The two are certainly not equivalent (except perhaps in the minds of a few Sunnis and Roman Catholics). While a man may have reasons, including good reasons, for being indifferent to the claims of various religious authorities, he can never have any reasons, let alone good ones, for being indifferent to God or God's claims. The problem here of course is that the indifferentist will, rightly, resent the current silence of God as being, if you like, a kind of indifference to man on the Deity's part. Hence, to go back to our earlier concerns, all the more need for a positive revelation that could dispel the apathy and indifference so rampant in industrial society.

We must leave it at that. I have argued, then, that the atheistic disavowal of God is a central and pressing concern on the modern agenda. The traditional religious explanation for rejection seems unconvincing in this secularised age. Is modern atheism indeed explicable solely in terms of a defiant hubris that never hesitates to abuse the prerogative of rational freedom? Is contemporary rejection simply and straightforwardly damnable, an exemplary embodiment of the will to perversity?

The problem of modern atheism is, as I have shown in some detail, essentially foreign to the koranic outlook. The issue of atheism was relevant to those in the age of revelation at best to a tributary degree via the concern with idolatry and iconoclasm. It is undeniable that the Koran was vouchsafed to a generation innocent of modern sceptical proclivities. It has, therefore, to be admitted, in fairness, at the risk of sounding unduly irreverent, that the sacred volume does not contain a single stretch of reasoning which could, even in alliance with minor extrapolation, be mistaken for the kind of argument that carries any weight with the modern sceptic. This circumstance should motivate the Muslim thinker to develop a natural theology, responsive to the intellectual pressures and assumptions of a sceptical age, which could be used to remove some kinds of conscientious doubts about the truth of religious claims. At the same time, and more generally, the traditional tendency to dismiss modern worries as bogus must itself be actively disowned. It is no solution to our predicament to say that if our modern sensibilities are outraged, so much the worse for our modern sensibilities. This is the voice of obscurantism; and we should call obscurantism by its name. Even if it is true that *God* is not concerned to make his views fashionable or credible to modern man, *we* should still be concerned to find out whether or not the views attributed to God are in fact God's views and hence, by implication, true, indeed necessarily true.

At another level, I have urged that it may well be reasonable for us to request God to reveal himself again openly and dramatically so that the autonomy of the secular outlook can be decisively destroyed. Surely God could disclose himself to all communities at once – in a global revelation rather than to isolated individuals and communities.[19] And certainly we can imagine a revelation that would put the truth of theism, or more narrowly, Islamic theism, beyond reasonable contention. I recognise that this is a grand proposal and have, throughout this work, tried to allay some standard religious fears. Thus, for example, there need be no fear that men's freedom of choice in matters religious would be thereby jeopardised. Assuming that the envisaged revelation was not utterly overwhelming (think here of Moses' encounter with God

[K:7:143]) men could continue to reject God, unreasonably, even after the great event. For men are as free to reject truth in favour of falsehood as they are to reject virtue in favour of vice. And the number who have regularly exploited that facility has never been small, least of all in the modern world.

The Brave New World

I

'Life is at an end where the "kingdom of God" *begins* . . . ' So Friedrich Nietzsche, unarguably among the most far-sighted of humanist thinkers of the nineteenth century.[1] The largest single ambition of western modernity has been to endow the notion of the intrinsic worth of life with a secular metaphysical foundation. Life, the humanists have argued, is no longer in need of a divine validation. The idea that we need a seal from Heaven to guarantee the worth of our lives is vehemently rejected by secular humanists: man is self-sufficient. There is no need for God in the brave new world of post-theistic man. Indeed, the contention continues, the concept of a divine ruler is incompatible with the possibility of a liberated and liberating intellectual and moral culture. If theism was a culture of revealed command, atheistic humanism is a culture of human liberation. In fine, men can and should learn to live in the godless universe – a universe deliberately and fully drained of religious purpose.

Hitherto, writes Nietzsche in his unjustly neglected autobiography,[2] mankind has on principle worried about precisely all the wrong things – an imaginary realm full of imaginary beings. As a result, continues Nietzsche, men have failed to undertake the really important task of living life as free and autonomous folk who seek to create norms with purely human and natural referents – who make a virtue of developing 'the whole casuistry of selfishness'.[3] Instead, human beings have been busy trying to constrain volition to suit the outdated dictates of an allegedly higher revealed morality; they have struggled to survive in the asphyxiating atmosphere of a life-denying idealism that was itself founded on a momentous error. The whole concern with a supernatural realm of benefits and burdens was, argue Nietzsche and the humanists, a pious fraud, the product of an age of gullibility and misguided enthusiasm. Theism as a creed has served mankind badly, even in its own time.

The death of God is, for Nietzsche, a picturesque way of enunciating the demise of the supra-sensible realm which is, in turn, the death-knell for the associated traditional system of ethical constraint. The purpose of life is not to make a good death – as the wise old men from Socrates to Muhammad would have us believe. It is rather to make a good living; we should exploit our purely human resources for achieving our destiny, a purely human destiny. Liberated then from the age-old tyranny of an oppressive metahuman order, men are free to develop a purely naturalistic philosophy of man and culture[4] and, in doing so, to celebrate the human condition.

II

It is axiomatic that atheism is the greatest inspiration of modern humanism. Indeed it is not merely a prejudice to claim that atheism has to its credit major accomplishments in societies in which it has some measure of public influence. Thus, in the western world, atheistic humanists have recently made great contributions to the self-understanding of our species, initiated some influential political programmes for the amelioration of the human plight, shown consideration for the environment and attempted to emphasise the importance of conservation of animal, especially wild, populations.

As a worldwide phenomenon with an impressive intellectual foundation and a defensible accompanying institutional structure, atheistic humanism has earned the right to a future. The humanist has in his atheism a satisfying world-outlook; he can hold up his head in the best ideological company. (In due course, atheists may even begin to 'proselytise' on a large scale.) In the past, the battle between religious faith and atheistic humanism was confined to the occasional rearguard skirmishes involving a few intellectuals; but it is possible that, in the coming century, this struggle will escalate into a major front-line war whose casualties may include a few of the prevalent convictions of the religious outlook.

The remarks and concessions in the previous paragraphs may have surprised some religionists. Even today most orthodox religious writers assume that at root atheism is irreducibly puerile and the atheist insincere and incapable of genuine commitment. In the past, of course, almost everyone, including relatively liberal thinkers, have refused to concede the sincerity of the atheist or the authenticity of his vision. John Locke was not out of step with his age when he disallowed atheists, in his perhaps inaptly named *Letter Concerning Toleration*, from effecting contracts with other social groups. In Muslim circles, both today as in the past, the view that atheism cannot possibly provide a basis for responsible social or individual conduct is held as one utterly self-evident to reason and, in consequence, absolved of the normal need for independent support. The very name atheist (*dahariyya*)[5] excites a peculiar dread among traditional Muslims. Indeed, so strong is the dislike of atheism among all religious believers that even in the modern increasingly secularised West, there is still a relatively powerful residual prejudice, particularly though not only in popular culture, that to disbelieve in God is *ipso facto* to align oneself on the side of immorality and laxity in conduct while to believe in God is *ipso facto* to side with decency and virtue.

The conviction, however, that belief in God is a condition of individual moral sense and of human moral community has, it would appear, been effectively refuted in this century. Countless individuals, sometimes entire tribes and societies, live apparently normal lives without professing belief in God. It is impossible, I would argue, to deny that such a belief-system as that of atheistic humanism is a 'philosophy of life'. Only an extremely facile apologetics would doubt this in the larger attempt to declare atheism a piece of childish, immoral and untenable confusion.

There is one important methodological remark, best made in this context, about the proper role of apologetics. So much religious writing about atheism is remarkably simplistic and naïve in its assumptions and claims. While apologetics is perfectly justified, it must be sophisticated, cognisant of atheism and its supposed grounds, aware of the issues and options. What is unacceptable is merely crudely apologetic material – of the kind common (and perhaps in its place) in Friday or Sunday homilies. Good apologetics is not only justifiable, it is necessary. We are, after all, all apologists for some cause or belief, if only the correct and true one. Nor will it do to say that truth needs no apology. For unfortunately the majority of mankind, including the professional thinkers, has never shown any marked enthusiasm for truth and reality, especially where some inadequate substitute has sufficed.

III

The humanistic approach which matured with the progress of secularisation has centrally contended that the whole of human experience, including moral and religious experience, is properly to be understood in purely human terms. One important part of the humanist programme has centred on the issue of the independence of morality from its traditional religious foundation. The atheist thinker is concerned to show that the traditional attribution of the authorship of moral codes to God can be disowned without sacrificing these codes – or at least some appropriately secular version of them. Christian theism, it has been argued, was the historical, not the logical, basis of moral values such as compassion, marital fidelity, and respect for the individual. Religion, the argument has run, was part of the teething process for morality. While many liberal thinkers in the West have sought to discredit the Christian heritage of western morality, few have seen it necessary – for that reason at any rate – to jettison all the values associated with that outlook.

There are some Christian writers, associated with the so-called 'Divine Command' school, who see God as the logical guarantor of morality. But this view is not as popular as it once was in the West. In Muslim circles, however, it remains influential. The Koran itself emphasises the point that virtue and vice both derive their characters from their relationship to the pleasure or displeasure of Allah. Indeed, it would appear that individuals and communities are rewarded or punished, in the first instance, for obeying or disobeying respectively God's messengers, not for the inherent rightness or wrongness of their actions. Thus adultery is wrong and punishable in the first instance not because it injures human relationships but because it offends God. To put all this in terms of western thought, the Muslim, like a Luther and unlike a Leibniz, would grasp the first horn of the misleadingly posed Euthyphro dilemma: 'Is the pious defined as what the gods love or do the gods love something because it is pious?' Grasping the first horn has, for the believer, particularly the Muslim believer, the welcome implication that virtue is a necessarily religious phenomenon. What makes an action X good is its relationship, perhaps conformity, with the will of God.

Is it then logically impossible to achieve virtue independently of religious belief? Is morality logically parasitic on religion? Now, *prima facie* at least, it would seem that virtue is not an exclusively religious phenomenon: it appears to be found sometimes in individual and social existence outside of any 'religious' commitment as such commitment is standardly understood. Assuming, importantly, that an engagement with moral value is not in itself equivalent to theism (a view implied by some versions of theological reductionism) it seems to be the case that secular piety is quite common. The standard way of radically undercutting the possibility of secular virtue is to deny the very coherence of the concept. And yet a 'virtuous atheist' no more implies a logical contradiction than 'virtuous theist' implies a pleonasm. Thus, it is entirely possible that, say, Marcus Aurelius and arguably Spinoza[6] were conspicuously virtuous disbelievers; and such staunch atheists as Nietzsche and Marx were good men who fought against heavy odds in order to contribute to the world's stock of philosophical insight and social criticism. Again, nearer our own day, Bertrand Russell, the secular prophet for the permissive society, was, some marital peccadillos apart, a man of intellectual integrity and sincere conviction.

The notion that atheists are incapable of moral sentiment is in fact odd, especially from a religious point of view. The Koran (K:75:2) insists that all human beings, believers and rejectors alike, are endowed with the 'self-accusing soul' (*nafs al-awwamah*), a faculty probably identical with the potentially upright conscience that, according to St Paul in Rom. 2:14–15, even the Gentiles possess. But if we allow the possibility that disbelievers can have a conscience at all, it follows that the capacity to discern the exigences of moral awareness is not always restricted to men of faith. And from here it is conceptually a short step to conceding the possibility of virtue, even conspicuous virtue, among rejectors. Couldn't then a man's behaviour be ethically praiseworthy even though he refused to believe in God? Suppose, for the sake of argument, that someone treats others around him with respect, refuses to condemn them unjustly, evinces active compassion for the dispossessed and the poor, conducts his sexual life with a care for the feelings of his partner (or partners), seeks to contribute to the world's stock of beauty, culture and insight before leaving the scene, endures patiently the lash of circumstance, and exercises mercy and restraint both in the moment of eclipse and in the hour of success. Wouldn't we say of such a one that he had integrity, had, if the expression be allowed, 'godly if godless' ideals? Would the mere fact that he refused to be agitated by fears and actuated by hopes of possible events beyond the grave be a sufficient basis for denying him the accolade of virtue? It is not at all clear that unbelief is necessarily incompatible with morally good dispositions.

Religion, it would seem, cannot claim a monopoly of human moral excellence. Certainly, unless one is morally hijacked by the religionists, one is hard put to deny the possibility, indeed the presence of actual instances, of virtue outside all religious commitment. Belief in God is not, apparently at least, the sole enabler of moral decencies. And it does seem irritatingly question-begging to the atheist to be told that somehow, deep down, every decent disbelieving person is really a believer after all. (Could the refusal to allow virtue to flourish outside the household of faith be itself 'immoral' in some sense?)

Certainly, the old legend that atheists are always incapable of moral commitment (or are always moral perverts) can safely be stored in the museum of theological absurdities – a monument to the pious desire to prohibit the flourishing of virtue and integrity outside religion. The view that atheism always or inherently has a morally subversive character invites comparison with Plato's absurd claim that listening to music makes men effeminate! Both are the kinds of legends that, like certain kinds of romantic rumours, are hard to explode precisely because they find their basis in some emotive and usually unevidenced *a priori* assumptions.

The religionist could, at this stage, argue that while an atheist can certainly possess fidelity to conscience, be vigorously conscious of the demands of moral awareness, and indeed even be of very good character, he cannot in general be as virtuous as a religious believer. What are we to make of this? There are several different claims implicit in this complex comparison. One of these claims is that atheistic humanism cannot boast of disciples quite so great as Moses, Milton, Sir Thomas More and Muhammad. There have been, it will be said, instances of unrivalled piety in the history of theistic faith. This is, I would argue, perhaps rather weakly, a defensible observation. Even if we make allowances for the fact that, in terms of modern moral sensibilities, some of the seminal figures of the monotheistic tradition were not necessarily great human beings, and even if we further allow for the relative infancy of the explicitly atheist humanist tradition,[7] it is still difficult to deny that it is the *religious* ideal that has retained the allegiance of some astonishingly conscientious and virtuous folk in our history.

When it comes to the common run of believers, however, things are embarrassingly different. While the pretensions of the faithful are certainly lofty, their lives, with very few exceptions, are not in any recognisable degree free of the selfishness and dishonesty that plague human beings in general. The moral superiority of religious believers may be an article of faith but it has, unfortunately, very little evidence in its favour. Indeed, the gap between profession and practice, as judged by observing believers both today and in the past, is wide enough to be scandalous. I suspect that at least one brand of unbelief is inspired by a distaste for a religious behaviour that is too pharisaic, too narrow-hearted, too much a product of religious provincialism – altogether one too capable of obscuring one's humanity to qualify as a gift of an other-worldly grace that seeks to widen the range of human sympathies.

The atheist is under no obligation to show that the believers are morally worse than their secular opponents: it is good enough to show that they are no better. And the fact is of course that the lives of those who are allegedly influenced by the grace of God are in practice rarely notably better than those of rejectors in the common run of humanity. To be sure, some atheists are indeed frivolous and shallow; but so are many believers. Laxity in conduct is no more a necessary consequence of atheism than domestic happiness is of marriage.

The religionist, especially if he is reflective and rationally cognisant of contemporary thought, will be sympathetic to these claims. Indeed, he may be only too willing, perhaps even eager, to emphasise the failings of our common humanity. But, all of that notwithstanding, he may still wish to insist that religious conviction alone can morally orientate man in his *social* role: religion is indispensable for preserving the *social* integrity of human beings. He may concede, of course, that individual men and women can have personal integrity and constraint even in a godless world; to contradict Dostoyevsky's sophistical atheist, everything is *not* permitted in the brave new world. But, he may add, atheism disrupts the socio-moral order: men cannot love and trust one another in their social and political relationships. Given what we know of human nature, it will be said, only certain kinds of eschatological sanctions could provide the motivation for preserving a morally tolerable social life. Without religion, it will be concluded, human society is impossible.

The question of the viability of a secular ethic is a large one. Suffice it to say here that the very operative existence of western secularised societies is an objection to the traditional claim about the subversive character of atheism. It is at least arguable that an ethic with an atheistic foundation could underpin a society. The social structure of advanced industrial communities in the West is not of course supplied exclusively by any genuinely atheistic ideology. Indeed it is true that western peoples live on the capital of the Christian tradition; but Christianity itself increasingly counts for little or nothing with many people of influence. And yet there are no signs of imminent social débâcle in the western world. In fact, occidental people somehow get along fairly well without their God – indeed better than many traditional societies do with their God. (Could this rather disquieting truth partly explain the ferocious critique of the West that is so popular with modern Muslim polemicists?)

I think it is not an exaggeration to say that the elimination of the supernatural warrant from morals has not seriously undermined morality itself. Scepticism about religious claims has not gone hand-in-hand with scepticism about ethics. Thus, for example, those who accept Nietzsche's doctrine of the demise of the Deity none the less reject his claims about the collapse of morality.[8] Ethics has survived the death of God. Indeed, it is not even clear that the alleged current decline in moral standards in the West is due to the rise of atheism as an organised socio-political force. In fact, it could be due to the experience of confusion and uncertainty caused by the rapid decline of the Christian faith.

I have argued, then, in this section, that empirically considered, virtue can be realised independently of belief in God. There seems to be no intrinsic relationship between religious faith and the achievement of a morally excellent life. The slogan 'no religion, no virtue' may well, like so much of conventional wisdom, have been adopted *a priori* – in the service, in this case, of a particular view about the centrality and indispensability of religion in human life. Indeed I have further suggested that it is an open question whether or not a society devoid of belief in God need lack an appropriate foundation for social morality. It is true that in the past atheism has been declared indispensable for both the personal and social integrity of men and communities. But the nature and direction of this inference are significant: it is not so much that atheism is shown, on the basis of empirical evidence, to be morally subversive but rather that nothing is allowed to count in favour of the claim that atheism can supply a satisfying and viable metaphysic.

One final remark to conclude this section. The Koran itself, like all sacred literature, is unfamiliar with the notion of an upright pagan, that is, someone who has heard and disbelieved the word of God while remaining recognisably virtuous. Rejection is traditionally thought to be, as we saw earlier, a fundamentally immoral posture sustained by an arrogant hubris that is itself rooted in wilful perversity. I have argued earlier that men could in fact conscientiously reject God in this secularised age, that the sincere rejector would not compromise his moral integrity. It looks now, if my arguments here are not wide of the mark, that the rejector could, theologically puzzling though it is, be virtuous without being faithful.

IV

I need now to widen the focus of the discussion. The crucial issue in the area of relationships between the secular and the religious life is not that of logical dependence or even of the mere viability of a secular ethic. The important questions here include the following: Do we need a merciful God to anchor our deepest aspirations as human beings? Can we live happily on atheism alone as long as we have our daily bread? Is the misery of our condition simply a changeable secular circumstance? Or is it indeed due to some unalterable malaise that requires supernatural grace for its cure? Is there any purely human guarantee that we can live with hope and without despair in the godless universe?

These are large and complex worries; we need to come at them indirectly. Certainly, with the decline of a belief in a benevolent force behind Nature, a dominant response has been an increasingly strident call for a personal revolution, a solitary defiance of the arbitrary tyrannies of an existence stripped of celestial foundation. The thoughtful modern person, unable to discern an order under a merciful sovereignty, looks back in anger and pride. Writing on the death of his father, Dylan Thomas's poetic refrain well catches the spirit of defiance so characteristic of the brave new world:

> Do not go gentle into that good night.
> Rage, rage against the dying of the light.

And yet significantly, this protest against the terminative power of death does not typically stand alone. Coupled with it is, often enough, an obscurely expressed longing for transcendence, a wish for a definitive triumph over the limitations of the mortal condition. Dylan Thomas again:

> Though lovers be lost, love shall not.
> And death shall have no dominion.[9]

The rejector wishes to surpass the human condition – after his own fashion. And that must be respected. The believer is simply contending that religion provides a realistic basis for the realisation of certain natural human hopes, such as the hope of transcending death. The religious thinker may argue that there are signs in our experience and history that suggest that death does not have the last word in life. He may insist that the secular sentimentalism that allows the dead to live in the memories of the living is, in a rival metaphysic of life and destiny, actually provided with grounds. Thus, the writer of I Cor. 15:55 can, given the assumptions that nourish his outlook, justifiably see death as a condition of eternal life, not an objection to it:

> O death, where is thy sting?
> O grave, where is thy victory?

Isn't every authentic philosophy of life a search for a vision that transcends the indifferent ravages of time and contingency?

V

In this secularised age, the atheist is likely to view the religionist's task as an impossible one inspired by a facile optimism that is sustained by an ignorance of the many lessons of secularity. The truth is, the humanist will urge, we should lay the last wreath on the tomb of theism – and get on with the task of living under an empty sky. After all, he may continue, the recent death of our monotheistic God is, from a purely anthropological point of view, only the latest in a whole series of celestial tragedies that began with the demise of the Egyptian and Roman deities; the only difference is that *our* tribe is now affected. The impartial student of religion must, he may conclude, reject as unworthy of credence even admittedly sophisticated versions of what is after all the same illusion.

This is no doubt too brusque. The danger for the humanist is the temptation to be prematurely dismissive of theism. Religious conviction is indeed sometimes unfairly derided in our increasingly religionless age. Thus theism has in recent years been attacked variously as morally degrading, cognitively senseless, and, by less radical critics, as merely pragmatically ineffective. To be sure, all of these different kinds of criticisms are, to some extent, justified. After all, who can any longer doubt that there are indeed sordid elements in the traditional belief-systems that atheism condemns? The atheist has every right to condemn a faith whose central shrine is occupied by a deity who patronises bigotry, prejudice and dogmatism. Furthermore, the humanist can fairly point out that even religionists have recently begun to acknowledge that metaphysical religious conviction in the old style often contained significantly large elements of sheer legend, even of oppressively incoherent fantasy. Unsurprisingly, he may conclude, such a religious belief-system has failed to satisfy modern enlightened man.

None of this can be denied without doing violence to fairness. But one has to put in the balance the fact that this allegedly illusory ideal has engaged the commitment of an astonishingly large number of exceptionally intelligent and virtuous people in our culture and history and continues to do so. While it is important that one should not be so deeply impressed with this fact that one makes it into a presumption, or worse an argument, from the start in favour of the theistic stance, it cannot be denied that theism has been a fertile and fundamental aspect of human life and thought in many cultures for many centuries. In view of this, humanists should be cautioned against simplistic accounts of the genesis of faith, such as, for example, the dismissive view of theism as being simply an illusion in the service of reducing our genuine anguish about the human lot. Let us never forget that there are as many bad reasons for disbelieving in God as there are for believing in him.

I want these remarks to be properly understood. The claim that a belief-system as extremely sophisticated and complex as theism is in fact inspired by the wish to secure certain mundane aims is in need of elaborate support. *Prima facie* at least, it is difficult to see why men felt the need for such an elaborately fantastic projection, a fantasy utterly disproportionate to the mere need for personal security in an unstable order. After all, the anthropomorphic deities of the Greeks and the Romans would surely have sufficed. Indeed, the belief in such deities provided a metaphysically far less problematic mechanism for strengthening personal and social life. The developed and mature versions of ethical monotheism – versions that essentially include a reference to a unique incorporeal being utterly transcendent to the spatio-temporal realm – are unnecessary for achieving such a modest end.

VI

This is too wide a mesh to catch the details; let me be more specific. Take the view, popular in one form or other among most kinds of humanists, that theism offers a large helping hand to emotionally crippled people. If one examines without prejudice religious faith in its seminal instances, one cannot fail to note that it is based on a vigorous rejection of all consolations, false hopes and the comforting illusions of self-deception. The most noteworthy feature of genuine religious conviction (and this is not a persuasive definition of such conviction) is its austerity: every kind of solace whether of the flesh or of the spirit is spurned with painful rigour. Even a cursory examination of the lives of the prophets and saints of the western monotheistic tradition gives the lie to the facile claim that courage is all that is required in order to abandon the deceptions of religious consolation.

In no sense is theism a soft option. On the contrary, it is a most demanding one: the Deity of St Paul, like the Deity of Muhammad, and unlike the Roman or Hindu deities, expects men to live up to uncomfortably high moral standards. The demands of religious morality, for instance, are exacting. The Ramadan fast, to take just one example from Muslim piety, levies a heavy toll on the ordinary human frame. More generally, the demands of theistic faith create a permanent mental anguish, contribute greatly to some kinds of fear,[10] challenge and effectively destroy the comforts of self-sufficiency – and warn us of a yet more thorough reckoning by an omniscient master after we shuffle off this mortal coil. For the believer, there is no 'solitariness where wounds are nursed';[11] he is always in the terrible hands of the living God. There are here none of the guarantees of success that ordinary life, in combination with the ironies of fate, sometimes renders possible; the affair altogether belongs to an inscrutable personality who is under no obligation to respect every human wish.[12]

It is not easy to discern the consolations of such an ideal. Would it not be more comforting to believe that we may live more or less as we please – within the increasingly relaxed moral constraints of humanist culture – and that the whole nasty affair terminates on this side of the grave? Isn't atheism our best bet if we really want consolation? The atheist could reply that theistic religion distinctively offers the prospect of immortality – a career beyond the grave – which serves to allay the natural human fear of extinction. Moreover, it will be said, religious faith offers a heavenly compensation for earthly wretchedness. To be sure, theism does indeed offer such hopes and reassurances. Like every ideology, whether religious or secular, it diagnoses our ailments and then offers a cure; it moves from a sense of despair to a kind of chastened optimism. And this of course is a defining feature of every viable style of living, of every *life*-style. Theism offers, according to its advocates, valid hopes grounded in a particular metaphysic of man and Nature. And in this respect it resembles every total belief-system, for without advertising such hopes it could hardly qualify as a way of life. The atheist is under an obligation to show that theistic conviction offers baseless reassurances which cater simply to the human need for security in a precarious existence.

VII

If theism is an illusion, it is certainly a grand one: reality is abandoned on a truly massive scale. Certainly no one need deny that the discrepancy between the mundane origins of religion, when viewed from the disbelieving perspective, and the elaborately metaphysical scheme it provides for the execution of relatively modest social and personal tasks, indicates at the very least the sheer fertility of the religious imagination. How did men manage to conjure from nothing, so to speak, a whole metaphysical outlook not suggested by anything in the world of experience? (Nothing in the austere Arabian desert even remotely resembled the voluptuous extravagance of the Muslim paradise.) Here, then, was an imaginary universe of false absolutes, pleasing to the religious impulse that seeks eternity, bearing no resemblance to the empirically known world of contingency and decay. 'A big lie', as Ernest Hemingway tells us, 'is more plausible than the truth', especially, one might add, when it is big and religious. The seminal religious figures of the biblical and koranic religions performed, it would seem, a major feat of imaginative literature beside which the literary fancies of a Shakespeare, not to mention a Plato, figure as mere experimental gestures in the art of fiction.

Theism is, it is said, like all transcendent religion and metaphysics, rooted in an inveterate hankering for false absolutes. Of all the controversial claims in this area, this is perhaps the most unconvincing. Theism is, on any showing, an exceptionally sincere attempt to escape from the government of illusory absolutes. The desire to uproot ultimately false ideals constitutes the impulse to iconoclasm, itself the religious vocation *par excellence*. Within theism, and particularly within Islam, the sheer severity of the iconoclastic conscience is striking and undeniable. In its very credo, this is laid down as a fundamental religious obligation, in a real sense the *only* religious obligation. 'There is no god,' says many a *surah*, 'but God.' What is this but an operative veto on the religious imagination from attributing ultimate efficacy to what are interpreted as false ideals? Religious idealism is, notwithstanding Nietzsche, based on a respect for reality, not on an escape from it.

There is here potential for polemic.[13] The theist is at liberty to announce that the place to find false absolutes, the impulse to unreality, is in the human, all too human world of modern humanist culture, art, fashion and academia. Such polemic inspires further polemic; and it helps no one's cause. But it is only fair to note that the aggressive disbelief of such institutions as the British Humanist Association exactly parallels the unreflective dismissal of atheism by religious orthodoxy. Dogmatism in either camp is the common enemy.

VIII

The claims in the preceding section are lacking in nuance and perhaps sound overly defensive. It would indeed be premature to rest one's case here and, accordingly, we shall return to these issues in subsequent chapters. In the meantime, the best way of handling this entangled skein of reasoning is by isolating one central concern, namely, humanism interpreted as the creed of the brave new world, and examining it in a deliberately general way.

'They that deny a god,' writes Francis Bacon, 'destroy a man's nobility: for certainly man is of kin to the beasts by his body; and if he be not of kin to God by his spirit, he is a base and ignoble creature.'[14] The humanist would retort no doubt that the divine is an external fiction that humiliates the deepest urges of the purely human condition – a condition that comes into its own, attains authenticity, only in the hinterland of a secure social order. We have here two ruthlessly opposed claims enlisting two opposed postures of the will. What, then, are the right ideals, the correct loyalties, for the achievement of an authentic humanity?

If in the past men wanted to overcome their humanity – surpass the human plight – today it is difficult enough to be human. Modern thought is only too familiar with the uncomfortable proximity between the human condition and a condition of unalloyed animality. Man is, as the social scientists say with routine indifference to the strange potential of the phrase, 'a social animal'. He is forever constrained to live in danger of sinking to a level where his purely physical (or biological) drives could dominate his existence. Indeed, it has been said, physical survival may not be a preparation for any higher end: it may well be an end in itself. The suggestion is repeatedly made in imaginative literature and in social theory that the human condition is itself a species of a purely animal condition graced with a few characteristically human delusions, such as the irrepressible wish for ideals with supernatural referents.

Modern humanism has supplied us with a new self-image. What is man? Religious people answer proudly that he is the apex of creation, made in the image of God and in consequence the epitome of God's fair handiwork. The humanist replies that man is a social being with a rather unflattering lineage in the animal kingdom. His faculties and natural endowments – reason, conscience, the impulse to altruism – are no gifts of the gods. They find their origin in human, purely human, needs and conventions. The human condition is, notwithstanding all its inspiring ideals, merely the outer veneer on an essentially animal condition to which we are firmly chained. The will to transcendence, concludes the humanist, must now seek a more modest aspiration that both begins and ends in the purely man-made condition.

It is no small irony that secular thought has, in attempting to aggrandise man by ousting God, managed to reduce man. Bacon's remark is not without a point. For certainly, man is not, for the humanist, on the pedestal in the way in which he was in the traditional religious vision that had assigned him the status of deputy of the eternal God, the crown of creation. If religion denigrates man by placing him under an external sovereignty, so does humanism – in its own way. And it is not at all clear which offers us the nobler humanism. For the atheist, man lives, dies and rots. For the believer, man lives, dies and lives for ever – under a merciful and omnipotent suzerainty.

In the last quarter of the twentieth century, there is a growing dissatisfaction with the humanist vision. The ideals of man's elemental goodness, the belief in indefinite progress, a trust in the efficacy of the purely human, a conviction about the exclusive centrality of man – in fine, all the ideals inaugurated by the European Enlightenment – are themselves now under the sceptical microscope. These normative principles, admittedly inspiring in the early eighteenth century are, after the darkness of our worst century so far, no longer capable of sustaining the old chiliastic hopes once associated with them. The result of this realisation has been a growing intellectual humility that is particularly marked in recent social theory. Has atheistic humanism succeeded where theistic faith had failed?

After post-war depression, the entrenchment of totalitarianism, the rise of organised crime, coupled with the general débâcle of the traditional outlook, many are finding it harder to believe in the inevitability of social progress, in unaided man's capacity for moral excellence or in the ultimate beneficence of the evolutionary process. To make things much worse, we have recently begun to live under the increasingly darkening shadow of universal holocaust. One cannot lay the blame for all this at the humanist's door; but, at any rate, the contemporary disillusionment with man has reached high proportions. We are easily disabused of the Enlightenment optimism about men's basic impulse to goodness and altruism. Even the exaltation of childhood and of the associated ways of innocence has become noticeably rarer in modern thought; contemporary misanthropy is not restricted to eccentric Englishmen or even to decent men whose daughters turned out badly.[15] The wave of humanitarian optimism has run its course.

In the secularised West, this is an age of disillusioned maturity. The decline of the Christian belief in a loving force behind Nature and the human world has gone hand-in-hand with the growth of a characteristically modern cynicism – a cynicism more intense in the quality of its conviction that any ancient variety. 'All is futile', said the old cynics. 'All is not futile: it is worse than futile', say the new cynics. For there is ignorance, prejudice, pain and failure; and these are worse than mere futility. To be sure, the most desolating variety of cynicism may itself be the product of a profoundly reverent and trusting humanitarianism. But it must be a humanitarianism internally frustrated. As a result, a chronic dissatisfaction with life's ordinary prospects has recently been gripping the secularised peoples of the western world. Gone is the zest for life *per se* so characteristic of both religious civilisations and of pagan civilisations in infancy. In its place one finds a gratuitous sense of doom that seeks ever and anon some temporary refuge in excessive self-absorption, in an increasingly sordid sensuality embittered by its own loss of natural eroticism, in crass commercialism, and in motiveless acts of unconstructive violence.

The decline of Christianity has certainly led to the dismemberment of western civilisation – a civilisation that has lost its old centre of gravity without having successfully found an alternative one. The overall result is a dangerous if creative experiment in cultural insanity. The self-satisfied rationalist credo of one brand of western humanism seems unconvincing. At any rate, it must accept responsibility for the current victory of commercialism and sensuality, for all the bitter produce of an increasingly irreligious society. At root, of course, our current circumstance in the secularised world is a signal defeat for those who initiated the Enlightenment project, firmly convinced both of the didactic value of history and of the inherent goodness of man.

Nietzsche was the greatest nineteenth-century critic of the Enlightenment. But his own brand of humanism, with its questionable emphasis on political inegalitarianism, has never been popular. The reasons for this are not far to seek. As a clear-sighted architect of western humanist doctrine, he carried his scepticism about religion to a maddeningly consistent conclusion. And then he turned back. For though Nietzsche had taken the axe to the root of one idealist tree, he still felt obliged to take refuge in an ideal – the humanist ideal – in which man was the only reality, to the delight of Protagoras, the measure of all things. And yet the final irony was that man also had to be transcended, not in favour of a divinity but in favour of an ideal. Nietzsche marked the normative crisis of human existence with a memorial – the Nietzschean corpus[16] – and then took refuge in the higher man, the *Übermensch*. It was difficult to live with the modern truth about our nature. Man, modern man, was not worthy of worship; we needed a new idealism to retain our allegiance. For in slaying all the old divinities, modernity had not spared man either.

The Kingdom of God

God,
There is no god but he,
The living, the everlasting.

Koran, *The House of 'Imran*

I

Visitors to the famous Cordoba mosque in Spain cannot fail to read
the ubiquitous inscription, 'He is the dominant (*Huwal-ghalib*)'. What
a revealing index to the Muslim mind! The twentieth-century Islamic
philosopher, Sir Muhammad Iqbal, is reported, on reading this inscription, to have exclaimed: 'Would that man were dominant somewhere
too!' The inscription and the philosopher's reaction to it together contain the germ of our concerns in this chapter.

Iqbal's comment betrays a characteristically modern impulse, one
that conceals a characteristically modern judgement on an older style
of religiosity. Those who built the mosque, one of Islam's architectural
glories, were of course expressing the perennial sentiment of Muslim
piety. They were men enchanted with the religious world, men who
had not tasted the forbidden fruit of modern scepticism. For them, man
is a pilgrim in this transient land always at the mercy of Heaven; the
earth, decked out in fair colours, like its mortal inhabitants, moves
inexorably towards doom and oblivion. 'Everything is in decay (*fanin*),'
says the sacred author, 'except the countenance of thy Lord'
(K:55:26–7; 28:88; interpreted).[1]

Iqbal's remark supplies a revealing index to the modern mind. For
us, including many religious believers, the primacy of the human and
the natural is almost second nature in a way that would be foreign to
the integrity of an ancient religious temper addicted to the supernatural,
reared on docility and unqualified obedience to faithful dictates. Certainly the instincts of traditional Muslim piety eagerly give way to God,
give everything to God, and nothing to Caesar. There is today, however,
a sophisticated seriousness about man, the purely earthly condition and

indeed about the autonomy of the human moral sense. Contemporary man is the measure of all things.

This current instinct is so difficult to dethrone; and it is wholly at odds with the dominant mood of Islamic religiosity. Islam, as the most absolute of the Abrahamic monotheisms, has a profoundly transcendental emphasis at its core. Indeed, it sees the transcendent as providing the true measure of the human. The divine, it is held, is fundamental to the truly human consciousness of the world; it alone *endows* – I use the word advisedly – man with a purpose that fully corresponds to human nature. Men must, the sacred author urges, confess the reality of Allah in order to be authentically human. Not only must the created being allow God to be the only sovereign – the creed of Islam – he must simultaneously allow himself to be human. And to be truly human is to be truly submissive to God.

II

'He is the dominant', says the inscription. God has the last word in the affair – every affair. This would no doubt seem to be the standard picture emerging from the Koran. Allah has inalienable sovereignty over human lives; rightful master of creation, man is his obedient slave (*'abd*) forever in danger of incurring his wrath.[2] Radically independent both of his creatures and of their response to his summons (K:35:15; 39:7), Allah has indeed honoured mankind by his free and gracious decision to reveal himself. Though the initiative here is divine, it is men who need, radically need, God. For idolatry does not debase Allah: it debases the created human being, making him into an inferior article.

The mysterious if gracious sovereignty of God allows no room for the presumptions of human expectation and understanding. Allah's ways are unaccountable, indeed doubly so for they are both ultimately inexplicable and morally absolved of the need for explanation – the need for accountability. 'Allah makes whom he wills enter into his mercy', runs the oft-repeated refrain (K:42:8; 48:25; 76:31, etc.). Indeed, God chastises whom he wills and forgives whom he wills, says many a *surah* with terminative emphasis. It is not in vain that God is God.

How should one live under such a conclusive and ultimate sovereignty? The Koran constantly advises men to 'fear' their Lord, have piety (*taqwa*) – live in constant awareness of their duty to God (K:4:1; 57:28; 59:18; 22:1). Believers are given the grim hint that there are trials which do 'not smite in particular the evildoers among you' (K:8:25). There is here no room for complacency. In unknown and creatively sinful ways, the human heart and mind can commit some secret treachery, unwittingly seek to usurp Allah's prerogative and thereby hasten on judgement and damnation. Take care, cautions *surah* 49 (v.2), 'lest your works become vain while you perceive not'.

Details of the creaturely obligations to the creator supply the Koran's dominant concern. The believer should seek to sanctify every circumstance of birth and biography, no matter how private, arbitrary, unholy, sordid; men ought to harness every faculty and its associated experience. There is no arena of human thought, sensibility, experience, volition or even creative imagination that deserves to be excused let alone exempted from the normative demands of Muhammad's all-encompassing master. From the cradle to the grave, human life is lived within the parameters of a righteous sovereignty that is careful, caring, concerned, observant, watchful. 'Allah is not unaware of the things you do', runs the quaint understatement (K:11:123). No indeed; he is not unaware. Nor is this mere talk. It is a startling feature of Islam as a way of life that it demands that its adherents take all the religious obligations seriously. Faith is as faith does. The sovereignty of God daily and ubiquitously weighs down on men, almost like the gravity of the natural environment. Even an arena of experience so instinctively private as sexuality is brought within the purview of divine dictate. Believers are to fear God and to seek to conceive their progeny in conscious, indeed humbling, awareness of the absorbing power and grace of sexuality as a divinely creative gift that perpetuates the human heritage (K:2:223). This is indeed a comprehensive suzerainty that leaves no room for 'a solitariness where wounds are nursed'.[3]

III

'He is the dominant', echoes the devout believer. If there be a single slogan that expresses the deepest impulse of Muslim piety, this surely is the one. For it turns up at each and every level of Islamic conviction. Thus, at the existential level, Muslims have allowed Allah to dwarf his creation. Sufi pantheism, to take an admittedly extreme example, has even seen God as the only being who truly exists[4] – exists by essence, as the Scholastics would say – welcoming, indeed celebrating the implied suggestion that he is the only genuine agent.[5] The ninth-century mystic Sheikh Abu Yazid al-Bistami is famous for an instructive witticism, still enjoyed in Sufi circles. When someone remarked that once upon a time there was nothing but God, the Sheikh soberly answered: 'There is still nothing but God.'[6]

The sovereignty of God is perhaps nowhere more importantly prominent than on the moral plane: he has the last word in the normative affair. Indeed, there is a reading of the Koran which would suggest that Allah is totally independent of the created dictates of moral norm. The divine is entirely immune from human moral appraisal or accusation. In so far as there is an ethical theme in the sacred text, this must surely be the one. It is a recurring subject providing one of the deepest convictions, embedding a central strand, in the Muslim or, more broadly, Hebraic experience. 'We did not wrong men but they wronged themselves' (K:9:69; 10:44; 43:76), declares the sacred author, lamenting the fate of the overwhelmed and destroyed. The prophet Dhul Nun, usually identified with the biblical Jonah, glorifies God while exercising severe self-incrimination, in a passage very dear to popular piety (K:21:87).

Muslim piety has always taken keen pleasure in giving Allah his due. If the preservation of God's perfect power and moral superiority requires the curtailment of human rights, so be it. God is king, owner, master; we are his servants, citizens in a world that is under the burden of a conclusive if deferred judgement.

IV

Huwal-ghalib, says the inscription. Contained within this concise exclamation is the unanimous verdict of traditional credal righteousness. And yet, of course, this is not to say that the rebellious impulse is totally dead within Islam. In 1911 Iqbal publicly recited a stirring poem that was interpreted by the religious authorities as in effect a blasphemous attempt to put Allah on trial – if the expression be allowed. The work itself, *The Complaint (Shiqwa)*, which is well remembered especially by some modern Muslims,[7] gives a moving poetical expression to the familiar human wish for an explanation of God's dark designs. *The Complaint*, rightly seen by many as a pinnacle of Urdu religious poetry, was banned by religious authorities but not before it had excited great interest in the learned world of pre-Independence India. While it is naturally impossible to convey here the beauty of Iqbal's writing, it may fairly be said that *The Complaint* is essentially an attempt to hold up God to the ordinary standards of moral accusation. If Muslims are faithless, is Allah indeed faithful to the Muslims? Why does he favour nations and communities in a manner that is to all appearances arbitrary? Iqbal fancies that he can, presumably, imagine coherent and morally superior alternatives to the ways of the Almighty.

Unfortunately, however, the great philosopher did not stay long enough in the whirlwind. Iqbal prudently wrote a sequel, the equally brilliant and justly famous *Answer to the Complaint (Jawabay-Shiqwa)*, in which he makes the infallible if enigmatic deity of Islam offer an incisive reply to the earlier implied accusations. The answers from Heaven were predictable in content if wrapped in Iqbal's unpredictably charming style. Those Muslims who were faithful to God, who took God to be God, were dead and gone; left behind were we moderns who know how to fold our arms and complain – like Iqbal. This was the orthodox line and the religionists liked it. Orthodoxy had won; only the sacred verdict remained in the field. *He* is the dominant.

Iqbal was rash enough to demand an answer out of the whirlwind; and sensible enough not to wait too long. The universal historico-human order remains firmly under a conclusive and blameless sovereignty. The potentially radical questions about the ultimate style of the divine art remain unanswered. Iqbal, like Job and other penitents, accepts the normal religious demand that the believer subdue his feeling of moral outrage against the unsettling features of God's providence – precisely what the satanic impulse incites. To be sure, some men do legitimately raise questions, it is conceded, about the divine commerce with the world. Moses complained about Allah's apparent lack of justice in giving the disbelieving Pharaoh a spectacular amount of wealth while visiting penury upon his chosen Children of Israel (K:10:88; interpreted) just as Noah was at a loss over the drowning of his son in the deluge given the divine promise of deliverance for the entire household (K:11:42–7). But such prophetic interrogation of God, if one may call it that, is not tantamount to any fundamental questioning of the divine art; it amounts merely to an expression of specific grievances from men whom God loves.

Iqbal didn't stay long enough to get an answer out of the whirlwind. This is entirely unsurprising. Men greater than Iqbal have done little better: even Job came out pretty badly from this ordeal. What is surprising is that Iqbal wrote a complaint at all. For not only did he know the answer before asking the question, he had no intention of suspending his orthodoxy long enough, or even seriously enough, to look in earnest for the virtues of heresy. Iqbal recognised, as every believer must, that the central mystery (*ghayb*) of Allah's choices and actions can at best be mitigated by recourse to further (if more comforting) mystery. But to recognise this is tantamount to accepting, for all practical intents and purposes, that God is God. He is the dominant for the orthodox – and for Iqbal.

V

For us, the central worry remains. 'He is the dominant' is no doubt the correct slogan but that still leaves on our hands the delicate problem concerning the right form, the appropriate kind of domination. Is God ascendant because he has the *de jure* right to transcend the dictates of morality? Is he ascendant – dominant – on account of his righteousness? (Does it make moral sense to ask these questions?)

To answer these questions, we need to pose another. Does the ordinance of moral norm operative in the created order, so to speak, breed a standard of potential accusation and vindication relevant also to the creator? The traditional Muslim (and orthodox Jewish) answer would seem to be that divine actions cannot coherently be assessed by use of the moral rules ordained for the human world. Indeed, the integrity of the distinction between right and wrong (fundamental to the operation of norm) is itself attained purely by divine arbitrium. That is to say, the validity of the difference between right and wrong operative in the mortal world is not intrinsic.

It is perhaps here that some modern sensibilities are most deeply outraged. The current awareness of the rights of humanity includes a rejection of the older amoral prowess of deity as unworthy of reverence. Any morally plausible portrait of God's relationship to man presupposes, it is thought, that both humanity and deity are somehow indifferently under the yoke of ethical dictate. The decree of moral regulation must necessarily be internally related to the ultimate nature of the divine art, much as sin – a revolt within the context of an essentially righteous order – is conceptually linked, on a religious world-view, to the deepest crisis in the human personality.

What are we to make of this? Certainly, Allah is a righteous being who loves the good. Is he, then, subject to moral assessment? One may say that any creative artist, including God, ought to be concerned with the soundness of artistic style. And a concern with the integrity of style, whether human or divine, implies at least a willingness to endorse internal demands engendered by the maintenance of such an integrity. In other words, God must in part answer to a sense of right and wrong already operative in a world that he has created. Nor is this to impose an external requirement – itself an act of presumption. Rather, it is to make explicit one central implied normative requirement of a creative art rooted in a concern with ideals of value.

In closing this section, let me try to put these deep and complex perplexities a little more simply if crudely. The divine being, I am suggesting, cannot properly be wholly absolved from the obligation to respect the moral norms ordained for the righteous government of the created order. For unless we accept that good and evil, right and wrong, or, more abstractly, commitment to and lapse from ideal, are authentic categories both for creature and creator alike, we cannot avoid making a mockery of the historic struggle, the creative tension, between the opposed forces of good and evil. Thus, if good and evil are illusory for God, illusory in the eyes of a superior wisdom (which implies that they are, in one way, simply illusory) then the drama of human history is, to put it in moral terms, a cheat. And it is unworthy of reverence to conceive of Allah as an impostor. In fine, then, God must share with man a common concern over the potentially accusatory power of normative demand.

VI

In quality of conviction, the sacred scripture of Islam may fairly be described as an amoral document, completely free from apology and justification. This familiar account of the Koran's dominant mood is, I believe, largely correct. But the Koran is a strikingly fecund literature capable of nourishing a large variety of religious moods, as is evidenced, incidentally, by the fact that Islam, a predominantly 'political' faith, has inspired a surprisingly rich mystical tradition. It is time now to explore briefly some of the uncharacteristic strains and emphases in the Muslim scripture.

The Koran frequently emphasises Allah's omnipotence, omniscience, and utter transcendence. While Allah is wholly independent of creation, men are wholly dependent on and answerable to Allah. Indeed, men must make themselves morally credible in the eyes of their creator – on pain of eternal torment.[8] The emphasis on the terrors of Hell is a characteristic feature of the sacred volume. The language used in this connection is often strikingly direct, peremptory, intensely sincere. Full of violent metaphors, it was a language that indelibly impressed the Prophet, his companions and consequently all subsequent generations of Muslims up to this day; the fear of God has always been unquestionably the dominant motive for Muslim piety.[9]

This is part, the greater part, of the story. But within the Koran, well under the surface, there runs, I believe, a kind of permanent meditative restlessness, capable of powerfully engaging the believing temper in some fugitive mood, and threading a kind of tenderness in a terrible tale. In a way, this is not surprising. Allah is not merely the God of Fire; he is also merciful, appreciative, forbearing, just, long-suffering. At the end, there remains in the field that characteristically firm Islamic refusal to slide into pity for man; any variety of mawkishness remains totally foreign to the Koran. But, and this is the central point here, one can discern within the sacred text not merely Allah's sheer strength or pure power – that would be a superficial reading – but rather a curious kind of *reserve* of strength, a potentiality that is the conclusive proof of moral integrity.

Let us now examine a few koranic passages in the light of these considerations. Take the passages which offer qualified assurances of success in the religious life, verses which exhort the pious and patient will to persevere in the firm hope of God's mercy. *Surah* 8 (vv.26ff.) contains a pledge from Allah, one expressed as part of what must be among the mildest of the many pleas for men to ponder their destiny:[10]

> And remember when you were few and abased in the land,
> and were fearful that the people would snatch you away;
> but he gave you refuge, and confirmed you with his help,
> and provided you with the good things, that haply you might
> be thankful.

O believers, betray not God and the Messenger,
and betray not your trusts and that wittingly;
and know that your wealth and your children are a trial,
and that with God is a mighty wage.
O believers, if you fear God, he will assign you a salvation,
     and acquit you of your evil deeds,
and forgive you; and God is of bounty abounding.[11]

What a far cry from the scornful indifference of *surah* 2 (v.105) where 'Allah singles out for his mercy whom he wills'! After enumerating his blessings, 'haply', concludes the sacred author, 'you might be thankful'. Haply – maybe – just maybe, says the verse. Again, consider a passage in which the Almighty conducts his interrogation of our species in a tone that is anxious, ruminative, almost aggrieved: 'O man, what has emboldened thee against thy gracious Lord, who created thee, then perfected thee, then proportioned thee aright?' (K:82:6–7).

What are we to make of these and other passages similar to them? Clearly, they cannot reasonably be interpreted as the outbursts of a dictatorial tyrant or as routine requests for information. Indeed, I believe that one can discern in them a sensitive application for a considered moral reaction from human beings. God is concerned about man; twice in *surah* 35 (vv.30, 34), Allah is said to be 'most appreciative' of whatever good men may do. The Koran contains, I would argue, genuinely moral literature in which there is a deeply felt awareness of the need for moral reciprocity. Man is not a slave or servant in any ordinary sense; Allah is certainly no ordinary master. Men are free moral agents who do good or evil and Allah respects their autonomy (K:16:75–6).[12] It is true that the Koran does suggest, in some contexts, that creatures are mere chattels (K:5:118; interpreted) but, I would contend, this suggestion is probably made in the larger attempt to dislodge human complacency.

One is tempted to warm to this thesis. Could the threats about Hell be deliberately hyperbolic, intended perhaps to jolt us out of our complacent negligence and heedlessness? *Surah* 20, v.113: 'Even so we have sent it down as an Arabic Koran, and we have turned about in it something of threats, that haply they may be godfearing, or it may arouse in them remembrance.' Haply – maybe – just maybe, says the verse. Could it be that the passages in which Allah is said to punish whom he pleases – passages exalting a kind of arbitrary prowess – were largely meant to anger the complacent and powerful Qureish whose conservatism, like that of all establishments, was too blind to see the efficacy of forces potentially greater than itself?

We cannot be sure of the answer. Certainly it can be said that threats alternate with milder pleas, that the language of the Muslim scripture is usually direct, even upbraiding, but occasionally coaxing, even gentle. It is possible, indeed likely, that the emphasis I have discerned is not dominant; it seems isolated, even incidental. We can, however, safely say, notwithstanding the complexity of the issue, that the God of Islam is no dictator with arbitrary powers. He is not simply the God of Fire wholly indifferent to men's interests or to purely human sensibilities. Such a conception of the Muslim deity does not fit the facts, though it certainly fits the prejudices of a very large number of critics of Islam.

It may fairly be said that Allah's power and transcendence are tempered with justice, mercy and deep concern for creation. The divine involvement with man is ultimately moral (as opposed to legal or political) in character. Unfortunately many Muslim writers sometimes celebrate the arbitrary prowess of deity (with a self-indulgence, incidentally, that invites comparison with the Christian celebration of paradox) and then complain if Jewish or Christian critics describe Islam as a power-centred faith. In one of his more questionable aphorisms, Iqbal tells us: 'Power is more divine than truth. God is power' and again 'God of Islam is power'.[13] Critics of Islam may indeed be occasionally excused for entertaining a mistaken conception of the Muslim God.

VII

'*He* is the dominant', says the inscription. To be able to allow God to dominate one's life – that is always the devout hope. And to do that, it is thought, men should, to put the matter in terms of a distinction alien to and unformulable in Islam, give everything to God and nothing to Caesar. Everything belongs to God; everything should belong to God. Nothing belongs to Caesar; nothing should belong to Caesar. God is the measure of all things.

When the issue is put in these terms, one can feel the full force of the central humanist objection to transcendent faith. The extrinsic nature of the religious ideal for human life, argues the humanist, comes out clearly when we interpret theism as providing a blue-print imposed from the outside and, consequently, suffocating men's right to prescribe their own aspirations and duties. To the extent that the human world is an imposed datum – imposed from an essentially non-human viewpoint – it cannot be, we are told, a world capable of fulfilling a truly humanist ideal. In so far as theistic faith is inherently an attempt at an external perception of human destiny, it must necessarily frustrate ambitions internal to an autonomous human nature. In truth, however, the objection continues, men should not expect some supernatural being to endow them with a destiny; they should make their own destiny, one that is human, all too human, purely human, proudly human.

This is a powerful objection; and the theist needs to answer it. The religionist's task is to show the humanist that transcendent religion alone can enable men to realise their true nature; that there is a viable kind of humanism which cherishes ideals of value themselves deriving from a concern with a transcendent point of reference. In other words, the theist needs to argue that our current attempt at self-realisation is itself optionally subsumable under the aegis of atheistic humanism or under the banner of faithful theism; to be a humanist is not in itself to be a rejector. Indeed, the religious task is to show that faith alone can perpetuate the noblest humanism.

To show that, however, in this day and age, almost necessarily requires that we give, deliberately give, Caesar his due. Our religiosity today must be reared in the hinterland of a seriousness, Semitic in intensity, but directed in the first instance not towards God but rather towards man. We must begin with man; the proper study of man is man – not God. That is inevitably the new style of religiosity in modernity. The human and the natural can no longer be relegated in favour of the world yet to come (*al-akhirah*); the world of man and mortality is the crucial locus of the supernatural.

To begin with man is one thing; to end there, another. To give Caesar his due is not to imply that one should usurp the rights of a divine sovereignty. Theism can never be, some Christian thinkers in the liberal wing of Protestant theology to the contrary notwithstanding, a doctrine about the affirmation of human autonomy. God must have the decisive word in the human affair. I am merely suggesting that he need not have the sole one.

Theism should be humanised if it is to win the allegiance of modern man. What does this mean? It certainly does *not* mean that religious faith should be seen as being of purely human origin. Genuine theism does indeed contain an integral reference to an other-worldly reality that secretes a significance for man in the natural world. Theism can never properly be merely an instrument for revising our self-understanding or just a useful tool for effecting radical anthropological criticism; transcendent religion cannot be in the service of providing merely enlightened comment on human nature. God must enter the scene and somehow or other dominate it.

One of the cardinal defects of Protestant Christianity in the liberal scholarly tradition has been its tendency to give everything to Caesar and nothing to God. We see this clearly in the misguided attempt to transform theism into merely a moral policy. Virtue may be its own reward; faith certainly is not. We can be moral for its own sake – perhaps we even ought to be. Moral conviction is purified by shedding external backings, sanctions and rewards; but a religion divorced from its supernatural setting of benefits and burdens ceases to be a religion. We cannot, then, meaningfully be religious for its own sake. Faith, as an objective rather than a personal reality, essentially requires a transcendent component in its definition and reference. For the goal of the religious life is neither virtue for its own sake nor even truth for truth's sake: it is the Kingdom of God.

To see religion in a human perspective is not, then, to reduce it to some purely human reality. Rather, it is to recognise that faith and rejection are both, in the last analysis, human choices. The central motivation today for embrace and rejection is, in general, exactly the same: namely, to make some purposeful sense of this whole nasty affair that life is. The central quarrel is over the correct interpretation of human nature, the right characterisation of the human plight. Is man radically independent of external supra-human parameters? Or is human nature properly to be seen as a reality necessarily subject to the scrutiny of a transcendent intelligence?

Rejectors do not 'make a just estimate of Allah', laments the sacred author (K:6:91; 22:74; 39:67). To render this thought accessible to the modern mind, the religionist would need to say that men, in rejecting their creator, fail to make, to alter the koranic phrase, a just estimate of themselves. For, on a religious interpretation, to reject God is to make an unfair estimate of man. Our problem today, then, is, in a crucial sense, man-centred, in and of this world, even when integral references to God and the transcendent are implied. Modern man is the measure of many things.

It is important, especially for orthodox Hebrew and Muslim readers, not to misunderstand these claims. I am arguing that the creaturely significance of man must today be assessed against the contemporary background of a new seriousness about the human ethos. The threads of our theological fabric all involve the natural, the mundane, the human. The possibility that our life has a meaning that is externally imposed and consequently independent of the sense it bears to human thought and ideal is one that can today be safely dismissed. It is our task to construct a religiously viable framework for giving Caesar his due: nothing more but nothing less. And to do that we must recognise the prerogatives of the human vocation, a recognition itself necessarily prefatory to the modern achievement of 'a just estimate of Allah'.

VIII

'Would that *man* were dominant somewhere too!' Iqbal's lament captures the characteristic mood of the sceptical, potentially rebellious, mentality. It is a mentality that rejects not so much the old religious solutions to life's problems but rather the old manner of posing the issues. The traditional thinker gave priority to revealed insight, seeing the world, his world, under the aegis of a supernatural dictum. The modern thinker instinctively interprets the world, his world, against the background of the primacy of purely human experience and opinion.

Since the European Enlightenment, the complex reality of human nature, rather than the transcendent reality of God, is at the hub of our knowledge of the cosmos and the special disciplines. Indeed, supernatural religion has itself been reduced by sceptics to merely a response to the anguish about our human lot. Our outlook has become largely anthropocentric.

This is indeed a seismic shift in human reflection and understanding. It is implicitly reflected in the manner in which we today pose many of the eternal questions about the central enigmas of existence. (Would any pre-Enlightenment author have posed various religious questions in a way even remotely similar to the way in which the present author has posed them?) The fact is of course that the religious thinkers of the Middle Ages usually saw God's (alleged) revelation as the starting point for human reflection about human nature and the Deity; a blue-print, vouchsafed by revelation, provided *a priori* the categories required for understanding the world.

A sceptical world-pattern, inspired by belief in a different cosmic geography, largely determines the direction and character of modern thought in secularised societies. Apart from the anachronistic style of neo-orthodox thought,[14] modern theology in secular culture is essentially empirical and anthropological in emphasis. Man and empirical Nature are at the centre of the contemporary stage. Indeed, the existence of God and the supernatural are today interesting because they supply the metaphysical hinterland to the religious contention about the true image of man. This shift of focus is characteristic of modernity discernible as it is on many different levels of contemporary reflection. Thus, the student of comparative religion recognises that the Crescent and the Cross are in effect battles over the true image of humanity and only derivatively over the true image of the Deity. (Think here of a Christian Crusader and his Muslim opponent of the Middle Ages both seeing their quarrel as essentially to do with the truth about God – and only in a lesser degree to do with man.) Again, many a modern historian, impressed by the darkness of the human saga, subsequently loses faith in some benevolent providence at work behind the mortal condition. Indeed, to light this candle from the other end, those moderns who have felt the need to retain God in their philosophies have often done so because they saw him as a human necessity, as, for example, a precondition of our moral sense.

I have indicated, hardly controversially, that the direction of much modern theological thought is from the mundane to the celestial, not vice versa. This is of course a consequential change of direction; and the clearest instance of it is perhaps discerned in contemporary religious reflection about Nature's relation to the Deity (one of the themes of chapter 4). In the past, Nature was thought to be rationally intelligible *because* God was conceptualised as an architect, an artist concerned to maintain the integrity of his style. Today, religious thinkers sometimes contend that there may exist a sustaining intelligence, God, *because* Nature is rationally intelligible. The primary matrix of modern conviction is human, not meta-human – physical, not meta-physical. These shifts in the focus and direction of contemporary thought, reflected in the increasingly anthropological emphasis that a Feuerbach would savour, have momentous implications. Even in themselves, they spell a signal victory for a humanism that dictates the prevalent mood of the modern mind.

IX

'He is the dominant', says the inscription. A humanism that insists on ideals of value totally immanent in the human world is religiously unacceptable. The religious task is to live *with* the fact of divine sovereignty, not against it, not in effective denial of it, not in spite of it. Can we, then, have an authentic humanism that derives its impulse from a meta-human point of reference?

The anti-humanist proclivity is in an important way irremovable from supernatural monotheism. (To what extent this is a bad thing will depend on what we mean by 'humanism'.) Certainly, to be more specific, the religious view of morality is, in Kantian terms, heteronomous. Theism necessarily denies the autonomy of man in so far as it fetters us with moral obligations to a superhuman personality. Theistic faith denies the autonomy of ethics in so far as normative imperatives are not seen to be, so to speak, self-contained but rather interpreted as being components of a larger lifestyle in which the impulse to gratitude and reverence seeks and finds a transcendent referent. A sovereign superhuman will, then, confronts man and demands moral response.

The root of genuine religion is neither hatred of the world nor love of the eternal; it is in fact an awareness of the insufficiency of human nature to fulfil the obligations it somehow internally engenders – aims that, it is thought, are properly achieved only by commitment to ideals of *religious* value. Islam, as a God-centred faith, frequently and fiercely condemns as sinfully presumptuous any unduly optimistic assessment of purely human potential (K:90:5–7; 96:6–7; 75:1–6; 75:36–40). It will come as no surprise, therefore, that it may well be impossible to remove from the genuinely religious consciousness a tendency to degrade – or better, downgrade – the values of secular existence.

'Allah dominates (*Allah-u-ghalib*) in his purposes', says *surah* 12 (v.21), during a dramatic hiatus in the tale of Joseph. It would be difficult for the believer to dispute this verdict. The inscription in the mosque well expresses the theistic sentiment.[15] It is a sentiment masking an attitude naturally very much at odds with the modern wish for autonomy and emancipation. But there we have it; such is the ultimate style of the divine art. It would be unwise to question it beyond a certain limit.

What the religionist can do is to show that the modern disbeliever's ideal of emancipation is itself chimerical – a characteristically modern illusion. For every liberation is merely a change of masters – at best dominion by falsehood to dominion by truth. There is here no freedom *tout court*; at most we are free to be slaves – of the truth. Of course, theism offers us bondage to a particular alleged truth, a truth that teaches us that we are finite, fallible, mortal creatures – slaves of the limit. But it also invites us to give allegiance to a reality that somehow escapes the bondage of contingency, lapse from ideal and the inexorable ravages of time and, in doing so, serves to 'gather [us] into the artifice of eternity'.[16]

The Riddle of Man

Surely we have created man in trouble.
Koran, *The City*

I

It is a central tenet of Muslim anthropology that man is the epitome of God's fair handiwork. Indeed, human nature may arguably be said to be semi-divine (K:15:29; 38:72; interpreted); man is certainly endowed with the capacity to attain a prodigious destiny. God has honoured man by elevating him above the angels, all of whom fell down prostrate in ready acknowledgment of his superiority (K:15:30–1; 38:73–4).

This is, however, only one side of the story. Men are created weak (K:4:28); their nature conceals a permanent emotional restlessness (K:70:19; interpreted).[1] Indeed, man is 'made of haste' (K:17:11; 21:37); he is impetuous, weak-willed, foolish and short-sighted. The human constitution as ordained by Allah's free decree contains a natural tendency to wrongdoing (K:12:53). These koranic passages are all elusive and there is learned authority for somewhat differing interpretations. But it would be agreed on all accounts that man is indeed a problematic article created, in the Koran's peculiarly suggestive but untranslatable phrase, 'in trouble' (*fi kabad*; K:90:4; interpreted).[2]

Human beings, then, are endowed both with the capacity to be genuinely pleasing to their creator and yet capable of distorting their own higher nature. This latter capacity explains the most characteristic of human faults; men are prone to infidelity to the better side of their nature – a tendency itself often rooted in the proclivity to heedlessness (*ghaflah*). The Koran's charge is that human beings often fail to cultivate and discipline a faculty that would serve to remind them of their normative endowment. In their heedlessness, men commit the intellectual error of associating false deities with Allah (*shirk*) which, when subsequently placed on the more serious level of volition, leads to sinful conduct. But the divinely implanted religious seed – providing the knowledge of Allah's radical uniqueness and of human accountability to the divine – acts as a heavenly counterpoise to man's natural waywardness. When men recognise the signs of Allah, the celestial side of the see-saw becomes heavy and they rise above the angelic; when men deny the divine portents, they 'gravitate towards the ground' (K:7:176), sinking beneath the animal as the heavenly side becomes lighter.[3]

We have here, then, the outlines of the Islamic portrait of human nature. Man is naturally inclined to accept Islam; the Muslim faith is the *deen-ul-fitra'*, the religion of human nature. (Those who embrace Islam often describe themselves as 'reverts', not converts.) Islamic doctrine is thought to provide a knowledge[4] satisfactory to reason, the integrity of which is unaffected by sinful proclivity, while the sacred law (*shari'ah*) lays down the details concerning the exercise of the will in the larger attempt to attain purity of heart. The laws and regulations of the faith, then, supply the appropriate moral tuition for human nature. Though men often come to grief through their heedlessness, they remain capable of attaining the highest good. The picture is a relatively optimistic one, at least when seen as an assessment of the human capacity for virtue rather than as the actual record of human conduct. The attainment of a virtuous destiny requires the patient struggle, the hard climb (K:90:11) of the straight path (K:1:5). But the achievement of good is not impossible although there simultaneously persists within human nature that inner, regrettably often dominant, tendency to evil, the fruits of which are gathered in the koranic world of unheeded messengers and the sombre ruins of the subverted cities.

II

'And when thy Lord said to the angels, "I am setting in the earth a viceroy" ... ' So reads the opening verse of one of the most influential passages in the world's literature (K:2:30ff.). The proposal is received by the angels – with uncharacteristically irreverent scepticism. Man, they argue, is a sinful creature given to corruption and bloodshed. Can such a one truly be a trustee (*khalifah*) on behalf of his righteous creator? Can the world be entrusted to him for responsible stewardship?

The obedient angels immediately apologise for their presumption in doubting the supreme wisdom of the Almighty. 'I know what you know not', says Allah, with convincing simplicity. The election of Adam and his descendants as vicegerents is affirmed; the angels unambiguously concede man's supremacy over them and over creation in general (K:2:30ff.; 17:70).

Iblis, the supreme evil being, refuses, however, to accept Allah's word for it. The divine decision is, he contends, extremely risky; man is an unworthy creature who will fall victim to temptation and hence humiliate his own higher nature. It is this satanic insistence on the impropriety of expecting human nature to be malleable in the service of moral excellence that sets, for Muslims, one part of the context of the historic struggle between good and evil. It is and indeed should be seen as a *satanic* insistence both in the descriptive sense – it is Satan's stance – and in the moral sense as implying accusation since it is morally improper to doubt the wisdom of Allah's decision.

God, then, has freely decided to sponsor the human project; the angels had temporary misgivings about it while Satan has registered a permanent, indeed culpable, reservation. Perhaps, men too sometimes wonder, in a heretical mood, about the wisdom of the divine undertaking. But this is a central temptation that must be resisted. For men are religiously obliged to see the locus of the human vocation within the attempt to demonstrate that Allah's confidence in man is not misplaced. Indeed one cannot appreciate the full urgency of the koranic message unless one recognises that God is inviting man freely to vindicate both humanity and divinity against the common satanic question-mark – one which is at once about the moral excellence of the human creature and about the wisdom of the divine creator.[5] Men could hardly, one thinks, be placed under a more crushing burden.

III

One of the most remarkable features of Islamic thought is its age-long ambivalence about the status of man in relation to his creator. Muslims frequently emphasise Allah's inalienable rights over man and the human world. 'He is the dominant', said the inscription in chapter 7. Allah is utterly independent of and from the created world. And yet, to record a different strand of conviction, the Koran insists on the centrality of the human contribution to the divine undertaking. Indeed, as the opening verse of *surah* 76 asks rhetorically: 'Has man ever been out of God's considerations?'

At any rate, it is a measure of the worth of man that his free actions could bring into question even the schemes of a transcendent wisdom. For unless we assume that the ultimate issue of the historical process is predetermined in Allah's favour, in which case the entire drama is morally a cheat, it remains an open question whether or not God had acted rightly in electing man against heavenly counsel. It is *men's* response to the call of the minaret, whether in penitent submission (*islam*) or in impenitent rejection (*kufr*), that will decide the final outcome of the human drama, that will vindicate the wisdom of God. Small wonder, then, that Muhammad's Lord so frequently stresses the moral seriousness of the human vocation (K:6:70; 7:51; 21:16; 38:27; 44:38).[6]

Unfortunately, however, rejection and perverse heedlessness litter the human saga. We have here the irrefutable testimony of the sacred volume itself. The picture is a lugubrious one, of an incorrigible humanity addicted to sin and ingratitude, never turning in repentance until their cup is full (K:34:15–19). An admittedly forbearing sovereignty will not tolerate disobedience and obduracy. God warns; men disregard; and again. And, then, Allah's judgement comes suddenly while the sinners sleep the sleep of heedlessness: morning finds a generation fallen prostrate in its habitation (K:7:78). This is God's judgement; and it spares no one. God repeatedly apprises human complacency that bitter indeed are the fruits of nemesis. A thoughtless humanity repeatedly ignores the warning. Allah's retribution catches up with the sinners while they are wrapped in the treacherous ease of the afternoon slumber (K:7:4). And yet the heedless Arabians walk unrepentant in the very ruins where powerful nations had once flourished (K:20:128; 37:137–8). Satan, concedes *surah* Sheba (v.20), found true his judgement about a rebellious humanity.

If sin and rejection tell the truth about mankind, they do not tell the whole truth. There is, the Koran tells us, embrace and piety too, including conspicuous piety. Many human beings have responded, sometimes enthusiastically, to the heavenly summons; indeed a whole community now and again surrenders and pays heed (K:10:99). God's servants include men of unusual moral integrity; over them, says the sacred author, Satan has no authority. God's judgement about them was true.

If sin and rejection do not tell the whole story, they tell most of it. 'Few indeed of my servants,' laments *surah* Sheba (v.13), 'are grateful.' Most men accept anything and everything but faith (K:17:89); it were as though every generation inherited the tendency to denial from its predecessor (K:51:53). Unsurprisingly, ingratitude and rejection – the same word, *kufr*, denotes both in Arabic – weigh heavy in the balance.

It is a dark picture. We have before us, as religionists, a vast picture of human folly – within both ancient and modern history. Hasn't our stay been marked by infidelity, waste and irresponsibility? Didn't man foolishly accept the trust (*amanah*) of the world (K:33:72)? It is true that we, as a species, have, when it comes to virtue and excellence, scored well above zero. But how rich and colourful is the repertoire of our vices! There is today, in the last few decades of the twentieth century, a very marked need to justify the election of man as God's appointee: the sceptical standpoint, the satanic reservation, has certainly much to feed on.

In saying this I touch on one of the greatest and, to me, the most impressively disturbing, of the many theological puzzles I have identified in this work. An assessment of the actual record of human behaviour may lead one to deny, absurdly, the wisdom of God; yet to affirm the ultimate wisdom of the divine being is, in effect, to deny the realities of human nature and history. One could, of course, short-circuit critical thought here by pontificating that such an admittedly peculiar circumstance finds resolution purely within the province of the mystery (*ghayb*) of Allah's doings. But the puzzle itself remains. And it is located on a high level of seriousness for it is, in a way, the central riddle of religious thought.

When men's piety, especially conspicuous piety, reaches Heaven, the traditional commentators remark, the angels actually apologise for their initial presumption in doubting man's moral potential. After all, the angels muse, men worship God despite the distractions of a world that abounds with opportunities for evil. They do remember God, if imperfectly and infrequently; they somehow struggle against their lower passions, subdue their evil whims, and seek God's pleasure. And indeed they do all this while contending with the enmity of the supreme evil being dedicated to their spiritual ruin.[7] Surely, the angels conclude, man's worship is truly remarkable: while angels worship in an evil-free environment, being indeed already naturally inclined to do so, men worship amid the varied temptations and tribulations of earthly life and do so despite an inherent tendency to neglect and heedlessness. Isn't then the occasional worship of the free human creature superior to the ceaseless devotion of the obedient angel?

The answer to this question is no doubt in the affirmative. But what is one to say about the angelic reaction to the darker side of human nature? The apologists are, understandably, silent on this point. Yet isn't this a signal (and rather obvious) triumph for bias? For if the record of human virtue vindicates the divine wisdom, the equally, perhaps more, impressive record of human vice vindicates the satanic reservation about Adam and his descendants.

Human history offers us a vast picture of both the good and the evil that men do. The devout hope is that we will somehow tip the scales in favour of the good on the fateful Last Day (*yaum-il-akhir*). It is a steady refrain of the Muslim scripture: men are constantly encouraged to cultivate virtue and subdue vice in the larger attempt to refute the satanic scepticism about human nature. To the extent that human beings are free moral agents, the option to do good (or evil) remains more or less within the prerogative of human volition. Will we, individually and socially, succeed in achieving a virtuous destiny? Or will failure dominate the human record? This is, within the koranic framework, a riddle for each of us and collectively the riddle of man. Only the Last Day will witness a decisive resolution of a permanently ambiguous destiny vacillating between good and evil – an event described unforgettably as the hour when even children turn grey-headed with fear at the sight of what their own hands have forwarded (K:73:17).

IV

To err is certainly human. Though conventional wisdom is often mistaken or ambivalent in its deliverances, this particular claim deserves the accolade of central truth in human history. If one doubted its truth accusing the sage of some pessimism founded on *a priori* foundations, cradled in solitude, it would be sufficient for him to retort: 'Have a look for yourself.'

From a theistic perspective, human history, from Cain onwards at any rate, is mostly bad news. A careful examination of the mortal record has, both in religious and secular perspective, inspired at times a pessimism and anxiety that only invincible faith in God or the self-perfectibility of the human circumstance could effectively overcome. The Koran laments often enough that men resolutely refuse to learn from their mistakes; they refuse to discern the didactic value of history and archaeology – the two disciplines that record the calamitous consequences of rejection. Tragically, men are deluded into thinking that the ways of sin will prosper;[8] rejection dominates the Adamic saga. And yet God's enemies always fail in the end. But it is only in the end. And typically, it is only on the further side of experience that men learn their lesson, if at all. Pharaoh, laments the sacred author, had the creed of monotheism on his lips as the waters engulfed him, making him an inhabitant of the eternal Fire (K:10:91).

It was too late for Pharaoh. But no one could say, within a religious framework, that he had not been sufficiently warned. The rejectors are usually well aware of the things they do. 'Forgive them for they know not what they do' is merely the verdict of a compassionate sovereignty. For they do know what they do; they know very well what they do. Ignorance is no more the main cause of disbelief than knowledge the main cause of religious enthusiasm.[9]

The human capacity for active opposition to the prophetic cause has long been a source of theological puzzles. It is indeed a characteristically human capacity; both the ability to resist grace and, more strongly, the desire actively to thwart God's purposes, are components built into human nature. To be sure, the capacity for submission (*islam*) also persists within us. And taken together, we have the characteristic paradox of human nature: to crave earnestly for ideals of piety and yet actively disown them. It is of course this very circumstance that generates the tension necessary to the achievement of virtue. But, to record the final twist of the dialectic, this circumstance is in practice more congenial to human failure than to human success.

V

Many a *surah* sympathises with Muhammad as he grieves over his compatriots' wilful tendency to prefer the ways of impenitence to those of piety (K:5:41; 6:33; 10:65; 18:6; 26:3). Earlier prophets were similarly comforted (K:5:26); the ways of sin are time-honoured. Why, then, is human nature so recalcitrant to guidance and virtue?

Part of the answer is of course that the life of rejection is usually easier and more appealing. To attain righteousness requires sustained labour; God's moral demands call for unwelcome privations and uncomfortable sacrifices. The Koran frequently emphasises the need for struggle; men should ceaselessly 'strive in the way of God' (*jehada-fi-sabillillah*), subduing their natural passions (*nafs*), restraining their will in the service of the moral excellence that divine dictate demands.

An instructive incident is recorded in great detail in the *surah* which is unique for its mysterious omission of the Invocation (K:9:38–99).[10] Word had reached the Prophet that the Christian Byzantines of Syria were gathering at a place towards the north of the peninsula in the hope of crushing the infant religion. Accordingly, in October A.D. 630, less than two years before his death, Muhammad began to enlist support for the so-called Tabuk expedition, one that may well have pioneered the later elephantine military successes of Islam naturally leading the votaries of the new faith to believe that they were under the special favour of God.

It was the hot season in the Hejaz and, owing to a drought that year, the heat was unusually oppressive. Though the ageing messenger himself and his devout followers were willing to go the extra mile to please their Lord, many were less enthusiastic, preferring to stay at home, gather fruits, and enjoy the benefits of female society. It is, said some, uncomfortably hot, only to receive the Koran's much-quoted response that 'Hell is hotter still' (K:9:81). Many were deterred by reports of the Byzantines' military prowess; and others vaguely complained that they would be 'tempted' in the new land – a temptation usually identified as being the beauty of Syrian women. Aren't such men, asks the sacred volume, already victims of temptation – the temptation to worry about worldly temptation? (K:9:49).

The picture here is familiar if instructive. The fervour required for the attainment of piety is hard to come by; the motive for enthusiasm is rarely knowledge alone. It is true that knowledge of important goals, especially short-term ones, can motivate some rational persons; but knowledge rarely suffices to actuate religious zeal. Enthusiasm minimally requires an active awareness of the goal – any goal. But awareness is not enough; and the Koran recognises that. Both in religious and secular life, even a lazy or indifferent person becomes active when he perceives danger or is seduced by the prospect of extreme pleasure. Fear and pleasure seem to supply more powerful motives for action than knowledge alone.

It is a recognised fact that knowledge of certain realities has no real, or if you like existential, impact on daily behaviour and decision-making. This is particularly true of long-term goals. Thus, for example, the fact that, say, death and judgement are inevitable, rarely alters our priorities in ordinary living. It is true that some men have, especially in the past, lived in constant fear of divine judgement. But such a perception and the piety it engenders are relatively rare among modern believers. There was a time when people saw death and the imminence of nemesis in such vivid colours that daily priorities were deeply affected. It would be fair to say that most of us, including believers, especially today, live as though we were destined to live for ever: the recognition of the inevitable circumstance of mortality and the possibility of damnation carry little weight.

The sheer remoteness of the religious goal is undeniable in this secularised age. The distant terrors of Hell are, particularly in the contemporary world, insufficient even to motivate deeply religious people. Certainly, in environments of great religious fervour, many human beings led tolerably excellent lives. (Virtue is caught – not taught.) But ours is not an age of religious enthusiasm; we do not live in a religiously charged environment.[11]

The Koran recognises the presence and immediacy of profane passions within the human soul. And it is their presence no doubt that explains men's failure in the religious life. Some of our most intense and powerful natural impulses are morally bankrupt: they can severely reduce, even humiliate, our humanity. Gandhi, to take an example from non-Muslim piety, divulges in his remarkably honest autobiography that he had found sexuality to be a tough opponent. Indeed, he tells us, he would never have risen above the purely animal stage had his nature contained another impulse as powerful as sexuality.[12] Small wonder, then, that men so badly need the wet blanket of ethico-religious restraint.

No one could reasonably deny the sheer strength of various outlawed impulses that include, prominently, pride, illicit sexuality and the desire for unfair privilege. For most of us it would be true to say that these potentially culpable tendencies sometimes completely subdue the small voice of conscience. Perhaps Nietzsche is right when he tells us, with characteristically disturbing profundity, that even our conscience bows to the strongest of our drives.

Given, then, the power of the human impulse to impiety and our natural proclivity to seek the easier option, it is not surprising that the mood for piety comes and goes. It does not stay. And precisely the attempt to *sustain* the mood of penitence is the central difficulty in the life of faith. How are men to live continuously on the moral heights?

'It is not the quality,' writes Nietzsche, 'but the duration of noble sentiments that makes men great.' This pithy remark has, as usual with Nietzsche, a full and coherent intellectual reality behind it. Almost everyone, with the exception of unusually corrupt or remarkably selfish people, has experienced exalted sentiments if only on rare occasions: wishing for the happiness of even those who may have been unjust to us, being moved to entertain a desire for conspicuous virtue by the experience of exemplary purity in the conduct of others around us, being chilled by the thought of the impermanence of our passage through the material world and forming a resolution to do good for the rest of one's days, and so on. But such sentiments do not last. The season of sinful impulse sets in; the moral temperature drops. We are suddenly face to face with our moral poverty; the spirit remains willing but the flesh is once again weak.

Muhammad was a great man because he felt every day what most Muslims feel only on Friday afternoons. St Francis was a great man because he felt repentant, found enough moral rope to hang himself, every day – not merely on Sunday mornings. In most of us, however, by contrast, the will to penitence comes and goes; it does not stay. The will to self-incrimination needs an outlet in the natural desire for indulgence in a pleasure radically free from ethical constraint. The instinct for piety must lie fallow, so to speak, for a while before it is replenished for more virtue. The mood for piety rarely stays long enough.

To be sure, as I have indicated, there are and have been many human beings who somehow successfully live in the active heat of a single pious emotion. The inherent sinfulness of human nature[13] is no argument against the possibility of cultivating virtue, even conspicuous virtue: there have been saints too.[14] And, in a familiar hagiographical maxim, the greater the sinner the greater the saint. But genuine saints are certainly rare – perhaps, given what we know of human nature, necessarily rare.[15] Nor is the achievement of a virtuous destiny an easy matter even for men of such saintly impulses. For every saint remains a sinner enough to be a failure in the eyes of a higher arbiter of value – a failing compensated only by the all-sufficient grace of God.

VI

When the Ramadan fast was initially instituted, it lasted from the evening meal of one day until the evening meal of the next. Apart from the physical hardship that complete abstinence entails in Middle Eastern climates, sexual activity was prohibited during Ramadan nights. Under this severe regime, a number of men had fainted and a few had come close to death by the time *surah al-Baqarah* (v.187) announced a welcome relaxation of the requirement. God, in his mercy, had relented: the duration of the fast was reduced and, in view of the fact that many men had already secretly broken the rule regarding sexual abstinence, that latter requirement was dropped.

The same *surah* counsels believers to pray: 'Our Lord, burden us not with what we have not the strength to bear' (K:2:286). How interesting an irony! For it highlights of course the peculiarity of deeply exacting demands on human nature. Why does God impose such demands on an essentially weak creature? Surely, one thinks, the divine mercy is properly occasioned by a willingness to overlook failures that are humanly avoidable. If the wrath of God is always strictly deserved, his mercy, it seems, is not even remotely within the range of our deserts.

I am not saying that religious demands should be easy to fulfil. Every faith needs to give its votaries certain ideals that require commitment and effort. But while the demands should be heavy and failure commoner than success, they must not be so heavy that failure is altogether commonplace and success well-nigh impossible. For rules that are impossible to obey are as pointless as those which are impossible to disobey. Surely, religion must command us to make those righteous choices that we actually have the strength to make. The magnitude of the natural impulse to good should match the quality of piety demanded. Only then can the requirements of religious ethics be authentic and convincingly relevant. Religious ideal must correspond to the potential resources of human nature.

Where there is a will – and a lot of sustained effort – there is a way. But, even so, not always. And that's the rub. The tragic discrepancy between the demands of piety and the realities of human nature is only too well known to most of us. For the overwhelming majority of well-intentioned folk, the wish for moral perfection remains simply a wish that cannot harness the resources required for its fruition. Indeed, even the saints found the achievement of a virtuous destiny a task necessarily and massively transcending human resources. St Augustine, in a sincerely expressed if unusually daring irony, catches the point: 'Thou [Lord] hast counselled a better course than Thou hast permitted.'[16]

VII

We know on the authority of Sheikh Muslim ibn al-Hajjaj al-Qushayri that a certain Hanzalah at-Tamimi had complained to the Prophet about the severe difficulty of sustaining an awareness of God after leaving the religiously charged environment of the mosque and enjoying the society of his wives and children.[17] The point I wish to make here emerges fairly naturally. God, like a jealous spouse, demands complete fidelity. And yet he had created a human nature that instinctively seeks the immediate, the contemporaneous, the natural, purely human satisfactions.

The Koran is no stranger to the ways of human nature. And its verses never lose an opportunity to promote the service of God above every worldly impulse and facility (K:3:14; 9:24). All the varied desires for property, wealth, power, commerce, progeny, love, sexuality, friendship, comfort, privilege, beauty, solitude, knowledge, wisdom, creativity, self-importance, self-sufficiency – all are under the axe. All the temporary bonds that separate man from God, be it kinship, communality, matrimony or filiation, all are under the divine axe. For here is a totalitarian if *de jure* sovereignty that relentlessly pursues, discriminates, catches, identifies, scrutinises, cauterises every piece of perfidy and rebellion in its corner. God knows the treachery of the eyes and what the breasts conceal (K:40:19). So the profane impulse withdraws to a yet more secure fortress within the heart – the last and central citadel of the sinful self. But even this chunk of solitude is not our own. God will besiege it until it too surrenders. *Allah-u-akbar.*

The religious rope is certainly tight. And it is around everyone's neck. We are *all* expected to restrain volition in the service of a proper righteousness. Yet, of course, even on a generous estimate, only two or three human beings in an entire generation are actually capable of putting God at the forefront of their loyalties, of actually loving God more than they love their wives and children. (Abraham was not typical even of seminal religious figures, let alone representative of the ordinary run of believers.) Certainly the overwhelming majority of human beings, both today and in the past, have fallen by the strict normative code of monotheistic faith. Unsurprisingly, hypocrisy has been their only refuge: a hiding place that may at best secure them against the indictment of other men but not of a God 'who is aware of the things you do'. (Recall here the Koran's fierce and frequent condemnation of all Janus-faced allegiances to God and his messenger.) By setting such a high standard God appears to endorse a certain kind of religious élitism: an entire generation frequently lives and dies while producing only a couple of saints.

VIII

The problem of the prevalence of human failure is not to be assessed or resolved *a priori* but rather in relationship to the larger question of the nature of humanity and of the context of human existence. More precisely, the significance of sin – of *zulm* in koranic vocabulary[18] – is itself to be assessed not *a priori* but rather in relationship both to the demands of religious morality and to the resources of a human nature under divine tuition. So, men are created frail; and their constitution contains an inherent proclivity to sin. Yet, despite their natural weakness and the force of their impulse to impiety, they are expected to fulfil the deeply exacting demands of religious faith.

It would be odd indeed if one refused to see in this complex circumstance a potential theological puzzle. For given the sheer variety and power of the corruptions to which the human will is (potentially) prone, it cannot be remarkable or surprising that the full achievement of *islam* (submission) is extremely difficult. Indeed it is only to be expected that all have sinned, all have fallen short of the glory of God. Is it a matter for surprise that a strict application of koranic justice would not 'leave a single soul unpunished on earth' (K:16:62; 35:45)?

Someone might, not unreasonably, be tempted to conclude that the religious ideal is, particularly in this age of secularity and indifference, an unrealistic one. Most traditional Muslims would no doubt reply that there is nothing wrong with the ideal; it's just that we live in a soft age that prefers the luxury of sin to the hard climb of the morally straight path. After all, the contention may run, life's edges are no rougher today than in the past. God had demanded much more of earlier communities (K:2:286) and always makes prejudicially rigorous demands on his chosen servants – though they have the offsetting privilege that divine grace confers. In any case, it will be concluded, the requirements of koranic piety – the five canonical prayers, fasting, comparative sexual restraint and so on – are already the product of a sufficient concession to an admittedly frail human nature.

Perhaps. And yet Islam, no less than Christianity, is fast becoming a Friday religion – our conscience on the seventh day.[19] This discontinuity within the modern religious life cannot, I believe, be fully explained without recourse to the fact that religious demands are indeed exacting. Voluntary religious obligation is, within Islam, now often ignored;[20] legally or socially enforced piety is, however, still largely intact. It is no exaggeration to say that Islam is now increasingly failing to keep the bulk of its followers on the strict traditional plane of ethico-religious demand.

There is some awareness even within early Islam that the requirements of koranic piety are harder to fulfil in an age far removed from the original age of incidence. Hence, the traditional concession that while those in the Prophet's era might be doomed if they disobeyed even a tenth of the law, those in more difficult times (like ours, presumably) need only perform one tenth to be saved from damnation.[21] Isn't this an implicit concession that the yoke of the *shari'ah* (law) may be too heavy for us today? Should one condone the occasional lapse from koranic piety? Or is this merely a disguised plea for self-indulgence uttered in a soft age?

IX

The practical demands of Islamic piety are rooted in a particular account of human moral potential – a particularly optimistic one. We can clearly see this (and other pertinent issues here) by briefly examining the related but significantly different Christian portrait of man. If the essential element in human nature is, for Muslims, an intellect endowed with the capacity to know and appropriate a salvifically significant theological truth, it is, for Christians, a will defiled by sin. The Fall, in Christian thought, was a unique event which fully determined the total nature of man: Adam's lapse from grace radically disfigured his true original nature and, hence, that of all his descendants. As a result, men, all men, are fallen beings with corrupted wills and irreparably damaged reasoning faculties. What they need, therefore, is not mere guidance but rather salvation, not merely a teacher but rather a saviour. We need to be saved from our own folly, not merely educated about the failings of a corrupt human nature. Education is not enough; we need redemption, reconciliation, transformation, in fine, salvation.

Islam, by contrast, sees the Fall as simply one powerful and contained manifestation of evil – more accurately, disobedience to God's will – that has no larger implications for human nature in general or even for Adam's nature in particular. Adam ate the forbidden fruit; Allah forgave him, for Allah does what he pleases. Indeed, Muslims view Adam's expulsion from Eden as the occasion for the 'Rise' of man. Adam's original disobedience to God's will is seen as being merely the joint result of ignorance and *akrasia* (weakness of the will). Therefore, men need only mentors and the grace of God. Though God gives out his grace as he pleases – he is not bound by the requirements of Judaeo-Christian theology – he has taken great care in selecting teachers for the moral and religious education of mankind. These teachers are simply men of larger vision and wider ken, blessed by God, whose mission is to caution their fellow human beings and attempt, if possible, to inaugurate the divine kingdom. In the final resort, however, we are all on our own: no soul already laden bears the burden of another (K:17:15).[22]

Christians, then, identify a far deeper crisis in the human personality than Muslims do and naturally adopt a far more radical solution to the problem of sin in human life. For Christians, man is known to himself only as a sin-infected creature; we do not know human nature in its integrity. Fortunately, however, we can regain that integrity. John 3:16 offers 'the good news' of a saviour for sinful Adam and his progeny.[23]

These fundamental differences about human nature are most clearly displayed in the contrasting attitudes that Christians and Muslims adopt towards the law. Islam is, famously, a practical law-centred faith. Faith is as faith does. Christians, however, believe that Christ delivered us from the tyranny of a law the demands of which no one could fulfil – with the sole exception of Jesus himself. The old Draconian law, inaugurated by a legalistic Yahweh has been, we are told, repealed by the grace of Christ. The new law accompanying the New Covenant is the law of love, a law that binds without bonds.[24]

It is important, particularly for (orthodox) Jews and Muslims, to try to understand precisely and sympathetically what Christians believe in respect of Christ's mission *vis-à-vis* the law. Now, we have constantly noted the Koran's concern with rejection: men refuse to desist from disobedience. God warns; a stubborn humanity disregards; God destroys. And again; and again. God wishes to educate; men refuse to learn; nemesis follows. And the cycle is often repeated. For two can play at this game – for a long time. Christians argue, quite reasonably, that God and man are in a kind of rut here. But we can break this deadlock through the transcending of the law coupled with the gracious gesture of condescension – in the strict sense – contained in the Incarnation.

Let us now examine this issue as carefully as possible. Kenneth Cragg has argued, patiently and coherently, that given the sheer depth and prevalence of human obduracy, itself reflected in the scale of rejection throughout history, mere education may not be enough. Men need much more than guidance – a fact which, in turn, according to Cragg, implies the inadequacy of messengership as the sole major institution for the divine tuition of a rebellious humanity. Given that the religion of Islam postulates an ultimate and resourceful sovereignty, continues Cragg reasonably enough, there is internal warrant for expecting the Muslim deity to take greater, possibly more radical, initiatives than merely those involved in law and prophethood. Only then can God successfully reach and cauterise human perversity and radically frustrate the will to impiety. For Cragg, predictably, the range of divine engagement with the human creature is, within Islam, more or less arbitrarily arrested at the level of mere guidance, the neglect of which entails divine retribution. Why shouldn't so comprehensive a divine Lordship find its fullest expression in an incarnate 'suffering love' – itself 'not as a compromise of transcendence but as its true quality'?[25]

The short and seemingly unsympathetic answer to Cragg's question is the one that is quite popular with non-Christian theists: the Christian solution is incoherent. Now, it seems to me, after due consideration, that this routine reaction is, for all its popularity and apparent shallowness, actually the correct one. For the fact is of course that Christians may well be bewitched by a particular picture, admittedly powerful and suggestive, of a sinless God come to earth at the sight of our enormities. All Christian writers, including Cragg, have a marked tendency to be overly impressed with the pathos of the Christian protrait of deity;[26] the result is that critical thought is, at this crucial juncture, short-circuited. It is, however, not enough merely to assert that human nature is redeemed through the self-sacrifice of a loving creator, beautiful and inspiring as that may sound to Christian ears. Christians are under an obligation, morally and intellectually, to rescue the concept of the Incarnation from the clutches of (apparent) incoherence. The moral appeal of this doctrine counts for nothing unless it derives its impulse from an intelligible and indeed true metaphysical foundation. The worry here is not whether or not the Incarnation compromises the unity of God as this is understood by Judaeo-Islamic thinkers. That is not the problem, since Jews and Muslims could be completely mistaken in thinking that the Incarnation effectively denies the oneness of the Deity. The problem is that the Christian tenet here seems to be, independently of standard Jewish and Muslim theological reservations, rendered incoherent on account of certain fatal logical infirmities. Have Christians got hold of the wrong end of the logical stick here? What sense is there in saying that God became man?[27]

It is possible that I have here begged the question against the Christian claim. The Christian could, one supposes, argue that the Holy Spirit has rendered coherent and credible certain claims that appear, to the limited human understanding unenlightened by grace, incoherent or incredible. The *exit in mysterium* is not necessarily illegitimate although critics of the Christian faith will no doubt discern evasion in any such move.

We cannot be certain that the Incarnation is a demonstrably senseless doctrine. But, for our present purposes, it doesn't matter. For the solution contained in the Incarnation, even supposing it to be a coherent one, is irrelevant. The problem of the recalcitrance of human nature – our ability and willingness to break the divine law – remains untouched. The obvious and correct response to the claim that Christ perfectly fulfilled the law is, of course, that it is easy enough for God. Nor will it do to say that Christ is not purely divine; for if he is also human, he is certainly not plainly or purely human. We, however, are men, just plain men. How, then, can the sinless God's moral deportment convincingly supply the appropriate exemplar for us human, all too human, purely human, sinners?

Cragg drew the correct inference that prophetic guidance doesn't quite seem to do the trick here. But he failed to note the much deeper implication about human nature implicit in the puzzling circumstance of God's (apparent) failure to cure men's recalcitrance to divine guidance. This deeper implication about the essence of man is well captured in the elusive koranic quotation that heads this chapter: 'Surely we have created man in trouble'. *Fi kabad*, says the verse. Human nature conceals the proclivity to disobedience on account of its permanently restless, tense, ambiguous, perverse component. A problematic residue always remains; there is a perverse remainder in our (and God's) calculations here. The human capacity for active opposition to prophetic summons is necessarily a liability, a potentially dangerous capacity. And the fact that we possess such a capacity in effect means a plague on all the theistic houses: men are as free to resist the grace of Christ as the grace of Allah. The Gospel is in no better shape *vis-à-vis* recalcitrance than the Torah or the Koran. For the fact is, of course, that in the face of the perversity of man, a certain kind of morally constrained sovereignty is always more or less helpless. One sees this most clearly in the proposed Christian solution. How extraordinary that even the crucifixion of a sinless God failed to teach us the ways of righteousness!

And yet the creation of the perverse element in man is itself the work of God. In exercising his prerogative as creator, Allah has made man in whatever form he pleased (K:82:8); and, as it happens, he has seen fit to create man with the potential for disobedience. The human form is capable of deteriorating into that which humiliates a human nature at its best. 'Surely we have created man in the fairest of statures,' reads *surah* 95 (vv.4–5), 'and yet debased him to the lowest of the low.' The passage is elusive and subject to interpretation. But its general import is clear. Such, then, is the ultimate style of the divine art, one that is, in the last analysis, not answerable to external rational or philosophical critiques. To question it any further would not only be blasphemous – as we have already arrived at the limits of the *mysterious* (*ghayb*) – but, as modern philosophy teaches us, *incoherent*.

Let me now return directly to the problem of law and run it to earth. The notion of a human nature subject to divine legislation is an inescapable part of Islamic (and Hebrew) theism. Christianity is alone in seeking to transcend the law.[28] I have argued that the Christian attempt to dispense with law not only fails, it would not have achieved its intended result even if it had succeeded.

There is one particular misunderstanding that often arises at this point in the discussions about the status of law in ethical monotheism. Jews and Muslims do not claim, notwithstanding Christian critics, that obedience to the revealed legislation is sufficient to attain religious success or salvation. Jews and Muslims, no less than Christians, emphasise the human need for the grace (and mercy) of God. Theistic religion, in all its varieties, integrally involves an awareness and endorsement of the poverty of man. The Torah and the Koran, no less than the New Testament, condemn any excessively sanguine estimate of the purely human potential for self-perfectibility through obedience to revealed legal norm. The fact is of course that theism is essentially a doctrine about the permanent discrepancy between the demands of piety and a human nature that is created by God in such a manner that it necessarily conceals a potential for failing to be fully malleable in the service of moral excellence. The capacity for frustrating the higher nature of man is an ineliminable component of human nature as created by God. That such a circumstance should require the grace of God to compensate for the occasional failing cannot be a matter for surprise.

X

It has been said, 'Law does not change the heart but it does restrain the heartless.'[29] Indeed; we need the law. In fact, given the strength, frequency and variety of temptation, men need the yoke of the law pretty firmly on their necks; otherwise, the chances are, as in the Christian West, it won't stay on at all. Christianity, particularly Protestant Christianity, has become, on a practical level, severely sentimental and religiose in proportion to its recent neglect of the law.[30]

Islam had originally aimed at effecting a balance between the excessive legalism of Mosaic piety, on the one hand, and Christian Pauline anti-legalism, on the other. In practice, it soon deteriorated, in the hands of the religious intelligentsia, into a law-obsessed religion often agitated by trivial details. Modern Islam is in some disarray at the moment but its central impulses remain very firmly legalistic.

The concern with law has always dominated the Muslim imagination. Indeed, it was the development of jurisprudence that more or less exhausted the genius of classical Islam. This is unsurprising. The Koran is preoccupied with the maintenance of justice in a divinely ordained order. God is the sovereign ruler, the just master; men are the citizens, the obedient servants. We have here Islam's characteristic tendency to place man face to face with God in that kind of sincere unsentimentalism that properly legal relationship presupposes.

The concern with divinely ordained legislation should not, I would maintain, blind us to the sheer complexity of human nature, of human inclination, motivation and experience. The tendency to over-simplify matters has been prevalent in Islamic circles and constitutes, outside the political sphere, the greatest failing of Muslim history. An unsympathetic moralism that the preoccupation with law so often inspires is, at all costs, especially today, to be repudiated. Any perfunctory analysis of the causes of our failure to live up to the demands of koranic piety will no longer do. We must recognise that we live in a world that is characterised by ambiguity of circumstance, unclarity of inclination and conviction and, in consequence, by the necessity of effecting delicate, sometimes tortured, choices. It would be nothing short of obscurantism to ignore all the lessons we can in principle learn by a perusal of the sophisticated body of theory about the personal and communal existence of men – itself a signal achievement of modern intellectual culture. Our dominant intuition today irresistibly has to be that the complexity of life is recalcitrant to the kind of routine normative resolution that the operation of law normally presupposes. It cannot be denied that so much that we see around us today is beyond the good and evil of our forefathers; we naturally know as little of their agonies as they knew of our modern aches. Many aspects of the contemporary circumstance elude the neat moral and religious categories of that less ambiguous bygone age.

XI

Muhammad's biographers, Muslim and non-Muslim, are unanimous that he was not a man cut out for tragedy. Therefore, he succeeded. Indeed it would be difficult to cite any comparable instance of so spectacular a worldly success among religious (or for that matter secular) figures. Islam's rapid yet largely permanent victories have up to this day continued to amaze observers. Certainly, Islam has always been, from its very inception, a faith that is clear, unambiguous, positive, assertive, dogmatic, defined, self-assured – in fine, lacking in all the accompaniments of tragedy. Apart from the heretical minority *Shi'ah* verdict, Islam has no truck with the kinds of messianic hopes of deliverance so characteristic of Christianity and, on a national level, of classical Judaism. Men are, according to Islam, on their own in this whole affair of life. If there be failure, one accepts it patiently. The only cure for failure is success. Nothing succeeds like success is a very Islamic sentiment.

Christianity has, however, famously seen the religious outlook as being a supremely tragic one – as tragic as the highest forms of the sentiment of love and no doubt as disturbingly powerful. The picture of the august and pure Christ of God amid a fallen humanity inspires in Christians, and indeed in others too whose temperament is congenial to the Christian impulse, a pathos born of the tragic conviction that naïve goodness has a severely burdensome if not impossible vocation in a world that harbours the perennial impulse to sophisticated impiety. Again, to turn to another fateful vision, humanism, particularly in its Nietzschean variety, is not free of a tinge of tragedy.[31] For it too is a vision wrapped in the peculiar pathos of an unconditional affirmation of the purely human interpretation of life – a life in which one learns to bear all the many burdens and ironies without succumbing to the comforting illusions of religious idealism.

Orthodox Islamic thought has always, by contrast, been characterised by its almost total freedom from the tragic instinct. Indeed, it is no exaggeration to say that for both modern and classical Islam, tragedy remains a foreign category of reflection. To be sure, there are incidental hints of both tragedy and constrained pathos in the koranic outlook. But, unlike the Greeks and later the Christians, Muslims have never taken refuge in tragedy. The Hellenic-Christian-Nietzschean sense of the tragic element remains totally foreign to the authentically Muslim sensibility. Even widespread political failure and disillusionment with the historical order in recent centuries have failed to drive Muslims to tragedy. The tragic mood remains, for the Islamic peoples, by and large fugitive and ephemeral, incidental and isolated.

And so it should. For the resolute determination to guard against the temptation to tragedy is Islam's distinctive contribution to religious anthropology. To be sure, this is not primarily a substantive contribution in the sense of an original doctrine about human nature. But it is a real contribution none the less, for it dictates the need for a particular kind of temperament. It is a truly astonishing feature of the Koran that it resists root and branch, on every occasion, at every level, the impulse to tragedy. The occasions are plentiful; the temptation is strong. But the Muslim scripture invariably says 'No' to tragedy.[32]

It is this feature that so radically distinguishes the Crescent from the Cross. Here is no superficial difference. The Christian sees the permanent and grand failure of the human condition as being a presupposition of Christian redemption; one that introduces a dominant inconsistency into the foundations of Christianity because it effectively denies the wisdom of a God who created man. The Muslim is religiously obliged, as I indicated in the opening sections of this chapter, to entertain a more optimistic view of the matter. He cannot consistently interpret the admittedly impressive record of human waywardness as a sort of omnibus if indirect condemnation of God's handicraft. Christians, then, believe that, on the level of description, failure and sin dominate the mortal record: and then build a theology on that foundation. Muslims, however, concede, what is undeniable, that humanity, including Muslim humanity, has often behaved foolishly and presumptuously in the world; and yet Muslims are religiously obliged simultaneously to resist the tragic conclusion that man has failed in some ultimate and irreversible way. For to admit that the human project is a failure is to endorse in effect the satanic, and hence culpable, scepticism about the divine decision to create and appoint man as God's representative. Christians need to presuppose, rightly or wrongly, the tragic failure of the human condition in order to operate the machinery of God's redemptive grace; Muslims must, rightly or wrongly, refuse to concede the tragic failure of man on pain of having no theology left to articulate.[33]

To see man as potentially capable of ultimate success under the auspices of a blameless sovereignty is not a way of saying that all is well on this side of the grave. Muslims must recognise the nature and causes of modern pessimism about the human ethos; they must discern the sheer depth of human chaos in a world which is not seen to be under that benevolent supervision which had once secured us against the caprices of history and destiny. In fine, Muslims must understand why so many thoughtful people both today and in the past have seen the category of tragedy alone as truly expressing our deepest conviction about a predominantly imperfect humanity aspiring to a perfection that often eludes it.

To see why men have felt the need for entertaining a tragic vision is not tantamount to endorsing it. In the final analysis, the Islamic vision is fundamentally and deliberately opposed to the tragic outlook whether this latter outlook is wrapped in a religious or a humanistic garb. But the rejection of tragedy is not a licence for offering shallow diagnoses of our contemporary ills. In considering the mystery of human nature in the twentieth century, Muslims must be prepared to abandon static and fruitless criteria of judgement and evaluation still so prevalent among a thoughtless orthodoxy trapped in the classical straitjacket. If Muslims fail to offer a convincing analysis of human ailments, including our current malaise, they should not be surprised to learn that Islam will certainly lose the current battle for the true image of man.

Part 3

MODERNITY AND BEYOND

Choice and Destiny

Travellers in the Kingdom of Saudi Arabia during the Pilgrimage season may have noticed the signs prohibiting non-Muslims from entering Mecca, the hub of the Muslim universe. In a justified religious apartheid,[1] instituted by the Prophet one and a half millennia ago and still in strict observance, the signs alert the traveller to the fundamental distinction Muslims make between Islam and all other ideologies, religious and secular.

If one needed a slogan to designate the post-war world, it might be 'the age of ideology'. There is a kind of ideological warfare that is at the forefront of modern sensibilities, exploiting ever and anon the contemporary impulse to belligerence, recruiting the media of mass communication and, in a different way, of academic scholarship. Incompatible ideologies share the globe between them; devotees gather for the glory of different 'gods' at many cities from Mecca to Rome, Jerusalem to Benares and Moscow. Unsurprisingly, the ideological rifts widen as each party claims a uniquely correct route to the heavenly city.

In this chapter, I turn my attention to the currently pressing need for ecumenical discourse among alien faiths and ideologies. Apart from some general comments about the nature and limits of ecumene, I restrict my attention to two major issues. These are, firstly, Islam's confrontation with Marxist humanism and, secondly, the problem of Christian–Muslim rivalry. I conclude with some remarks about the conceptual location of Islam in the current setting of irreligion and religious pluralism: a concern that conveniently leads us to ponder yet again the theological puzzles which the current circumstance of religio-ideological pluralism brings in its train.

I

It is a characteristic feature of the self-understanding of any orthodoxy, whether religious or secular, that it views its own constitutive beliefs as uniquely and fully true while regarding the convictions of those outside its pale as being wholly or partly false. Since about the nineteenth century, however, claiming truth for one's own belief-system to the exclusion of all others has become deeply problematic. Indeed, in recent years many writers have argued that there is no such thing as absolute truth, that truth is relative to culture and era.

The rise of metaphysical pluralism with its implied threat of socio-cultural and historical relativism has tended to erode the absolute authority of any given religious tradition. Pluralism itself has roots in the nineteenth-century development of historical perspective; and the twentieth century has witnessed a spectacular growth in our knowledge of other faiths and ideologies. There is a prevalent opinion these days that different visions are brought to prominence by a fortunate combination of social causes linked with some individual will fired with enthusiasm for reform, and fully matched with the hour of its appearance on the historical rostrum. Observers have been impressed by the apparently fortuitous manner in which history hands out its patronage to various causes. Certainly, individuals like Moses, Marx and Muhammad have turned the world – or rather their world and hence our world – upside down; but they, like lesser men, have remained prisoners in a historical process that seems sovereignly indifferent to normal human ambition.

The self-image of every ideology as uniquely authoritative is, of course, created retrospectively. And that is just as well. For no great world ideology, no matter how established and influential it became, was impressive in its origins. But success alters perspectives. (People are interested even in one's failures – after one has succeeded.) Karl Marx was at first an obscure intellectual scribbler; and yet at the height of its power a third of the world's people lived under what was termed Marxist government. That a first-century Palestinian teacher of humble origins and a seventh-century Meccan merchant should together continue to influence the hopes and aspirations of almost half of the human race is remarkable. In fact, it is astonishing; for there is a huge difference between famous ideals at their most potent and their necessary obscurity when they first entered the socio-political arena.

II

A notable feature of religious debate in modern western society has been the avoidance of unduly pejorative language for describing the convictions of those outside the pale of orthodoxy. Castigation of dissidents as 'heretics' is much rarer in most Christian circles, particularly liberal scholarly ones. The use of epithets like 'infidel', in descriptions of non-Christian believers (particularly Muslims), as of 'heretics', in descriptions of those of dubious orthodoxy, has declined very noticeably in published theological literature in the last few decades. Moreover, many Christian writers, usually Protestants, now disown the insularity of Latin Christianity and of the more recently fashionable Barthian neo-orthodoxy.[2]

This new politeness among Christian thinkers is the result, at least in part, of the decline of religious enthusiasm coupled with the rise of the secular disciplines such as the philosophy of religion and the comparative study of religion. Liberal and sceptical influences of various kinds, associated chiefly with militant humanism and its political counterparts, have together helped to curb the excesses of an older Christian fanaticism. This has, in turn, paved the way for a more critical and balanced self-assessment as well as a more impartial assessment of other faiths, particularly of related religious rivals, Judaism and Islam.

Most Muslim writers still remain largely indifferent to the kind of sceptical and liberal trends that have so radically altered the provincial attitudes of some Christian writers towards other traditionally rival patterns of piety. One result of this is that, by and large, Islamic thinkers resolutely refuse to treat, even for purely academic purposes, religious rivals as autonomous modes of religiosity. Jews and particularly Christians are thus often prematurely dispossessed of their faithful heritage: Islam alone, it is said, contains true Judaism and true Christianity.

Bearing in mind these general trends and attitudes, let us now clear the ground for the development of ecumenical discussion among alien ideologies. We can conveniently do this by making three related preliminary remarks of a methodological character. Firstly, I take it that neither the range nor the content of ecumene is determinable *a priori*. It could be that we can hope for a tolerable community of doctrinal belief among Jews, Christians and Muslims but not among *mono*theists and their *poly*theist detractors. Or it could be – as I am inclined to think – that the picture is even bleaker: even the possibility of a unified theology of the western faiths is questionable. Related to this, there may well be different kinds of possible ecumenical community among faiths: a given religion may attain doctrinal (i.e. metaphysical) ecumene with another related religion but fail to attain a moral or political community of sentiment. Thus, for example, Islam may occasionally and temporarily have a partial unity of political obligation with Marxism while retaining a metaphysical association with the Judaeo-Christian tradition. Christianity may, to take another example, seek moral ecumene with a faith like Buddhism while rejecting any doctrinal unity. And so on.[3] There is a further worry here about the ranking of different kinds of ecumene. Is doctrinal ecumene more fundamental, so to speak, than political ecumene? Arguably, ecumene should denote primarily metaphysical unity of conviction since ethico-political communities of sentiment are ultimately derivative from – parasitic upon – doctrinal similarities.[4]

Secondly, someone could argue that the range of ecumene is, once we take seriously a particular scripture, zero: the very notion of ecumene is a disguised form of compromise, one of the subtle ways of destroying genuine faith. The theological position with which such an isolationist view may naturally be associated is, of course, Christian or Muslim orthodoxy or neo-orthodoxy. Arnold Lunn, a convert to Roman Catholicism from Protestantism, speaks eloquently for this attitude:

> The modern theory that you should always treat the religious convictions of other people with profound respect finds no support in the Gospels. Mutual tolerance of religious views is the product not of faith, but of doubt.[5]

This objection to ecumene, clearly religious (as opposed to philosophical) in complexion, is likely to be of some importance for a large number of orthodox religionists, whether Christian, Jewish or Muslim.

Thirdly, someone could, rather unrealistically, suggest that the range of ecumene is broad enough to encompass a global theology. Only a little need be – only a little can be – said here about this unlikely possibility. In effecting a harmonisation of various religions, we might effectively jettison all recognisably religious content. The result may well be a philosophical, purely humanistic, alternative to the admittedly insular religiosity associated with each of the established religious traditions. To put it another way, there is no reason a priori for entertaining the assumption that the least common denominator among all religious faiths is itself a religious faith. Perhaps, the only common thing here is our common humanity. (Should humanists be included in such an ecumene?) The problem of course is that such a syncretistic view is likely to be even at best only superficially religious.

III

Every contemporary religious faith must present some kind of official position vis-à-vis an increasingly influential humanism. Accordingly, I shall now examine Islam's relationship with one particular variety of naturalistic humanism – namely, western academic Marxism. The discussion here is deliberately general and details would need development in a different context.

Typologists of religion usually classify Islam as a western religion. I think this classification is, by and large, a correct one; and it does provide a useful starting point for our discussion. But this classification has some potentially misleading implications. It suggests, for example, significantly, that the relationship between militant humanism (a product mainly of western reaction against Christian theism) and Islam is essentially similar or identical to that between Christianity and militant humanism.[6] And yet this suggestion is only partly true. For Christianity is significantly different from Islam, as both Christians and Muslims themselves recognise and often seek to emphasise.

One might say, at the risk of misleading the reader, that Islam, unlike Western Christianity (or Buddhism) is a 'political' faith.[7] What does that mean? Well, we can imagine Muhammad face to face with Pilate: the Roman would have had a lot more to do than merely wash his hands. Islam is a religion of action, albeit morally constrained action. The Prophet of Islam inculcated in his followers a very firm sense of the colossal social responsibility that faith incurs: fidelity to God entails political activism here and now.

This is a significant observation. It may indeed have taken Marxism to teach Christians that private salvation is futile in a world of large-scale political failure; but Marxists can claim no such didactic favour with respect to Muslims. Far from dulling men's political consciousness, Islam has, in general, called for action and revolt when required. Certainly, there is something amiss about the familiar socialist criticism, often levelled indifferently at all theists, that the religious promise of heavenly compensation for earthly wretchedness has effectively imposed on human society a passivity in the face of gross injustice. This criticism is almost entirely based on experiences in western Christian lands.[8] It is no exaggeration to say that the attitude of passivity is totally foreign to the very instincts of Islam, as recent political events have amply indicated, if demonstration were needed.[9]

The morally constrained use of power is seen by Muslims, no doubt rightly, as an intrinsic demand of an all-encompassing and genuine faith, not – despite their Christian detractors – as a lapse from moral integrity necessitated by recalcitrant circumstance. This is clear in the case of Muhammad's own ministry. Islam began in Mecca but, for complex historical reasons, first found adequate political expression in Medina. The Prophet, rightly, saw no good reason why a resourceful sovereignty should be denied ultimate success in the world merely on account of certain utterly baseless qualms about the recruitment of force. As long as coercive methods were legitimately and properly applied, the use of political power was not only not wrong, it was positively right. Muslims have, unlike their detractors, never pretended to be waiting for history to patronise good causes.

At root, the involvement with power is, in both the Islamic and the Marxist visions, the outcome of the conviction that human suffering, to the extent that it is not inevitable, remains essentially an exclusively political phenomenon. Islam, like Marxism, recognises the possibility of a prosperous social order here on earth. Christianity, to take another vision, sees – or rather should in principle see – the radical sinfulness of human nature as imposing an operative embargo on the possibility of a heaven on this side of the grave. Men's sinfulness entails a permanent social disability that no political order could remove. Christianity, like Buddhism,[10] views much of human suffering as an apolitical feature of our plight transcending as it does purely political resolution.

Both Islam and Marxism, then, are characterised by an integral concern with the morally conscientious use of power in the service of social change. To an extent, therefore, they are temperamentally similar. To discern the details of a unity of political obligation, however, is a difficult, even involved, matter. Islam currently prevails in lands which Marxists consider, not without reason, to be right-wing and reactionary – a circumstance that explains the political odium Marxists reserve for Muslim conservatives.[11] In any case, this situation is not congenial to the task of establishing a unity of social obligation, one that would cut across the right–left political divide. To be sure, Muslims and Marxists are in agreement over the issue of eliminating obvious injustices of the kind prevalent in, for example, the 'Christian' society of contemporary South Africa. But such cases of consensus are relatively rare.

Even where Muslims and Marxists tread on common political ground, several complications arise from the fact that the ecumene is at best purely political in complexion. Metaphysically the two parties are of course worlds apart. To the Muslim, Marxism is blindness and spiritual error of the worst kind. To the Marxist, notions of a celestial order are merely a dangerous fantasy. Thus, while the Muslim continuously entertains thoughts of Heaven and faith as a necessary backcloth to social struggle (think here of the Afghan fighters taking off an hour for prayer during fighting) the Marxist sees in religious faith merely an unnecessary and indeed dangerous obstacle to a proper recognition of the true nature of human existence and destiny. It is not surprising, therefore, that any temporary and partial unity of political obligation is in constant danger of collapse as the metaphysically motivated tension comes to the surface.

Perhaps it would be best for each party to do its own share separately, thus avoiding the complications that the quest for unity among rivals sometimes brings. At any rate, it is clear that there can be no metaphysical ecumene involving Islam and Marxism. For Marxists, the idea of a supernatural haven is a preposterous legend which comforts the alienated man. Marxism sees itself as the new way and the truth for enlightened man in industrial society. The promise of our salvation does not lie in the religious myths and tyrannies of a bygone age. Rather it lies in the political struggle that would emancipate men and encourage them to inaugurate the classless Utopia.

In the final analysis, then, Islam is on the same side of the metaphysical struggle as its sister faiths of Judaism and Christianity. All three faiths centrally endorse the reality of a spiritual order. This is clearly a very basic similarity. For the Marxist, however, this is a fundamental mistake. There is no divine lawgiver, no supernatural order superimposing a normative significance on the natural and human order. All our benefits, all our burdens, are human, purely human.

All theists, then, argues the Marxist, are mistaken and, in a significant way, alike mistaken. The ideal of a God-governed universe in all its various forms – Jewish, Christian or Islamic – is an illusory one; the theological details that divide Jews, Christians and Muslims are, for the Marxist, of little or no consequence.[12] All the theistic, or for that matter the polytheistic, faiths come out on the wrong side of the border. The Marxist's rejection of Christianity is not simply a rejection of specific Christian doctrinal beliefs but also, and more broadly, a repudiation of an outlook that routinely relies on and appeals to superhuman authority, revelation and ultimate transcendent mystery. Religion, all religion, is a discredited superstition.

I have laboured this perhaps rather obvious point because it has one extremely important corollary often overlooked by Muslim apologists. In a triumphant mood, Muslims sometimes boast that Islam will win the allegiance of western secularised man once Islam is properly presented. To be sure, Islam is indeed regularly misrepresented in the West. But it would be idle to suppose that western humanity will embrace Islam once the virtues of Islam are properly noted and recognised. My own view is that if Christianity has largely failed to anchor the hopes and aspirations of an increasingly secularised humanity, Islam must fail too – if not to the same extent. Only a mistaken diagnosis of the secularised consciousness could lead anyone to imagine that Islam will win the loyalty of secular western humanity. In this matter, as it happens, all the theists are sailing in the same boat. If they survive the storm, they do so together; if they sink, they sink together.

IV

Islam's confrontation with its old religious rivals, Judaism and Christianity, is a hugely involved issue. I shall now concentrate on some aspects of Islam's relationship, including its rivalry, with Christianity. The main reason for this focus of interest is that Christianity and Islam are currently the two major imperial powers, so to speak, in the religious world.

One brief remark first, however, on the relationship between the Jewish and the Muslim religions would not be out of place. Islam's theological and temperamental similarity to Judaism hardly needs elaborate proof.[13] But this circumstance makes for hatred rather than love. For, in matters of ideology, affinity breeds contempt. Although Jews and Muslims, particularly Arab Muslims, have always had frequent commerce throughout history,[14] the current state of Jewish–Muslim relations leaves much to be desired.[15] Theological exchange between adherents of the two faiths is extremely rare.[16] And although Jews and Muslims have often lived in uneasy harmony, there is currently little ground for optimism.

Islam's encounter with Christianity, however, is, and has always been, a perennial source of interest, misunderstanding, mutual accusation and bitter polemical exchange. The major reason for this is fairly easy to identify. Islam, as an historical religion, claims to be in the same prophetic tradition as Christianity and Judaism. Indeed, the Muslim scripture offers its own account of its two ethical monotheistic predecessors. The Koran offers a distinctive account of the status of 'Jesus ('Isa), son of Mary', as he is typically called. The scripture of Islam is concerned in part to retrieve the truth about the nature and ministry of Jesus, who is described as being no more than a particularly important messenger steeped in Jewish piety. Christians are seen as errant monotheists who commit a basic error in regard to the status of their spiritual leader; they are sternly warned against indulging an over-developed sense of devotion to an admittedly great prophet. Steering between the Jewish rejection of Jesus and the Christian deification, the Koran asserts, with clarity and force, that Jesus was no more than a distinguished and strikingly righteous prophet sent to reform the impenitents among the House of Israel. Needless to emphasise, the Jesus of the Koran would have found foreign if not blasphemous the views attributed to him by the Church and the Christian community.

According to the scripture of Islam, Jesus preached absolute and unqualified submission to the will of God, i.e. Islam in the generic sense. Allah empowered him to perform miracles, from the very day of his birth,[17] in support of his claim to be the Messiah whose advent had been predicted in the Old Testament. Most of his Jewish contemporaries, predictably, rejected him; a party among them, however, recognised him to be the promised Messiah. The rejectors among the Jewish establishment intended to crucify (*salabu*) Jesus and he was prepared to die in this manner if required by God. At the last moment, however, Allah intervened to rescue the obedient Christ. The Jews were misled by the substitution of another person in Jesus's place on the cross. In this way, Jesus was not (successfully) crucified though 'it was made so to appear unto them' (*wa la kin shubbi ha lahum*; K:4:157; translation disputed).[18] The Koran implicitly concedes that this was an unusual manoeuvre. Although lesser messengers had been allowed to be martyred, God translated Jesus, that is, removed him by arbitrium (K:4:158), without death, into Heaven where he still enjoys close community with the divine. Islamic tradition has additionally maintained that Jesus will return in the latter days, live as a Muslim, refute Christian interpretations of his mission, subdue the Antichrist and then finally die.[19]

This is the standard Muslim account of Jesus of Nazareth. The Koran insists that he was theologically a true son of Israel, upholding the uncompromising monotheism of his prophetic predecessors. The Gospel (*Injil*) of Jesus the Jew was fully Hebraic. Jesus wished, according to the Koran, to recall his people to the high standards of the Torah and the Mosaic law.[20] He did not intend to establish a new religion.[21] His mission, continues the Muslim contention, was to confirm the only faith – the faith of submission (*islam*) – which Allah had inaugurated, through his messengers, at the very beginning of human history. Before leaving the scene, however, Jesus, according to the Koran, predicted the coming of a messenger, among 'the Gentiles', who would complete God's favour on mankind (K:7:157; 61:6).

Unfortunately, however, continues the author of the Koran, Christians (like Jews) deliberately sought to 'distort'[22] their own authentic scriptures in order to avoid acceptance of Muhammad and of Islam. Partly out of motives of envy, the revelation vouchsafed to Jesus was, it is claimed, subsequently altered or wilfully misinterpreted, thereby obviating the need to acknowledge Muhammad's claim to prophethood. (Jews and Christians secretly recognise, says *surah* 6, verse 20, the truth of Islam with as much ease as they recognise their own sons.) The overall result of these complications was that the ministry and nature of Jesus became the province of purely human (and hence fallible) opinion and conjecture (*zann*) (K:4:157). Allah has subsequently commissioned Muhammad to vindicate the reputation of the Christ and, in doing so, set the record straight once and for all. Pristine 'Christianity' is found only in Islam.

This is, I believe, a fairly accurate description of the orthodox Muslim stance on Jesus and the faith he is alleged to have founded. Post-koranic Islam has, in expatiating on scriptural charges, identified Saul of Tarsus, the apostle Paul, as the main culprit.[23] He is accused of having wittingly or unwittingly 'de-judaicised', to put it clumsily, the faith and practice of the very Jewish Jesus. The main basis for this accusation is that, as far as the message of Jesus is concerned, St Paul should not and cannot be treated as a principal witness since he did not know Jesus in any uncontroversial sense. Pauline Christianity is, it is concluded, not truly Jewish and hence not Islamic.[24]

Christianity, then, is, according to Muslims, the religion of Paul, not of Jesus. As for Jesus, his Gospel, it is argued, is no longer extant or, at any rate, not traceable.[25] Muslims see the interpretative tradition of the Christian faith – the New Testament, the patristic literature, the pronouncements of the early Christological councils and theologians – as more or less human and hence fallible work. The New Testament itself is often seen as being based on an unreliable oral tradition, subjected to extensive later revisions and apocryphal additions; some of the materials are interpreted to be simply anecdotes amplified in transmission.[26] The only truly revealed (and hence infallible and authoritative) literature is the Gospel (*Injil*) of Jesus the Jewish prophet who preached in the Aramaic language. This document, however, unlike the Arabic Koran, fails to meet the canon of literal transmission (which orthodox Islam demands for the transmission of sacred messages) and hence cannot be appropriately appealed to in current theological debate. The New Testament in Greek or in Latin, as it is now possessed by Christians, does not, it is maintained, contain the *ipsissima verba* (the literal words) or, if you like, *ipsissima vox Jesu* (the literal speech of Jesus). The Christians no longer belong, it is concluded, to a truly scriptured society.[27]

Muslims, then, see themselves as insiders, so to speak, with respect to Christianity. Jesus, it is said, was a prophet of Islam foretelling the advent of the Arabian Prophet. Christians naturally resent this interpretation since it effectively dispossesses them of their faithful heritage. How, then, is the impartial scholar, whether Muslim or Christian, to avoid begging crucial theological and historical questions?

Clearly, it is important for both Christians and their Muslim (and for that matter Jewish) opponents to examine first-century Jewish history independently of the later (including contemporary) demands of both Christian and Muslim (and indeed Jewish) creed and tradition. If one can successfully suspend specific religious assumptions, then presumably a fair assessment of the life and opinions of the historical character Jesus of Nazareth can be attained. In what follows I first try to suspend orthodox Muslim claims about Jesus in order to do justice to specifically Christian convictions; subsequently, I offer a critical assessment of these convictions.

I begin by offering an account, impartial and perhaps sympathetic, of a set of core Christian doctrines that are frequently parodied by unsympathetic Muslim and Hebrew critics. Leaving aside, provisionally, the purely historical but deeply relevant question concerning Jesus's own views about God and his relationship to God, let us look now at the two related doctrines of the Incarnation and the Trinity. These are, by any standards of religious originality, among the most fertile and indeed influential ideas in the history of faithful conviction. Though easily parodied, I know of no Muslim writer whose polemical attacks meet the issues on the current level of sophistication among Christologists. That Christians are 'associationists' or polytheists needs much more careful argument since Christians condemn, as Jews and Muslims condemn, certain crude interpretations of the Trinity and the Incarnation – interpretations that would palpably compromise the divine oneness or the divine transcendence respectively.[28]

Every faith possesses – and is possessed by, as it were – a basic inner genius. (The theologians are paid to supply the remaining doctrinal obscurities.) In the case of Islam, as we saw in chapter 8, the inspiring impulse is supplied by the creation and maintenance of a kind of moral distance between man and God in the larger attempt to frustrate the will to tragedy. In the case of Christianity, the inner religious genius is contained in the gesture that closes the gap between the Creator and the creation while rendering humanity into an episode within the divine career: the radically tragic episode in which a merciful God pitched his tent among a sinful generation and graciously disclosed himself as self-sacrificial love.

If Christian students of Islam have been struck by what may be described as a rather emotionally jejune portrait of man's relationship to God, Muslim students of Christianity have been equally struck by what may plausibly be described as a profound pathos at the core of

Christian conviction – a pathos bordering on pity for sinful man. This picture of a God come to earth at the sight of our enormities, of a sinless Christ amid a fallen humanity, has evoked a deep sense of the sheer tragedy of the human circumstance.

The notion of divine purpose for mankind without the corresponding notion of divine need (and of the involvement that such a need may entail) is *prima facie* one of the central oddities of transcendent theism. While Jews and Muslims are theologically obliged to be inured to this peculiarity, Christians have actively sought to defuse it. God, it is urged, became incarnate in man and, by implication, rendered himself morally credible to a rebellious humanity. He tasted the Adamic tragedy; he experienced suffering and all that seeks to humiliate human nature. The good news is precisely that suffering is not an exotic feature in the experience of an almighty spirit. Yet in taking responsibility for the darkness of human existence, God retained and indeed vindicated his own moral integrity. The divine humility, then, counteracts the human hubris. If the fulfilment of the divine purpose necessitates self-sacrifice via entry into a condition of mortality, then so be it. For God is not above – does not disdain – such a supreme gesture of humility.[29]

Most Jews and Muslims would put all this down to a puerile search for excessive pathos. And yet this is a shallow reaction. For it is not at all clear that Christians simply enjoy creating an unnecessary spirit of mawkishness. Certainly, it is no childish kind of sentimentality at work here. Rather, it is a deeply serious and morally passionate concern that is trying to emerge and, in doing so, express albeit in an elusive way, the theological significance of the ultimate crisis in the human personality, namely, the tendency to wrongdoing. This is a feature of human nature that has long been responsible for certain lamentable consequences both for our personal and communal existence and for our relationship to a morally perfect creator.

It seems to me that the doctrinal complexity of Christianity is intimately tied up with its concern to record and partly resolve a central perplexity, namely, the riddle of God's moral involvement with a human nature that is so strikingly recalcitrant to divine guidance. It is very much to the credit of the Christian faith that it recognises – feels and lives in creative tension with – this puzzle. The scandalously intricate collection of Christian doctrines is in fact the direct result of taking seriously the characteristically human threads of the theological fabric: sin, suffering, our moral sense, and the human demand for a divine accountability to the human. The God of the New Testament has begun, if you wish, to experience the tragedy of man, the central tragedy within the created realm. Not only our offence against a perfect sovereignty but also that sovereignty's normative debt to us, so to speak, has reached Heaven; and both are to be remitted by what had seemed a hard and unrelenting Lordship. One might say, then, that the Deity of St Paul is concerned not only with educating mankind about the nature of the divine but also with taking the full measure of the human. We – ordinary human beings – can, as it were, address God; we can have the right to a profane rage. Here is a sovereignty that is humane enough to render itself human.

Among the monotheisms of Hebrew origin, Christianity alone fully explores the issue of God's implied normative engagement with creation. This concern with the moral interface between creation and creator is highly characteristic of the Christian faith. Indeed it is this concern which, especially when probed beyond the level of dogma and doctrine, singles out Christianity as the odd man out in the Semitic trio. Certainly the emphasis on God's moral engagement with man, in the radical sense in which Christians interpret it, is clearly foreign to the Abrahamic tradition in its inception. And it remains largely extraneous to Judaism in its later development. It has to be said that the God of the Old Testament seems by and large indifferent to men's sense of moral outrage. God's designs may be dark and incomprehensible. But there we have it. Think here of Job's 'dialogue' with Yahweh: both came out pretty badly from that ordeal but poor Job had lost right from the start.

The dominant mood of the Torah and the Koran, then, is very different from that of the New Testament. In the Jewish and in the closely related Islamic vision, God appears to be a fully sovereign will wholly in control of a world that is admittedly full of sin and disobedience. But the God of the Covenant, like Allah, is fully aware and capable of ruling a stubborn humanity. To be sure, reading the tedious details of the exchanges between Yahweh and his people in the Old Testament gives the impression, on occasion, that he is a somewhat incompetent tyrant. But there remains the notion that none can outwit him; those who ignore his dictates do so only at the risk of terrible consequences. Here is an ultimately ruthless sovereignty whose passionate desire for human success and welfare is offset by an equally passionate wish for due acknowledgment of divine supremacy.

Much of this changes in the New Testament. The same God suddenly appears in a morally tame posture, ready to come to earth, ready to condescend – in the literal, not pejorative sense. Here is a sovereignty that is ready to suffer every humiliation to which the creaturely nature is prone. God enters the human condition in the larger attempt to reach the last citadel of human perversity and, in doing so, transform creation. The God of Love is not merely concerned yet distant; he is concerned and engaged. The radical division between a morally perfect God and a sinfully presumptuous creation, the old gulf between humanity and divinity, is now bridged.

There is much that is new about the New Testament. Many of its dogmas and attitudes suggest that things had gone radically wrong on earth, that the creation of man and the calamity of evil had fundamentally destroyed the integrity of creation. One might say, in that familiar colloquialism, that things had got out of control. Hence, of course, the need for the radical measures of the New Covenant. And yet all these new dogmas and proclivities are wholly at odds with the temperament that permeates the Old Testament. God is there masterfully in control of a world that produces sin and perversity; though concerned, God remains disengaged. The oddity in any juxtaposition of the Old and the New Testaments is, on a sympathetic understanding, part of the religious genius of Christianity. Those who reject the New Testament claims are naturally scandalised. Nietzsche well speaks on behalf of the rejectors when he remarks that conjoining the Old and the New Testaments in *one* volume constitutes 'the greatest literary rape on the conscience of Europe'.[30]

I need now to explore briefly the Islamic (and partly related Judaic) reservation about some central Christian claims. It seems to me that part of the scepticism here is centred around the historical foundations of the Christian religion and part of it around some perceived conceptual difficulties with central Christian beliefs.

It is now widely recognised, even by a number of Christian theologians, that some Protestant churches' perspective on Jesus contain several strands in apparent conflict with the best available historical evidence. Thus, for example, it is highly improbable that a Jew concerned to fulfil rather than abolish the law (Matt. 5:17–18) would have violated its most central dictate. The idea that Jesus claimed to be God incarnate finds almost no historical support, even in the Christian scripture. Of course, a self-indulgent ingenuity can always discern, even in the most innocent of remarks, unequivocal support for later ecclesiastical theories. But such a procedure carries little weight or persuasion outside circles of faith. Some Christian theologians have, in the latest round of speculation, claimed that the 'Christ event' (*Christusereignis*) is merely implicit – embryonic – in the Synoptic Gospels, waiting for fruition in the Pauline corpus. Such a view is, however, likely to carry conviction only with devotees for it is, by definition, devoid of independent support.

And the search for independent, particularly historical support is frustrated both by the unavailability of the relevant scripture in the language of its original incidence and by the existence of an apocryphal tradition. It is uncontroversial that Jesus spoke in Aramaic, the language of Galilee in first-century Palestine. But the Gospel allegedly vouchsafed to him and his early disciples has never been traced. In view of this circumstance Muslims remain, not without reason, sceptical about the interpretative tradition of the Christian communities. Are the Protestant churches' *ex post facto* interpretations of Jesus's reported sayings indeed theologically legitimate? It seems to me that the Muslim insistence on the *ipsissima verba* is not at all unreasonable in view of certain recognised complications, such as the fact that the contemporary Bible has evolved by a process of addition and deletion of certain edicts. What did the historical character Jesus of Nazareth say and believe?

We cannot be sure; we do know, as an established fact of historiography, that the intellectual ethos of the ancient world was very different from our own. Thus, for example, for many classical eastern writers, putting speeches with a purely imaginary if thoroughly edifying content into the mouths of actual historical figures was not considered to be a violation of the canons of historical veracity – a liberty now generally restricted to popular journalism. Did the Gospel writers take liberties with respect to what they placed in Jesus's mouth? This is not intended to be a flippant question. Did Matthew, Mark, Luke and John allow some purely personal whims to creep into a text originally faithful to the Christ's teaching? These are fascinating queries; we may never know the answers.

Whatever Jesus's own views may have been – and no one should pontificate here – there is little doubt about the views of the Christian churches' great hero, St Paul. The Muslim view about Paul, held also by some Jewish scholars, is simple: Paul effectively transplanted the Hebrew religion into Gentile soil. Paul, the argument continues, saw himself as a delegate to the Gentile constituency (Acts 9:15; Rom. 11:13); after the founding of the Gentile mission (Acts 15), the Jew–Gentile distinction, so central to Jesus's own ministry (Matt. 7:6; 10:56; 15:24), was dissolved.[31]

Along with this dissolution of a religiously central distinction, the Pauline corpus gave warrant for a certain kind of radical denigration of Jewish legal norm. Rom. 10:4 contains the influential comment, 'Christ is the end of the law'. This remark may well be the product of Paul's own religious enthusiasm; certainly, it would seem foreign in its impulse to anyone steeped in Mosaic piety. Would Jesus have endorsed Paul's verdict? It is true that Jesus was no legalist: his emphasis on the interiority of motive and the purity of inner intention is proverbial. But the idea of abolishing the law would, one might fairly say, have been utterly alien to the thinking of a man reared in Hebrew credal righteousness. The abolition of the Jew–Gentile division, the radical change in the status of Jewish legal norm in alliance with the semi-Hellenic ethos of Pauline thought may well have served to sever Christianity from its original Jewish roots.[32]

I cannot here explore further the reservation concerning the historicity of the Christian faith. There is an entangled skein of historical reasoning here that is perhaps best left to experts in the field. When we turn to the conceptual problems, we have difficulties that are by no means noted only by religious scholars. It is true that many orthodox Christians are inured to the oddity, the strange potential, of phrases like 'the Son of God' or 'God incarnate'. But every reflective Christian believer has, in one mood or another, found some central Christian claims extremely difficult to believe in and, particularly in recent years, even to grasp.

And it is indeed difficult to avoid being impressed by the peculiar content and sheer incredibleness of some Christian credal claims.[33] It may fairly be said, at the risk of sounding polemical and unsympathetic,[34] that among monotheistic creeds, embrace of Christianity requires assent to the largest collection of highly implausible beliefs, requiring at times – what a Tertullian or Kierkegaard would welcome – an unusually dramatic suspension of critical powers.

Christians themselves do indeed sense the sheer complexity of their own doctrines: a fact that no doubt explains the Christian churches' justified wish to entrust the faith to a body of religious professionals.[35] And these professionals have certainly developed a body of complex and sophisticated doctrine. It seems clear that, in itself, the fact of doctrinal complexity does not count against Christianity (Muslim critics notwithstanding). There is no guarantee, scriptural or secular, for the view that the ultimate truth is bound to be a simple one. Indeed, if anything it is likely to be complex, involved and multi-faceted. If one complains about the sheer intricacy of Christian theology, the Christian is at liberty to respond that life is intricate. Shouldn't doctrine reflect – be true to – our involved experience of existence, sin, ideal, norm and transcendence?

Complexity, however, is one thing, incoherence another. Paradox is one thing, nonsense another. The doctrine of the Incarnation does appear, even in the eyes of sympathetic critics, to be incoherent. Clearly, the paradoxical notion of God becoming man while simultaneously remaining God is not easily intelligible. Jews, Muslims and atheists have often sincerely expressed their inability to understand, make sense, of this central Christian doctrine. Though atheists often claim that the doctrine of the Incarnation is cognitively suspect, they believe that it supplies an excellent example of our natural liability to project the human will on to an allegedly superhuman referent. It is true that Christians interpret the direction as being from God to man: God condescends towards man. But the atheists see that claim as simply a delusion that masks the truly Feuerbachian direction, so to speak, of the humanisation of the Deity.

Almost all those who reject the Incarnation and the associated doctrine of the Trinity sincerely find it difficult to resist, in some moods, the suspicion that there is an element of sophistry in the reasoning behind these central orthodox claims.[36] Some kinds of statement that appear paradoxical are actually incoherent. And though the firmness of men's intellectual loyalty to two opposed claims may excite our sense of pathos, it cannot atone for the poverty of logic.

It is a truth not always noted that in matters close to the heart (as in matters of the heart) it is judicious to suspend, when required, not only the judgement but also the emotions. Christians should, I suggest, suspend temporarily their deep emotional attachment to the 'gesture' in the Incarnation and examine, in the clear light of day, precisely what they mean – or is meant – by this orthodox claim on which Christianity rests. Leaving aside the pathos it evokes in the religious temper, what does it really amount to? Could it be that Christians are, to use Wittgenstein's idiom, bewitched by a picture: that of a sinless God crucified by sinful men?[37]

At any rate, the claim about God becoming incarnate in Christ suffers from a variety of conceptual difficulties that would appear to be insuperable. To be sure, *if* the doctrine of the Incarnation were free from certain apparently fatal logical infirmities, *then* it could provide useful theological resources, lacking in Judaism and Islam, for explaining in part the nature and origin of evil. But, as it happens, the belief in the Incarnation seems to be the outcome, in large part, of a particularly tempting variety of sentiment that somehow overpowers the purely rational impulse to seek theological truth. The impulse to pathos has most to feed on when a religion is practically and doctrinally in eclipse; but the presence of pathos does not in itself tell against the truth of a faith. Yet, in the last analysis, the moral – or aesthetic – appeal of a view counts for little unless it is also metaphysically true.[38] It is important to be clear about my point here. I do not say, in the manner of many unsympathetic critics, that the Christian remedy for human ailment is worse than the disease. Christian doctrine may well be morally appealing. But is it coherent? Is it (factually) true?

I cannot here do justice to the extraordinary complexity of the problems in the area of Christological research. I have indicated my reservations about some central Christian convictions; I do not claim to have shown that these convictions are demonstrably unintelligible. And certainly Christian readers are entitled to dispute some of the assumptions (prejudices?) in the previous section; many would no doubt appeal, perhaps rightly, to the possibility of a coherent explication of the doctrine within the mystery of God's knowledge. No human author, however, has ever succeeded in rendering the Incarnation (and the Trinity) entirely free of what may be termed conceptual confusion.[39]

The idea that God decided to become human, condescended (in the non-evaluative connotation of the term) is one that Islam seeks to unmask, in its very credo, as an illusion. Yet it is of course the very notion that the Christian churches have laboured so hard to maintain and invigorate in the face of the accumulated abuse and scorn of sceptics and rejectors. Unsurprisingly, therefore, the Crescent and the Cross have often been seen as being radically opposed in their claims about the character of the Deity. Thus, for instance, Muslims do not see God as their father or, equivalently, themselves as the children of God. Men are servants of a just master; they cannot, in orthodox Islam, typically attain any greater degree of intimacy with their creator. This conviction is also reflected in the extent to which God is thought to be accessible to human knowledge. The Koran, unlike the Gospel, never comments on the essence of Allah. 'Allah is wise' or 'Allah is loving' may be pieces of revealed information but, in contrast to Christianity, Muslims are not entitled to claim that 'Allah *is* Love' or 'Allah *is* Wisdom'. Only adjectival descriptions are attributed to the divine being and these merely as they bear on the revelation of God's *will* for man. The rest remains mysterious.

Given the fact that both the Christian and Muslim faiths are often professionally entrusted to men of aristocratic impulses, both religions have sought hegemony and triumphant monopoly. The unfortunate results of that circumstance both historically and now hardly need comment. In recent years, however, Christian writers have initiated the attempt at effecting harmony and reconciliation among members of different faiths. There have recently been calls for a serious and sympathetic engagement with Islam; Christian thinkers have expressed a desire to eschew polemic and belligerent exchange. Christian–Muslim relations have currently spawned something of a boom industry in the United Kingdom and the United States. It is time now to examine some of the central issues in the area of Islamic–Christian exchange.

The idea of dialogue is not of course an exclusively modern one. Christians, Muslims and Jews have, for many centuries, debated the alleged merits and demerits of their respective faiths. Indeed the world of the Prophet was already pluralist in perspective; and the Koran treats disputes between Jews, Christians and Muslims as essentially sectarian – which they are indeed – a fact that explains the tensions and hostilities among the various parties. In religion, as in politics, the most intense struggles occur among groups holding similar, not widely different, convictions.

I need to investigate here one central problem in order to get our bearings and to decide whether or not Christian–Muslim dialogue is likely to endure as a serious and integral mood of western theology and experience. The issue can be simply stated: what are the major hindrances to the attainment of a genuinely constructive Islamic–Christian encounter? There are predictably two parts to the inquiry here; one dealing with the obstacles rooted in Muslim attitudes towards Christianity and the other in Christian attitudes towards Islam. Let me take these two concerns in the order given.

One severe hindrance to Islamic–Christian dialogue is the Muslim tendency to see Christianity as an *obvious* distortion of Islam – one that must be tolerated for various reasons. The view that Christianity is a perversion of Islam is generally held to be self-evident to reason and hence released from the normal need for independent historical or rational support. This attitude offends all Christians, including those sympathetic to Islam. Christians feel, not without reason, dispossessed of their rich faithful heritage by 'outsiders' who claim, with irritatingly routine conviction, that genuine Christianity is found only in Islam.

This conviction derives ultimately from the Koran which, as I indicated earlier, portrays Jesus as preaching the *shema' Israel* (K:4:171;

5:116–17; cf. Deut. 6:4; cf. Mark 12:29). The Koran proffers an interesting exchange, of an obviously edificatory nature, between Jesus and
Allah: Jesus explicitly disowns what looks like a very simple Muslim
interpretation of the Christian doctrine of the Trinity (K:5:116–18).
Elsewhere the Incarnation is rejected (K:5:17). It is clear that the author
of the Koran sees the Trinity and the Incarnation as prejudicing respectively the radical uniqueness[40] and the absolute transcendence of the
divine being. Thus, the teaching of the churches[41] is seen by Muslims
as being unfaithful to those of the Master; *de facto* Christianity has
been and remains a perversion of the teachings of Jesus who preached
islam. Christianity is not only a Jewish but a Muslim heresy.

To make things much worse, most Muslims, including educated ones,
know next to nothing about Christology. Few Muslims can distinguish
clearly between the view that a man claims to be divine – a blasphemy
– and the entirely different view according to which God volunteers to
become human – the orthodox Christian conviction. And both of these
views are routinely confused with the heretical doctrine that God
'adopted' a son – the heresy well known to the early Church as 'adoptionism' and alluded to in *surah* 18, verse 4. To be sure, the doctrines
of the Christian religion are by nature complex so that the occasional
confusion in the minds of non-Christians (and perhaps even of lay
Christians) could be thought understandable and hence forgivable. But
a Muslim cannot reasonably claim to be seriously engaged in dialogue
with Christians unless he can possess a thorough knowledge of the
Christian faith and, if at all possible, exercise imaginative sympathy
with the ideals of that faith.

I am not saying that a Muslim should believe in Christian doctrine
– that would be absurd. But I am saying that Muslims need, in some
contexts, to treat Christianity as an autonomous expression of religiosity. They need to respect, though not accept, Christian ideals. For a
long time, Muslims have complained, no doubt rightly, that Christians
judge Islam by totally extrinsic standards. It is only fair to light this
candle at the other end. Most Islamic writers resolutely refuse, even for
purely academic purposes, to lay aside distinctively Muslim perspectives
on Jesus and his nature. That Christianity is a perversion of Islam is a
claim rarely lifted beyond the level of *a priori* religious assumption. A
detailed exposition of the Christian faith in all its diversity has rarely
been attempted by any Muslim writer.[42]

Let us turn our attention now to other obstacles to responsible
Christian–Muslim exchange – those created by Christian perceptions
of Islam. There are, broadly, two related major areas of concern here,
namely, the Christian attitude towards the scripture of Islam and the
Christian assessment of its alleged author, Muhammad. I take these in
turn.

Christians have in the past and, by and large, continue to treat Islam
as a rather inferior and unoriginal faith. Much of the literature produced

by modern Christians, including that from the pens of some very able Christian students of Islam, is saturated with the familiar but wholly self-indulgent assumption that the Koran is a hotch-potch of Old Testament materials mixed with fervent denunciations of Christian heresies and all wrapped in some legendary if exotic materials of purely local Arabian origin.[43] Thus, Islam has been variously denigrated as 'Judaism for the Arabs' and a Christian heresy. (For a Christian heresy, Islam has done remarkably well!) Unsurprisingly, Muslims are often dispossessed of their religious heritage: Islam, it is alleged, is a faith which, to the extent that it is authentic, derives its inspiration more or less exclusively from Judaeo-Christian sources. As for the many, sometimes very significant discrepancies between Muslim claims and the Judaeo-Christian statements that predate the Koran's incidence, these are, it is said, to be explained as being the natural outcome of incompetent plagiarism.

Many committed Christian (and a few Jewish) writers assert, with a dramatic dogmatism as offensive as unfounded, that Muhammad selectively appropriated biblical ideas into the Koran and simultaneously enriched his version with a few curiously original incidents: Noah had a son who drowned in the deluge (K:11:42–6), Joseph's female admirers inadvertently cut their hands while gazing at him (K:12:30–1), and so on. That Syriac Christianity heavily influenced the formation of the koranic outlook, that to make the Arabs into members of a scriptured culture was the personal and calculated ambition of a Muhammad impressed indelibly by his Jewish neighbours – all such opinions, expressed with sapient confidence, indeed pontificated, are no less nonsense for being so often repeated. The stock charge of theological unoriginality is wholly misguided when directed at a faith which openly intends to base its credentials precisely on the confirmation of a scriptural record. The Koran, it should be noted, explicitly claims to be the final and definitive edition of revealed scripture incorporating the truths of the Jewish and Christian dispensations, reopening the Ishmaelite lineage of sacred history, and in doing so, exploiting the prerogative of making appropriate additions and corrections.

Muslims often need to shake Christian (and Judaic) complacency by explaining that Islam also possesses a scripture of integrity that embodies an autonomous expression of religiosity. Christians wish to remove altogether this card from the pack; and Muslims rightly detect a deplorable cynicism in the view that the Prophet of Islam deliberately appropriated biblical claims into the koranic corpus. No impartial student of the Muslim scripture would endorse such an opinion or indeed, more importantly, any of the more sophisticated versions of the same absurdity. It is a fortunate peculiarity of Muhammad's plagiarism that it happens to omit all the questionable elements found in the biblical predecessor.

Closely related to the Christian perception of the Muslim revelation is the Christian perception of its alleged producer – Muhammad. The estimate of Muhammad has never been favourable in the West. The earliest Christian polemic had described him variously as the anti-Christ, an unscrupulously ruthless political opportunist, and a debauched sensualist. Denigrated as a false prophet, his experience of 'revelation' was attributed to attacks of epilepsy.

These are, of course, accusations made to mislead – as most recent western thought itself both recognises and seeks to emphasise. That the figure of Muhammad should inspire such Christian rage is, in one way, a matter for amazement. Certainly it gives the lie to the popular fiction of western 'objectivity' with respect to alien conviction. There have, of course, been more sympathetic critics too. Many of them held the view, as remarkable for its historical naïveté as for its moral absurdity, that Muhammad was initially a candidate for prophethood on account of his sincerity and genuine religious quest in Mecca during the hour of trial and (worldly) failure, but he subsequently forfeited that right because of his Machiavellian policies in Medina during the hour of political achievement and worldly triumph.

A large number of propagandist biographies of the Arabian Prophet (which are still produced regularly, incidentally)[44] have contained in one form or another the assumption that his initial moral integrity was undermined, after his fiftieth year or so, by base passions leading to a serious deterioration of character. This accusation has been supported by an appeal to the fact that the literary quality of the koranic corpus had suffered change as a result of the move from Mecca to Medina, from worldly failure to worldly success. In this manner, Muhammad has unwittingly been accorded the unique privilege of being the only exception to that otherwise universally valid biographical maxim, 'Once a villain, always a villain'.

There is, within the writings of past western theologians, a very clear *a priori* prejudice against Muhammad and his faith, a circumstance that fully justifies Muslim reservations about orientalism. Indeed, my own view is that almost all Christians of the previous generation secretly thought atheism better than Islam as a candidate for western allegiance in post-Christian society. (Such are the ways of religious prejudice!) At any rate, critics eager to malign Muhammad and his religion have left few stones unturned in their efforts to obscure any recognition of the Koran's crystal purity of vision, its most impressively authentic genre of religiosity – one that offers a total contrast to the superficial and debased variety often attributed to Muhammad by many of his allegedly impartial non-Muslim biographers.

Recent western writing on Muhammad is hardly much better; indeed it is much worse if in subtler ways. Diluted versions of the older polemic are becoming commonplace as Christian sensibilities assume the garb of outward politeness. Part of the reason for this inveterate hatred is the Christian fear of Islam – a fear increased by recent developments in the Middle East and in the West. 'Nobody,' concedes the distinguished German Islamicist Josef van Ess, 'is afraid of Buddhism or Hinduism; *vis-à-vis* Islam, however, fear is the normal attitude.'[45] This fear, though both natural and justified, ruins all perspective from the start. Almost all recent works about Muhammad by Christian writers, including those by sympathetic ones,[46] betray a prejudicial rigour in assessing his moral character.

All this is demonstrably clear when we note the remarkable reluctance to concede, in any unequivocal fashion, that Muhammad has as much right to be classed as a prophet as any of the Old Testament figures do. Christians rarely miss an opportunity to compare unfavourably the Arabian iconoclast with Jesus and various other Jewish figures; the suggestion is usually that he fails by the allegedly higher standards of the Gospel. But it is not at all clear what the grounds for this claim are. For surely the fact that, say, Muhammad was a polygamist who ruled a state cannot in itself serve to detract from his claim to prophethood: many Israelite and Hebrew predecessors, notably Moses, were heads of theocratic states and several, notably Abraham and Solomon, enjoyed multiple matrimonial alliances. That Muhammad was different from Jesus is neither here nor there. For David, Solomon, Abraham, Jeremiah and so on were also significantly different from Jesus. It is true of course that Jesus's mission has several unusual and characteristic episodes, both in Christian and Islamic perspectives. But to focus upon some peculiarity of his mission as supplying the essential criterion of prophethood would be akin to the case of someone who argued that, say, Nietzsche and Descartes fail to qualify as philosophers since, unlike Socrates, they were not martyrs for the cause of philosophy. Such reasoning would universally be seen as idiosyncratic at best and, at worst, arbitrary in its foundations.

That western writers, Christian and otherwise, have a deep-rooted antipathy towards Muhammad and his religion is a fact wholly beyond the range of reasonable dispute.[47] The hatred of Christian detractors of Islam is fairly easy to explain. Muhammad is seen to be a usurper of Christ's kingdom. It has to be said that this is a sentiment most Muslims find difficult to understand for it seems to them so utterly religiose, indeed unworthy of genuine religion. Certainly, it is a sentiment that is totally foreign to the Koran. The Kingdom belongs to God; and no one can usurp it. Jesus and Muhammad are both servants of God, not usurpers of his sovereignty. This conviction, peculiar to Islam, no doubt explains its strikingly (and indeed characteristically) magnanimous portrait of all religious figures including Jesus, for whom the Koran reserves some unique accolades. The Muslim scripture contains a profoundly respectful estimate of Jesus and his mother; the miracles of the great Jewish teacher are recorded without a trace of rivalry or envy. Whence the envy when all credit belongs to God?[48] While proffering a high estimate of Jesus, however, the author of the Koran does not fall into the Christian error of attributing gross immoralities to all other messengers in order to exalt Jesus by contrast. Every prophet, whether junior or senior, has his own status in the eyes of the Creator.

It used to be an axiom of Christian resentment about Muhammad that he had deliberately and consciously exalted himself above his prophetic predecessors, particularly Jesus. This is a sentiment which, like almost all other Christian sentiments *vis-à-vis* the Prophet, is remarkably bereft of the benefit of evidential support. To be sure, the Koran asserts that some prophets have, by divine arbitrium, been exalted above others (K:2:253); but very wisely it does not give details of this ranking, the implication being presumably that these belong properly to the province of the mystery (*ghayb*) of Allah's cognisance. Moreover, we know on the authority of the traditionist al-Bukhari that Muhammad explicitly denied that he was 'better' than Moses or Jonah;[49] and, in general, it seems that he never lost an opportunity to discourage all forms of misdirected zeal, fearing, not without reason, that his followers would fall into the same trap as the followers of Jesus.[50]

For Christians, Jesus was much more than a prophet or even a great prophet. In an attempt to celebrate this conviction, Christians seek to emphasise Jesus's superiority to other prophetic figures, particularly Muhammad. Although Muslims are often indifferent to the comparison between the two – God knows better, as the pious formula has it[51] – it is, I believe, a comparison at best unfavourable to Jesus and at worst senseless. For if Jesus is taken to be simply a human prophet, like Muhammad, it is not merely triumphalism to say that Muhammad's own achievements are, considering early Islam's swift yet enduring victories, probably far greater. However, if one sees Jesus in a particular Christian religious perspective – namely, as the third Person of the three in the Trinity – then on account of his divine status the suggested comparison with an admittedly (and purely) human Muhammad is rendered baseless.

It would be fair to say that western writers have, by and large, failed to give the Arabian Prophet his due. But, oddly enough, they have been very eager to give him *more* than his due. This is implicit in that offensive label 'Muhammadanism', now generally recognised to be entirely unjust and self-indulgent.[52] The Koran preaches, as I indicated earlier, an uncompromising monotheism that is incompatible with worship of human entities. And Muhammad was a man, a great man, an unusually great man – but a man none the less. Muslims have famously claimed that Christianity is founded on a basic error in regard to the status of Jesus: he is not worthy of worship. Naturally, therefore, Muslims have always been concerned not to make the same mistake in regard to a human Muhammad as Christians (allegedly) made in regard to a human Jesus.

In the past, of course, Christians made this mistake on behalf of

Muslims: the followers of Muhammad were called Muhammadans. In recent years, this label has ceased to be popular. But, it seems to me, the impulse that inspired it is still alive and well. The attempt, often tortured, to find 'Christ figures' in Islam is partly the direct result of the same kind of misguided perception of the status of koranic monotheism.[53] For if Islam has a Christ, it is Allah – not Muhammad, not the Koran, not even Islam. The slogan is *Allah-u-akbar* (God is greater), not *Muhammad-u-akbar*, not *Koran-u-akbar*, not even *Islam-u-akbar*. *Allah-u-akbar*. Islam has no human or partly human reality that can correspond to Christ for the simple but sufficient reason that no such reality could properly deserve worship. God alone is divine; God alone is worthy of worship. Therefore, God alone could correspond to Christ – the reality worshipped, rightly or wrongly, by Christians.

I have just briefly examined some of the major impediments to the achievement of harmony among Christians and Muslims. To focus our discussion, we can now ask: what kind of attitude should one have while engaged in a dialogue with someone from a different religious persuasion? Why should a Christian or Muslim engage in dialogue? Should he seek to demonstrate the superiority of his faith? Is the posture of responsible exchange a good one? Why would a religious person seek to terminate dialogue? Would he be justified in doing so?

There is nowadays, beneath the surface, much genuine tension and disquiet in the area of Islamic–Christian exchange. Though both Christians and Muslims continue, at religious conferences, to talk very enthusiastically about the need for eschewing polemical critique in favour of eirenic exchange, it would be no exaggeration to say that neither party trusts the other.

Muslims do sometimes suspect the motives of their Christian counterparts. And there may be grounds for suspicion. Why, after all, should Christians whose forefathers have opposed Islam root and branch, by means fair and foul, for well over a thousand years, suddenly wish to effect a peaceful reconciliation? This is an important worry. For the current liberal attitude towards Islam prevalent among some Christians is either the result of a betrayal of a principle held tenaciously for centuries or else it is a realisation of past errors. Neither of these possibilities is sinister: nations can sometimes owe allegiance to false ideals and do so for centuries; to realise one's errors or those of one's ancestors is an act of humility and, as such, worthy of respect. What is troubling, however, is the possibility that dialogue is merely part of a new strategy to deal with an old enemy. (Remember that Islam has been, remains, and will remain, far and away Christianity's most successful religious rival.) Could it be that some Christians are merely putting a different bait on the old hook? Could it be that dialogue is sometimes undertaken in deference to the maxim 'Know thine enemy'?

These are not meant to be rhetorical questions; and I do not wish to impugn the motives of all Christians engaged in dialogue with the

Muslim faithful.[54] My own answers, to be given here without regard for the rules of professional diplomacy, will, I fear, seem rather harsh and unpleasant, especially to a people who regard the demands of politeness as overriding those of truth. It seems to me that the practice of Christian institutions by and large gives the lie to the claim about desiring a genuinely impartial or sympathetic study of Islam. There are grounds for this accusation, though I do not expect Christian readers to agree with me. It cannot be a coincidence that in western universities Islam is rarely if ever taught by someone who embraces its inspiration. Christianity is taught often enough by Christians, Buddhism by Buddhists, and so on. There is, notwithstanding the liberal ethos of western intellectual culture, a strong operative bias against the hiring of Muslims, especially well-informed Muslims, to teach Islam.[55] The motives for this are fairly easily identified: a vigorous Islam poses a great threat to the historical and religious foundations of an apparently disintegrating western Christianity. But while this fear is understandable enough, it cannot constitute a defensible ground for disallowing Muslims to teach Islam – or even Judaism and Christianity.

To refuse to see unfairness in the present arrangement, deliberate as it clearly is, requires some degree of sophistry. Nor will it do to retort that, for purposes of teaching, adherence to a faith prejudices one's outlook. For while that is usually true, it is equally the case that rejection often prejudices one's outlook in a different direction. And, in any case, it is indefensible to single out Islam for special, indeed prejudicial, treatment. One could argue that Christianity should be taught more or less exclusively by Christians in a seminary just as Islam is always taught by Muslims in an Islamic seminary (*madrasah*). But it is odd to prohibit Muslims from teaching their own religion in 'liberal' western universities while allowing Christians to teach Christianity. Indeed, Christians often teach Islam in such institutions, while it is difficult to find a Muslim teaching Christianity or Judaism alongside his non-Muslim colleagues.[56]

There are, to widen our discussion, certain attitudes that tend to cause friction between Christians and Muslims engaged in dialogue; and some of these threaten the continuation of organised exchange. Christians, to focus on one particular attitudinal issue, frequently accuse the Muslim protagonists of 'triumphalism': Muslims, it is alleged, complacently pretend that a good few of the problems facing Christianity are peculiar to that religion and have no relevance to Islam. Thus, modernity is to most Muslims, Christians contend, simply a Christian problem.

This is a partly just accusation. Many Muslims do boast, as I indicated in chapter 1, that Islam is immune to the many challenges of secular modernity. This is indeed triumphalism (in the pejorative sense) and ought to be abjured. It is an attitude nourished by an ignorance (or at least an inadequate understanding) of the nature of the modern secular sceptical reservation about *all* transcendent religions. As I have argued in this book, Islam may well have to consider seriously the possibility of making concessions, albeit minor ones, to the secular temper. (One good result of Muslim obscurantism here has been that Islam remains Islam: there are no revised versions, no 'neo-Islamic' doctrines or trends.) To refuse resolutely to recognise even the need for any such concessions in the case of Islam while recognising, even emphasising, such a need in the case of Christianity is tantamount to a species of triumphalism, though, to be fair, Muslims are rarely guilty of this particular variety of it. Their attitude is often simpler: Christians are having problems controlling the subversive sceptical developments within their own culture; Islam can take care of these developments if only Christians will hand over their difficulties to the Muslims.

Such a pretension is, of course, to put it minimally, quite silly. When it comes to the challenges of a secular reason fully emancipated from age-old theistic strictures, all the theists are in the same – and, as it happens, currently rather leaky – boat. To make concessions to secular modernity, however, is one thing; to make concessions to Christianity quite another.[57] And it is here that the charge of triumphalism becomes problematic. We can easily see this when we note that 'triumphalism', like 'reductionism' or 'revisionism', is a term of opprobrium, and one that readily finds its place in the polemical lexicon. What, then, is triumphalism? And what is wrong with it? Now, surely to mention one's strengths, to argue that Christianity may have weaknesses absent from its great religious rival, is not in itself culpable. Perhaps, Islam is, when all is said and done, genuinely superior to Christianity (and Judaism). Perhaps, just perhaps, Islam has all the strengths of Christianity and none of its weaknesses. In fact, of course, all of us, Christians no less than Muslims, talk of our strengths. Could it be that when the other party does it, it is tempting to call it 'triumphalism'?

The charge of triumphalism is an interesting and revealing one. It offers us an insight into the evolution of Christian attitudes towards Islam. In many ways, this accusation may actually be the residue of that much older, much more crass, charge of fanaticism – a charge still in vogue in popular and intellectual western culture. Muslims have been, and still are, accused of fanaticism sometimes solely on account of the fact that they, unlike many Christians, refuse to compromise on matters of principle. And yet if adherence to principle be fanaticism, then fanaticism is an admirable trait – and one in rather short supply among modern Christians.

Fanaticism is of course other people's passion. (What the English newscaster calls suicide may still be martyrdom in God's eyes.) All nations are fanatical about one thing or another, whether it be elevated matters such as religion and honour or trivial matters such as football and sensuality. We can all live with some prejudices – but not with others.

To get back to our theme, not all Muslim claims about the alleged relative superiority of Islam *vis-à-vis* its great religious rival can reasonably be dismissed as triumphalist in a derogatory sense. We must allow conceptual room for the possibility of recording one's strengths just as we should allow room for recording one's weaknesses. And Muslims are, I believe, perfectly justified in seeking to argue that Islam has a relative strength, for example, in the areas of canon and intellectual appeal. Christianity has in the region of canonical formulation a weakness well documented even by its adherents. Many Christians have been attracted to Islam's exceptionally powerful intellectual foundations. Why should a believer be prohibited from mentioning the strengths in his vision?

Christians, particularly those committed to the proselytisation of Muslims (and Jews), are naturally disturbed by Islam's powerful hold on the minds of many Muslims. But the dexterity with which committed Christian apologists and missionaries continue to mix poison and praise with respect to Islam simply has not produced the required results. The rate of conversion from Christianity to Islam is relatively high, often attracting highly distinguished Christians; the rate of conversion in the opposite direction is very low indeed, often attracting only undistinguished Muslims. It is true that conversion from Islam to Christianity is usually fraught with dangers: Islamic societies have strong disincentives, formal and informal, against conversion.[58] But in the modern secularised West most Muslims can convert to Christianity, and do so usually with relative impunity. And yet in spite of that liberty, few Muslims of any distinction have gone over to join the Christian Club. The stock Muslim claim, that *all* Muslims who convert are merely insincere opportunists rescued from poverty by the missionary's dangerous gift of financial assistance, is unconvincing. It is indeed unfair to doubt the sincerity of most of these conversions, especially when one notes all the isolation and suffering often entailed.

Sincerity aside, one can safely say that most conversions from Christianity to Islam are based on some measure of intellectual reasoning; often reasoning about Christianity's glaring weakness in the area of scriptural canon. Conversions in the opposite direction are almost always based on subjective religious experience, itself often inspired by the wish for a kind of guarantee about the attainment of salvation.[59] Islam, it is thought – and this is a correct understanding of Islam – offers no guarantees of success in the religious life; Christianity famously offers a kind of 'insurance policy' for sinners. The attractions of the Christian view, deceptive though it clearly is, are not difficult to discern.[60]

To record facts, such as these in the sociology of conversion, is not in itself either polemical or triumphalist. Indeed, it seems to me, we *should* record unpleasant facts. (Or is honesty in religious dialogue – as in business – the worst policy?) Certainly there are grounds for genuine disquiet here generated by the current circumstance of rivalry. Christians and Muslims are both in the same business: that of religious success. And it would be absurd to pretend that such a circumstance is not often radically divisive.

There is a tendency among educated Christians and Muslims to sail under false colours in order to keep afloat a liberal ecumenical enterprise. And yet such a strategy is religiously unacceptable, for it sacrifices, sells short, the virtue of truth merely for the sake of attaining a false if comforting sense of community. Of course, dialogue (or, in the latest fashion, 'trialogue', with a few liberal Jewish thinkers lending a helping hand) does achieve genuinely educational ends if only for a handful of academics. But one should put in the balance the fact that Christianity and Islam co-exist in an atmosphere of fundamental and native anxieties about questions of moment. The gulf between the faiths, like the gulf between the dualist's mind and matter or the conservative politician's East and West, is not likely to be bridged merely by dialogue undertaken by a handful of expensively educated academics.

I do not wish to deny the importance of responsible exchange between members of different faiths. But it must be responsible: well-informed, cognisant of the tensions, ready to acknowledge rift and difference, concerned to record realities.[61] And this is indeed a tall order. Will Christian–Muslim dialogue endure into the next decade? My own view about the future of such dialogue – a view denigrated by some as unduly pessimistic – is, I believe, surely realistic. I myself find it difficult to attend an inter-faith conference without thinking that religious exchange will indeed endure into the next century – but merely as a fashion. It could be that religious liberalism of the kind exhibited in dialogue may not survive the currently widening ideological rift between the Crescent and the Cross in many parts of the globe. If it does survive the trial, it is most likely to do so, like modern optimism, by relying on increasingly unclear generalities.[62]

It is not recent scholarship alone that has noted the deep, perhaps irresolvable, doctrinal incompatibility between Islam and Christianity. The problem had already been felt and recorded as early as the seventh century. In fact the Koran itself invites Christians to a prayer duel (*mubahilah*) in the larger attempt to break the deadlock. According to this arrangement, sometimes known as 'trial by imprecation', the contending parties invoke the wrath or adverse judgement of God expecting it to 'fall' immediately and visibly on the dishonest, guilty or otherwise misguided party. The trial by imprecation can also be invoked by one individual against an alleged religious impostor or heretic; and it was invoked in the nineteenth century by orthodox religionists against Mirza Ghulam Ahmad, the founder of the Qadiani sect, now expelled from Islam. The results of this procedure are difficult to interpret.

Muhammad had set out, in accordance with koranic instructions (K:3:55–61), to meet his Christian detractors in a large open space.

The Christians, according to the Muslim account,[63] arrived on time, but were deterred by the sight of Muhammad and his party's sincerity and confidence. The Christians declined the challenge.

That method of imprecation is, whatever its merits in the age of revelation, clearly unsuited to our current circumstance. Given the silence of God today, the deadlock between any given faith, such as Islam, and its rivals, is not so easily broken. To be sure, there may well be an intellectual process transpiring beyond death in which the ambiguities and doctrinal stalemates of this life are finally resolved and broken just as the moral imbalance of mortal existence will, according to ethical theism, be eventually and satisfactorily rectified in a world yet to come.[64] But this view, even supposing it to be coherent and true, still leaves all the important theological puzzles on our hands. Why does God allow many large portions of mankind to remain in doubt, hesitation, or even outright error concerning matters of moment? The Koran sternly warns us that confession of the monotheistic credo *after death* may not suffice to escape damnation: we had better find out while we are still living. If so, isn't God morally obliged, so to speak, to make clear, especially in an age of confusion, his existence, will and purpose for men on earth?

As the various doctrinal deadlocks in Christian–Muslim debate become increasingly prevalent, the critique of the religious rival is likely to become purely moral. Each faith has an associated normative outlook; Christians and Muslims naturally argue that the ethical scheme associated with their faith is superior to all other such schemes. It is felt that religions can sometimes be ranked for plausibility in terms of their moral, as opposed to purely metaphysical, appeal. Such a shift of focus is, it might be argued, a welcome one indicating the direction in which a possible resolution of the Christian–Muslim deadlock lies. It is worth exploring this suggestion before eventually widening our discussion to include the more general problems of religious pluralism.

For many centuries, Christians have been eager to criticise the behaviour of the Prophet of Islam and of his followers, often castigating Islamic ethics as demonstrably inferior to the moral code allegedly preached by the Jesus of the Gospels. Muslims have in turn responded not only by denigrating the Christian ethic as totally unrealistic – out of touch with the reality of a human nature under its tuition[65] – but also by casting an accusing eye over the normative record of so-called Christian nations, particularly *vis-à-vis* other faiths and cultures. The resulting exchanges have been marked by bitterness and acrimonious commentary from both sides. There may well be another potential deadlock here – on the moral plane, so to speak – but let us keep this question an open one for as long as possible.

All learned authorities are unanimous that the first koranic revelation (K:96:1–5) had ordered Muhammad to 'recite' certain words, an act from which the sacred volume derives its title. 'Recite in the name of thy Lord', reads the *surah* – a Lord who 'taught man that which he knew not'. The emphasis here is straightforwardly educational; certainly, there is no mention of fighting or using force for the sake of one's convictions. Some time later, after a painfully barren hiatus familiar to prophets and mystics, the Voice from Heaven ordered Muhammad to warn his compatriots about Allah's impending judgement against an unjust generation (K:74:1ff.)[66] The audience remained largely impervious to the prophetic threats; some of the more powerful members of the Meccan establishment began to mock and mildly persecute Muhammad's weaker disciples. Being naturally averse to militant struggle, the infant Muslim community bore with patience the increasing threats of persecution and extinction. Certainly, the sacred volume had made no mention of fighting even in defence let alone in aggression. The Muslims recognised that the pagans were guilty of no minor offence: they were ignoring the word of God. The question of the relationship between religious truth and the role of (secular) power in defending, confirming or establishing it remained unresolved.

There is some dispute among students of the Koran concerning the date of revelation of the first passage that sanctioned militant struggle.[67] But *surah* 22 (vv.39–40), the classification of which as Meccan or Medinan is debated, offers a characteristic picture of the Koran's attitude towards the (legitimate) use of force in political conflict:

> Permission to fight is hereby granted unto those against whom war is made, because they have been wronged; God is indeed able to help a people who have been unjustly expelled forth from their habitations merely on account of their saying 'Our Lord is God' . . . [68]

The rest of our story here is familiar. It fell to the lot of the later theoreticians of Islam to justify the use of force in the service of extending the witness to the dominion of Allah – far beyond the confines of Arabia.[69] At any rate, the Koran had settled the problem of the theoretical relationship between power and truth.

It is the use of force in the service of religious ends that most enrages Christian critics of Islam. Muhammad, it is charged, succumbed to the temptation to use political power; unlike Jesus and some of the other suffering prophets who cried unto death in the wilderness, Muhammad, at the watershed of spiritual biography, betrayed his vocation. The Arabian iconoclast, the accusation continues, wanted God's purpose to have the upper hand, to remain in the field despite human perversity. But he misunderstood the nature of victory in matters of the spirit: God's aims are sometimes vindicated even in, indeed especially in, the pattern of defeat. For even, perhaps only, the (apparent) failure of the divine task can take the full measure of men's obduracy. Islam's emphasis on the need for seeing God's cause victorious in some unequivocal way –'a clear victory', as the Koran has it (K:48:1) – betrays, the charge continues, a false, religiose concept of triumph itself reflective of purely profane values. Indeed, it is urged, such a victory is no victory at all: the sinful impulse merely withdraws deeper into the heart much as a frightened child hides himself in the mother's bosom. The last citadel of the sinful, hypocritical, self-betraying man remains unconquered: the sinner's heart remains within the province of a profane sovereignty. God has failed to reach that inner seat, the deepest, the most inaccessible, the most secure part of the human person.[70] Thus what is victory to the God of Islam is yet failure in the eyes of a higher arbiter of success.[71]

Muhammad, then, had misunderstood the logic of divine triumph. This is the Christian indictment. The issue here is one close to the hearts of Muslims (and Christians): many doors are slammed over it in interfaith gatherings. It is important, therefore, to examine it as dispassionately as possible.

The Christian view of the role of power is, given the assumptions that nourish it, perfectly intelligible, perhaps even justified. Certainly, it is unsurprising once we note that Jesus, unlike Moses before him and Muhammad after him, never founded a polity. It is true that there is some rather equivocal support – in a speech probably attributed to him by the clergy at a later stage – for the establishment of a Church. But the Church, as *corpus Christi*, is properly to be seen as an institution proclaiming the power of the Spirit, so to speak, rather than as laying the foundations of a socio-political order in the standard sense. The idea of such an order has always been suspect in Christianity. It is quite likely that Jesus himself, given the significance of eschatological expectations and the perception of the imminence of divine judgement within the outlook of first-century Palestinian Judaism, saw the suggestion of an established political state as a superfluity. At any rate, much of subsequent Christian thought has characteristically been of the opinion that since the integrity of human nature was destroyed by original sin, men are incapable of attaining a prosperous order here on earth. Power cannot remove or mitigate the disability entailed by radical sin: as long as men are corrupt at heart, they cannot establish a fully just society. Unsurprisingly, then, Christians have discerned a religious sanction for entertaining a moral suspicion about the use of worldly power in the service of socio-political ends.

The Islamic story is of course a very different one, the differences often rooted in differing theological preconceptions about the nature of man and God. Men are expected to establish the Kingdom of God on earth: a just and prosperous social order. They are endowed with the capacity to recruit power in the service of faithful ends: human nature is not inherently corrupt. Islam, in principle, recognises no distinction between the religious and the secular spheres of life: everything, including the political, is placed under a righteous sovereignty. Men are actively encouraged to cultivate the correct use of all facilities, including power. Every resource, every impulse, must be harnessed in the service of God.

Let us explore now the problem of the relationship between religious truth and (secular) power. Certainly, power can be, indeed often is, misused. There is a morality in this affair. (All is *not* fair in war – whatever may be said of love.) But the mere fact that power is liable, is even particularly liable, to misuse is neither here nor there. For almost every facility, and particularly every facility of genuine worth, conceals, in the nature of the case, a potential for misuse. Is the fact that, say, knowledge can be misused, an argument then in favour of cultivating ignorance? Knowledge can indeed occasionally lead one astray; but ignorance never fails to achieve that end. Of course, power, like knowledge, can be used for good or evil. Powerful men are as capable of virtue as of vice. It is, I would argue, morally a truism to say that power should be used properly; but it is morally absurd to say that power should never be recruited even in the service of an admittedly good cause. There are times when the end justifies the means.

To embrace if reluctantly the political arm in a harsh and difficult world is not to make an idol of it. Power is, in the Muslim outlook, not an end in itself. The end is peace: one of the meanings of the word *islam*. The Koran contains, to the surprise of Christian critics, as much support for peace and reconciliation as the Gospel, if not more.[72] But Islam has always, and rightly, rejected peace where such a circumstance was effectively contaminated by injustice. 'Peace – only with justice' is the Islamic motto. To talk about peace even in the face of overwhelming injustice, to insist on passivity in the face of unmitigated evil, is anathema to Islam. Some Christians have found religious support for pacifism even in an arena of tyranny. But Islam sees that as a moral absurdity of the worst kind – one that no religious sanction could sanctify.[73]

I have here stated very baldly the standard Muslim – and in my view wholly correct – attitude towards the use and abuse of power in social conflict and struggle.[74] This kind of directness about the morality of coercion often leads Christians, especially given the current state of political tensions on a global level, to accuse Muslims of being unscrupulous warmongers. Seen in one way, this is a truly remarkable accusation. Though Christians have failed to strike any theoretically coherent posture *vis-à-vis* secular power, they have, in practice, rarely if ever hesitated to prostitute their faith in the service of reasonably modest as well as wildly Utopian political schemes. (Think here of Calvin's Geneva.) Certainly, for a faith whose votaries have subdued much of the globe in the hope of saving others' (and presumably their own) souls, the willingness to claim none the less the privilege of an otherworldly apolitical impulse must itself be inspired either by genuine naïveté or a private sense of humour.

That Christians should here cast the first stone is, in every way, a matter for amazement. Christianity's own moral record in matters of tolerance and coercion, judged by internal Christian standards, is, as many fair-minded churchmen themselves now concede, utterly deplorable.[75] For though the Christian community has never defended intolerance as an ideal, it would be difficult to find many among its members in the past who have avoided intolerance in practice.[76] Islam, however, judged by standards intrinsic to the faith, has always had a strikingly good record. Indeed, in general, Islam's actual record is, even when judged by exterior, allegedly higher Christian standards, honourably distinguished by its relative tolerance of alien conviction.

Recent years have witnessed some trenchant critiques, often by impartial churchmen themselves, of the churches' political mistakes both within and outside Christendom. A large part of this self-accusation has, quite rightly, centred on the concern to condemn the focused brutality directed against people of Hebrew origin settled in Christian lands – a people historically under the burden of the charge of deicide. We need not dwell on that. It is, certainly, an unacceptable bias for a Muslim to make heavy weather of the churches' wrongdoing while refusing to put his own faith – also a missionary faith – under the moral microscope. And when we do that, there is little room for complacency. It is true that Muslims, in an age of intolerance, did grant limited political autonomy to religious rivals; the ideal of partial tolerance preached by Muhammad in the seventh century was in sharp contrast to the contemporaneous fanaticism and intolerance so prevalent among the scriptured societies of Jews and Christians. It is also (and importantly) true that the very fact that Christianity, Judaism and Hinduism continue to exist at all in the lands of their origin, after Islam's lengthy domination, is a signal tribute to Muslim tolerance. But while Muslims have every right to make much of Islam's lenient ascendancy in Spain in the Middle Ages – particularly of its comparative forbearance towards its religious cousins[77] – it is only fair to put in the balance the undeniable fact that Muslims have often persecuted not only heretical minorities but also, in one of the most shameful episodes of Islamic history, Hindus and Sikhs living in the days of the Moghul Empire in India. (Was Hindu polytheism indeed equivalent to the Arabian paganism so fiercely condemned in the Koran?)

It is sometimes said in mitigation of these kinds of criticism that it is unfair to expect Muslims to be tolerant in an age in which no one else was so. But this observation overlooks the moral rule that those, like Muhammad, claiming to be *ex officio* in advance of their times, must expect to be judged by a standard somewhat higher than the prevalent one. And in any case, why should we Muslims be permitted to light our candle at both ends: to be admired for introducing an ideal of tolerance in a largely intolerant age and yet excused for our occasional intolerance on the grounds that it is merely a reflection of the times?

Before finally widening our discussion to encompass the larger issues of religious pluralism, let me briefly complete this one. The suggestion was that the normative attitudes associated with the doctrinal schemes of Christianity and Islam should also be examined and assessed in order to effect valid comparisons and contrasts. This area of Christian–Muslim exchange is likely to be marked by fierce disagreement over the proper resolution of fundamental questions. What is the correct relationship between power and religious truth? Though there is some measure of consensus among Christians and Muslims concerning the historical details of political rivalry, the proclivity to intolerance and so on, there is a deadlock between the protagonists concerning the status of (secular) power in an order under divine sovereignty. Whether or not the moral deadlock can be broken is naturally a matter for legitimate dispute. Certainly the more basic deadlock concerning doctrine is likely to stay.

V

Once upon a time it was reasonable to say: 'Every religious controversy is due to someone's ignorance.' No longer though. It is possible now to understand various faiths in a comprehensively cross-cultural way; there has been a spectacular recent growth in our knowledge of rival views and ideologies. But, as I have already had occasion to remark, there is currently a stalemate among ideological opponents. And the Christian–Muslim deadlock is an especially intractable one that is likely to endure for a long time. In the end, we may all do well to take Father Robert Caspar's characteristically charitable advice, deriving from the Koran (K:2:148; 5:48): instead of being rivals in the negative and harmful mode, Muslims and Christians should cultivate rivalry in good works.[78]

The theme of inter-religious dialogue, to widen our discussion, is likely to occupy the centre of theological concerns in this and the coming century. Many characteristically modern religious puzzles are generated by a growing realisation that the doctrinal elements in any one given faith cannot reasonably maintain a universality of normative claim upon modern human allegiance. The presence of authentic religiosity outside one's own tradition of faith seems undeniable if religiously disconcerting. Indeed, enlightened opinion among theists – Jews, Christians and Muslims – is more or less unanimous that scripture contains irresolvable puzzles with respect to the existence of plural pieties.

I shall now try to identify some of the theological difficulties to be experienced by a Muslim sensibility. It is convenient to begin by noting the existence of moral excellence among the adherents of non-Islamic faiths. Only prejudice could motivate a denial of the existence of instances of conspicuous virtue among Jews, Christians and members of various non-theistic faiths. And if one examines, say, traditional Christian piety, it would be difficult to believe that Christians intentionally wish to dishonour Allah (God) when they proclaim in all sincerity: 'Christ is our Lord!' To be sure, that there should be such a virile piety outside Islam may indeed be religiously unsettling. But its presence cannot reasonably be denied. Again, to turn to Judaism, one cannot fail to be impressed by its many men and women of proverbial piety, whose lives have had a deep influence upon the human pursuit of holiness, an influence absurdly out of proportion to their number. And, finally, when we cast a glance at the non-theistic eastern religions, we have a different metaphysic yet a strikingly similar wish to seek moral excellence. Thus, though the eastern sages entertained a cyclical (rather than linear) view of history and saw their destiny as being caught in the wheel of rebirth awaiting final emancipation, their lives displayed many of the virtues associated with the theistic faiths.

Can Islam in principle accommodate these concessions, irresistible as they surely are today? Well, there are some religious resources within the Muslim scripture that do apparently facilitate to a considerable extent the resolution of some pluralist difficulties. Although Islam as a specific historical religion begins in seventh-century Arabia, the Koran traces the origins of the Islamic tradition back to Adam. The religion (*deen*) of Islam – the religion that centrally advocates submission (*islam*) to the will of God – begins, in koranic perspective, at the very beginning of history, receives a formulation with Abraham, is repeatedly enunciated by a long line of Hebrew and Israelite Patriarchs and lesser figures, and culminates, in one of its branches, with the appearance of Jesus the Messiah. In parallel with this, Arabian figures arise in various 'Gentile' communities: a process that culminates, through the reopening of the Ishmaelite lineage, in Muhammad the Apostle of God. This conquest of the past is a characteristic, indeed favourite *motif* of the Koran: the faith of Muhammad is merely a restoration of the pristine faith of Abraham and Adam.

If we temporarily lay aside the important reservation that the koranic conception of the origins of Islam may offend certain criteria of critical and historical objectivity, it would appear that at least all the theistic faiths, possibly all traditions of whatever religious complexion, come within the orbit of 'Islam'. But, of course, this is not Islam – the historical faith embraced by members of *al-umma al-Muhammadiyya*. And it is precisely this realisation that lies at the root of one's dissatisfaction with the orthodox religious claim about Islam's radical comprehensiveness. For the notion that Islam is the primordial faith of mankind is not so much an historical-empirical claim as a normative religious judgement about the monotheistic proclivity of human nature. The scriptural axiom of man's inherently theistic tendency – the view that all men are inclined to accept Islam – may well here be parading as an empirical scientific claim. Certainly anyone who believes that Islam is the only faith that God has ordained since history began is almost certainly bound to be a Muslim. For such a claim is fundamentally religious, indeed Islamic; it is not in the first instance empirical or historical, though it may enjoy some independent historical and factual support.

If we are to develop the Muslim response to other faiths, we must begin by examining the Koran's own sentiments about Islam. 'The religion (*deen*) with God,' says *surah* 3 (v.19), 'is Islam.' When God wishes to favour a man, he 'expands his breast to [contain] Islam' (K:6:125; 39:22). With the complete establishment of Islam, God has completed his favour on mankind, announces *surah* 5 (v.3), a verse that is generally held to complete the revelation of the koranic corpus. Predictably, anyone who seeks a faith other than Islam will not find acceptance in the eyes of God: such a choice would entail a radical loss (K:3:85).

Of course, the Koran uses the term 'Islam' in a very broad sense.[79] But there is a residual exclusivism, especially when we examine the sheer range and variety of actual religious conviction in human history. Many traditions are outside the orbit of Islam: a fact that will certainly plague the labours of those Muslim believers advocating an authentic religious pluralism. It can be defensibly asserted, however, that if Islam is true, all the various theistic faiths, particularly Judaism and Christianity, are at least partly true, reflecting as they do irregular forms of Allah's varied grace.

Though the Koran declares Islam to be the only faith-style fully acceptable to God, it nowhere restricts salvation (or, rather, religious success) to Muslims in the narrower sense of those who endorse Muhammad's claim to prophethood.[80] The only conditions of obtaining God's forgiveness seem to be belief in the unity of God and his judgement coupled with the intention to perform good deeds (K:2:62). If this indeed be so, the Muslim Paradise would probably be a kind of commonwealth of pious souls all accepting the ultimate sovereignty of God. (These relatively liberal koranic sentiments have not stopped Muslims from effectively restricting entry into Paradise to other Muslims, indeed even to members of their own sect.) Beyond that, Allah reserves the right to 'do whatever he pleases', forgive whom he wills – a right utterly central to the divine nature as depicted in the Koran. Such a caveat introduces the possibility of universal salvation albeit at the risk of trivialising the clash between faith and rejection, between piety and impiety.[81]

Whatever the correctly Islamic stance on other faiths may turn out to be, the case against complete religious exclusivism has, I would argue, largely been made already. The liberal view, adopted notably by Professor John Hick, seems to be the one most likely to gain, implicitly at any rate, widespread acceptance in the coming years in religiously pluralist cultures.[82] According to this view, a certain kind of exclusivism with all its isolationist corollaries is to be shunned, and to be shunned for religious reasons. Every established faith, argues Hick with characteristic open-heartedness, is properly to be seen as merely one among several authentic but partial and culturally relative approaches to the knowledge and experience of the divine. After all, would a merciful God indeed restrict guidance and salvation to only a portion of the human race? Hick's view is no doubt, like most theological opinions of this kind, open to devastating criticism, especially from orthodox religious quarters.[83] But it is based on the plausible observation that no religious belief-system raised entirely from the ashes could yet give convincing sense and direction to the lives of countless human beings for many centuries. And it seeks to establish the attractive conclusion that large sections of our species somehow find salvation and religious fulfilment in different, creatively variable ways under a unique, all-encompassing divine sovereignty.

VI

According to orthodox Islamic belief, immediately after death the soul undergoes preliminary interrogation by the angels. The catechism involves standard and simple questions: Who is your Lord? What is your religion? The answers come easily to the lips of the pious believer. The rejectors are quickly caught out variously on account of hesitation and confusion, silence, or else incoherence and falsity. Those who pass the doctrinal part of the test are then subjected to a further test about their deeds and actions. Few indeed pass this part of the examination. The sinner, according to some authorities, then requests Muhammad to intercede on his behalf. In any case, the appeal is presented to Allah; the final decision rests entirely within the divine prerogative and is, naturally, not subject to dispute.

This orthodox doctrine best serves to illustrate the temperamental gulf between the innocence of traditional attitudes and the sheer complexity of choice in the pluralist ethos. The faithful man who has worked hard all his life in the hope of attaining Paradise finds that his battle is not yet won: accordingly, he is here being given the final details. The relevant answers are as defined, direct and clear as the questions. There is no room for unclarity, confusion or hesitation. The pious man has already done his homework; he has nothing to worry about. Indeed his piety and innocence even take pluralism in their stride: 'Let everyone worship God in their own way; I'll worship him in his way. And death will reveal unto the others the error of their ways.'

But what is the way of God? It is indeed difficult to know. Even within faiths, opinions abound; and all faiths now exist, co-exist, in conscious proximity to alien convictions. Thus, for example, Islam is no longer exclusively the vision informing the lives of people in traditional lands. It is in fact one of the religious choices for modern man. Given the multiform religious experience of modern man, every faith is to some extent, within pluralist cultures, a potentially live option.

Modernity has radically altered the total context within which men make choices and decisions. Indeed one need no longer live and die in the tradition of one's forefathers. Conversion need no longer occur by dint of chance contact with alien conviction; it can be effected through research, itself undertaken in a spirit of organised interest in other belief-systems. Even mass conversions are, in principle at least, possible: large numbers of people could come to recognise that their allegiance to a particular religious ideal was largely an accident of birth and geography.

It is highly likely that most people's actual choice of religion is partly governed by cultural bias. It is unsurprising that most modern Swedes are Lutherans; it is equally unsurprising that most modern Saudis are Sunnis. There is, of course, one obvious corollary of this point: some people may, after due consideration, decide that they are members of a particular religious community (as opposed to another) by chance rather than choice. If so, conversion is the natural step. Yet there is a significant harm in conversion which the potential convert would do well to bear in mind. Every religion is concerned in part to lend unity, create community among human beings by supplying a more or less uniform self-image. To the extent that conversion often emotionally deracinates a person from the community of his birth and initial allegiance, it creates confusion and disruption and is, therefore, perhaps to be discouraged. (Think here of the angels questioning the convert.) It is, however, no doubt, a questionable policy to abjure what one takes to be the truth merely for the benefits of the unexamined life.

The Road to Mecca

'There are two ways of getting home,' wrote G.K. Chesterton, 'and one of them is to stay there.'[1] No doubt that is the safer option; for some it is the only option. But there is another itinerary too. In this book I have urged Muslims to leave, if temporarily, the House of Islam, to venture through the alien world of rejection and rival patterns of religious conviction: to venture beyond dogma and unargued assumption, in the larger attempt to become acquainted not only with the *a priori* theologies of scripture but also with the sometimes recalcitrant realities of a world and human nature under their usual tuition.

The journey thus far has not been easy; and the rest is harder still. For we must now make our way back to the household of faith, back on the road to Mecca. And yet we have, of course, traversed the forbidden ground; we have seen the vast disarray of conflicting beliefs and ideologies vying with one another for our allegiance. An untested faith that prefers the security of unargued assumption, a faith whose votaries never lift their heads above the dogmatic parapet – that is no longer for us. 'Thou shalt think!' is the first commandment of a characteristically modern piety. For in seeking to come to terms with modernity, we must develop a new rationalism, one that must reverently and conscientiously refuse to cherish the unempirical or otherwise questionable assumptions still so innocently enjoyed by a traditional piety. Can we, then, find a way back to the House of Islam and take our place in it as authentic members and genuine adherents?

I

Perceptive western listeners to Arab radio services relaying the Koran in the month of Ramadan can sense the competing noise and impact of more powerful neighbouring stations as these intermittently drown out the reciter's voice. A somewhat fanciful observation; but it may well serve to symbolise Islam seeking an audience in the contemporary world of profane leisure, irreligious confidences, opposed values, and most characteristically, louder voices.

The voice of God in the daily life of Muslims is often only faintly and intermittently heard. But it is, at least within the range of transmission, still heard. It is rare that the noisy turbulence of the vicinity drowns out the entire recited sequence; the partial segment reaches the alert ear. But it has to be an attentive intelligence, given to what the Koran calls reflection (*tadabbur*).

Equally, one might say, it has to be a message worthy of our attention, couched in a relevant idiom, voiced in an appropriately attractive way. The Koran, like proper Christian preaching, has an exceptionally intelligent earnestness at its core. The art of beautiful recitation of the Koran is a mature and extensively cultivated one in Islam, especially Arab Islam, giving Koran reciters the same kind of kudos in Muslim society as opera singers have in western culture. The concern with achieving a dramatic impact upon contemporary audiences is utterly central to any attempt to repossess the legacy of Muhammad for the needs of the age of reason. Yet the message seems increasingly irrelevant. Even its intelligent earnestness these days is often mistaken, particularly by outsiders, as being at one remove from, if not identical with, unworthy passion: in a word, fanaticism.

Yet the need for the preacher and the reciter has rarely been greater. For religions are not saved or even best served by intellectual efforts alone. If the thinker has *a* word in this affair, the preacher has *the decisive* one. It is the preacher who is forever exhorting, warning, advising in the accents of scripture – thereby creating disciples who are, by God's grace, inwardly repentant and outwardly concerned to effect social righteousness.

The scripture of Islam aims to persuade and educate us and thereby motivate right conduct. In its striking Arabic eloquence, it registers powerfully even on the rejecting and uncomprehending mind. But the full force of its compassionate coercion, if we may so term it, is felt only by the thoughtful listener.

The Koran frequently calls upon its audiences to give heed to its sequences. And much is done to facilitate its reception in the wayward human constituency. Thus, for example, the Koran weaves backwards and forwards into the fabric of the present a concern with the past – a past that is dead as history yet alive as a source of guidance. The text is sprinkled with heart-searching meditations that serve to give the reader pause – and the text, too, as it were – in midstream for deliberation. The result is the concise argumentativeness of prosaic literature but the charmingly incongruous effect of poetry in the dramatic impact of the sentences. In fine, the author has found the right tone of 'voice' for preaching to the unconverted.

The voice from the radio conveys the word of God, received as proclamation and directive, delivered as sermon and imperative. It is piety and devotion in the highest sense, a reminder of mission and vocation. Through it breathe the allied ethical accents of demands unfulfilled, the intimations of nemesis, and the urgency of repentance, both individual and collective. The interval between birth and death – life itself – is to be properly punctuated by reflection on its elemental seriousness. Reminder is needed here constantly. Profane distraction must be subdued; the voice of mission must speak even when the listeners refuse to listen or when pressures, external or internal, conspire to silence, absorb or deflect it.

II

'Don't bother about being modern. Unfortunately it is the one thing that, whatever you do, you cannot avoid.' Can't you? This remark of the late Salvador Dali, in his rather pretentious autobiography *The Diary of a Genius*[2] is oddly thoughtful, even discerning, especially if we may borrow it for our purposes here as a comment on modern religious conviction. For even 'traditional' believers are far more secularised today than they themselves might imagine. Modernity, the circumstance of being 'modern', is, in a central sense, inescapable. It is the necessary context for every tolerably well-informed life-journey undertaken in the contemporary world.

Yet there is a choice. One need not be too eager to catch up on the facts; one can cultivate a kind of deliberate and bloody-minded will to obscurantism. Indeed even that is unnecessary once innate security of mind strikes alliance with laziness. The results, in the case of Islam, are well known. At least since the end of the nineteenth century, the entire House of Islam has been surviving on an intellectual overdraft.

A signal hindrance to the development of Islamic thought in the West in the coming years is what may be called 'the problem of temperament'. An ideology, especially one aiming at the common good, must avoid reactionary and polemical impulses as the chief sources of its motivation. Unless Muslim reflection is actuated by motives nobler than an undifferentiated dislike of the West and all things western, it has no chance of a hearing. (Remember that 'the West' is no longer some amorphous realm, some abstract foe, out there in some distant land: Muslims are *in* the West.) We are all in search of an audience these days; and it is not easy to get anyone to listen, let alone to listen for long. A modern preacher either captures or loses an urbanised audience within the first *three* minutes of his sermon.

To cultivate 'rejectionist' and isolationist attitudes is to invite accusations of apology. Moreover, such attitudes severely sap the energy of the faithful intellect. In any case, a shrill voice is an unworthy accompaniment of truth.

Many Muslims believe that contempt for our current situation of secularity and religious pluralism is an adequate substitute for an intellectual reckoning with it. Throughout this work, I have excoriated such a conceit. Here it is sufficient to pass summary judgement and pass on.

That Muslim believers have always placed a sturdy trust in the ultimate truth of the Islamic scripture is all well and good. But such security of conviction must itself reckon, if it is intellectually aware and morally honest, with the facts of post-Enlightenment culture. Modern faith should properly allow room for a pertinent variety of anxiety: an anxiety free from contempt for hostile challenge, an anxiety devoid of hatred of alien belief. For there are secular and religious groups whose members sometimes reject Islamic presuppositions for reasons that cannot be dismissed as shallow or trivial.

The reason for this 'new' style in Islamic religiosity is itself specifically Islamic in complexion. The didactic element in Islam is least properly presented in a shrill and unreflective tone precisely because it is then deracinated from the Islamic scripture's own deeply meditative context with all its constant calls for reverent reflection (*tadabbur*). The current Muslim tendency to discuss narrowly dogmatic issues in an unrelievedly authoritarian mood is the best way of imprisoning latently massive scriptural powers. A cramped and degradingly minor Muslim intellectual ambition today effectively gives the lie to the Islamic claim that the Koran is a 'miracle of reason and speech' vouchsafed to 'the best community ever brought forth among mankind'. There is work to be done; and, notwithstanding Dali, there is merit in being modern, for it is possible to continue to live in the past – a past that is both a fetter and a release.

III

Is contemporary man then indeed the measure of all things? Should he be? I have argued that the starting point of our modern attempt to achieve an eternal perspective – a modern theology – must be an attempt to take the full measure of man. We begin with men and women under an empty sky. Such an emphasis is categorically foreign to a traditional Islamic piety that both begins and ends with God. But there is, as I argued in Part 2, some koranic warrant for taking the human condition seriously, if only as an index to God and the transcendent. Within the Koran of course any attempt to give man his due necessarily involves giving God his due, so to speak.

This new style of religiosity may strike one as entailing an unduly large concession to modern thought. But there is no real cause for alarm in the Muslim theological camp. Wherever we may begin, we religious thinkers can safely be trusted (as Marxists well know) to arrive finally at God. Naturally, one supposes; for that is our job. And, more seriously, because a correct theology must contain in its premises (and hence in its conclusion) a true statement about *man* and hence about God. There is a really good conceptual mix here: if theological conclusions about deity are false, the implied theological statements about humanity must also have been untrue. If theological statements about the nature of God are true, a valid anthropology must already have been implicit in the premises.

To understand the nature of God is not equivalent to providing a sound anthropology. But any full understanding of the nature of God will involve some understanding of the created order placed under a divine sovereignty. The theist will argue that any full understanding of man would imply some fundamental if implicit reference to God. For the consciousness of the divine alone constitutes the authentically human.

The starting point is of great importance. But, as in the formation of some systems of mathematics, we should begin where we need to begin. Thus, for example, if we are engaged in the development of Muslim theology and expounding it for the needs of the traditional pious mind confident of faith's claims, there is no harm in beginning – and even ending – with God. For many deeply religious people, man is, at every level, tributary to the divine Creator. However, in other areas, the starting point may well have to be different. For example, in Christian–Muslim dialogue, it is preferable, though not necessary, to begin at the level of the human condition and then explore as to which of the two faiths gives the most 'satisfying' characterisation of the human and hence of God. God can enter the picture indirectly or, if you like, as an inference from the premises implied or stated. When it comes to the non-theistic faiths and atheistic humanism, God cannot be the starting point of responsible exchange with the rejector. There, man is necessarily, in the first instance at least, the measure of all faiths. We must begin with man; the theist hopes, naturally, that we need not end there. But that must be the hope of a valid epistemology, not the presumption of a dogmatic temper.

Wherever we may begin, we must end with God. Modern Protestant thought, of a reductionist and revisionist vintage, has sometimes lost God in the intricate procedures of theology. Fortunately the supernatural emphasis remains integral to Islam; the human and natural remain tributary and derivative.

A due recognition of the importance of man is likely to be misunderstood in many ways. For example, to say, with Christian thinkers like the Rev. Kenneth Cragg, 'Let God be God' is to endow man with an excessive significance and thereby misunderstand Islam or, for that matter, any theism.[3] For God is God – independent of our recognition or acceptance. Even if God's truth can, at worst, fail to be accepted in a sinful human constituency, it remains truth none the less. On every score, this is the Koran's message. 'Let man be man' is the true creed of Islam. For *man* is debased, denatured, disfigured, devalued by *kufr* (disbelief) and idolatry; *man* attains authentically human stature via Islam. It is man, not God, who must submit his will. God is not a Muslim; he does not need anything and certainly not anything from us in order to be truly divine. He is, in a manner of speaking, necessarily Himself.

To come to terms with modernity is one thing; changing a revealed Islam to suit human whim shaped by passing fashion is quite another. It is a rarely noted tribute to the authentic conviction of the religious intelligentsia of Islam that they suppressed the very conditions in which a neo-Islamic belief could take root. Islam is Islam and remains so. An Islam moulded under the concentrated pressures of secularity and inter-religious encounter must nevertheless be recognisably a faith bearing a family resemblance to traditional Islam. My attempt at a reverent scepticism in these pages is in the service of rediscovering the old Islam, not of inventing a new heresy. The only dogmatism which is charming and profound, in religions as in individuals, is the one at once aware both of itself as well as of alternative patterns of belief. To learn to face fully the sceptical gaze of modernity is not a licence for any wholesale disowning of authentically Muslim dogmas in the tradition. It is only because we today still wish to retain Islam as a complete vision that we need to identify, record and religiously contend with various new theological puzzles. Once we simply sacrifice the problematic parts of revealed scripture – as some Protestant Christians do – we either alter altogether the grounds of our puzzlement or else feel no need to be puzzled at all.

IV

A true Muslim is never a man of many dogmas. For, at the end of the chapter, there is only one dogma, concerning which he has no option: *Allah-u-akbar*. This confession of the greatness of God is central to the Muslim imagination. It punctuates the prayer and, when sincerely confessed, transforms the heart and mind. Indeed, even the most obscure and flickering recognition of its worth adds dignity to a life being lived in a complex industrial-commercial society that sets great store by worthless ephemera.

The confession of the overwhelming greatness of God is by no means distinctive to Islam. Every theism is grounded in such a recognition. But it is the manner in which such a conviction continues to leaven the whole of an authentic Muslim life which seems to set Islam apart today as a pre-eminently practical faith.

There is no necessary triumphalism about such a claim. For one can state the strength of Islamic conviction as a fact rather than as a boast. In any case, the Koran is concerned with both sides of the idolatrous coin: if the profane is to be repudiated as profane, the sacred is to be wor-shipped as sacred. If we should categorically refuse to worship forces unworthy of it, we must equally categorically embrace worship of forces worthy of it. 'There is no God but God' is a twofold declaration, vigilantly denying the efficacy of purely profane realities while categorically enjoining a trust in the power of the unique Deity. To utter, therefore, with meaning and conscious intent, the creed of Islam is to discover the full nature and bounds of one's duty as a created being.

Modern living is a tall order: a personal quest for fulfilment limited by all the tortured choices of an age of uncertainty, an attempt to recognise and fulfil obligations to oneself, the family, the nation and the global society of mankind. For the Muslim believer these attempts are themselves secondary to a larger attempt to please his Creator, who is to be actively recognised as being greater (*akbar*) than this purely human network of expectations, duties and hopes. A tall order indeed! In such a context, the Muslim sees his Islam as a unified enterprise of private faith and public practice, which cultivates the fullest appreciation of whatever is good and wholesome while actively inviting the most permanent quarrel with the forces of what the Koran calls *zulm* (wrongdoing), whether personal or communal. For what is the worth of a piety that retires from the real world of varied voices, whether innocent and caring, or, more frequently, irate and tired?

What, then, is it to be religious today? To be religious is to see oneself continuously as an exile in the midst of natural existence. This is not to say – it would be plainly untrue – that one is not of this world or in this world nor, most importantly, that one is under a religious obligation to entertain hopes of a false Utopia here or elsewhere. Nor is true religion a warrant for uprooting oneself from the soil of existence by refusing to give personal passions their due: faith has its own resources for easing the burden of private emotion, such as the natural desire for legitimate power and (licit) sexual gratification. It is certainly not for Islam to undermine the normal aspirations of human beings by demanding some deliberate and sustained detachment from the sensuous, the natural, the immediate and the temporal. No; the truly religious ideal involves an intense effort to pass through ordinary human experience and sanctify *every* episode, whether immediately or retrospectively, by celebrating the good while turning the realisation of wrongdoing into an occasion for repentance. In doing that, one is merely practising the conviction that 'God is greater'.

V

Such a religious view of the universe would merely indulge our speculative ingenuity – unless it had practical consequences. And these are legion. Choice here settles on three motifs that are dominant in any contemporary discussion of the Islamic religion as a relevant charter for human society. All three are authentically koranic, proclaiming as each does the greatness of God; all are increasingly significant as this century draws to a close: man as custodian of Nature and technology, man as a socio-sexual creature, and man as a tenant with a fixed lease on physical life in this world. We may, for convenience, call these the problems of technology, sexuality and mortality, respectively. The first two are explored briefly here, the third in section VI.

Some of the Koran's comments on the religious significance of Nature and an auxiliary technology are profound in a way we today more readily appreciate than did Muhammad's own contemporaries. Within the scripture of Islam there is, in the Rev. Kenneth Cragg's apt phrase, 'a theology of ecology'.[4] Unless technology is itself placed under a constraining sovereignty − unless *Allah-u-akbar* is also the scientists' slogan − all our scientific achievements may well radically come to grief. A merciful creator has placed the natural world in our trust. Do we know the duties of stewardship? Can we discharge these properly if we recognise no responsibility to forces greater than the human? The Koran's implied verdict is unequivocal. A science and technology freed of all reference and responsibility to the transcendent will cause irreversible damage even while, paradoxically, aiming to confer immeasurable benefit. For a generation that lives under the increasingly darkening shadow of global nuclear holocaust, such a verdict is neither extreme nor rooted in some outdated dogma.

Man too is part of a universal order of mercy and provision. The inaugural revelation already, if we may move on to our second theme, makes a reference to the basic mystery of procreation. 'Recite in the name of thy Lord who created man from a blood-clot (*'alaq)*' (K:96:1–2; interpreted). Throughout the Koran, there are many reverent allusions to human sexuality and its consequences as among the signs of God for a people given to sustained reflection (*tadabbur*). The male–female division and the benefits of mutual love and compassion flowing from it are divine portents.

Within the Muslim scripture, the sacred and the sexual are often discussed in association. It is as though sexuality is next to godliness in the Islamic lexicon! There is no doubt that the sexual act hides within it deeply religious significances, notwithstanding its essentially legal as opposed to sacramental status in Islam. At the very least, it is an invitation to reflection. For the koranic confidence seems to be that a destiny brought close to the texture of its own origin and dependence (its biological root and the promise of the human fruit) could hardly fail to register the power and caring wisdom of its creator. Humility is certainly not out of place in an area of deep mutual vulnerability. Given the large and varied liabilities and significances of the sexual office − the delicacy of an intimacy that conceals temptations to exploitation, the inevitability of far-reaching consequences of our choices here − the koranic stress is surely salutary.

This is particularly true today. For within the area of the sexual demand upon the human frame, the koranic warning against reducing 'the best form' (*akhsani-taqweem*, K:95:4; interpreted) to 'the lowest of the low' (*asfala-safileen*, K:95:5; interpreted) acquires impressively contemporary meanings. When we survey the opposed modern view of sexuality as an arena for the celebration of our emancipation – a form of recreation – we can well understand why the fear of God is an appropriate concomitant of the will to sexuality. The prostitution of sex, serving and served by profane interests, notably commercial pornography, is an almost inevitable consequence of the rupture of the traditional liaison between the sexual and the sacred. Given the peculiarly powerful proclivity of the sexual demand to degenerate into what is, stripped of the garment (*libas*)[5] of piety and compassion, merely base and humiliating, the fear of God, in recognition of his greatness, is the best possible background to the activities of the sexual instinct.

It is in this context that one should broach the vexed subject of Islam's legal charter for a truly erotic society. The traditional Muslim custom of segregating men and women in order to protect women against aggressive kinds of male desire, has led to charges of sexual apartheid. But one must not judge too hastily here. The aim of Islam's admittedly paternalistic provisions for women is to secure valid norms of modesty, male and female, so that sexual appetite can be indulged with wholesome enjoyment. Within recognised and appropriately liberal limits, men and women can develop a sexual potential, enjoying it without fear of private sin or public reproach. Beyond that there is a clear and legally enforced recognition of the dangers of injury to the dignity of involved parties. Given the power of sex as an instinctual energy, the need for control and harness is virtually axiomatic. Any kind of irresponsible adventurism here spells disaster. Certainly, the recent western experiment, with all its auxiliary techniques for sexual gratification, has produced an increasingly sordid sensuality retrospectively embittered by its own paradoxical loss of natural eroticism.

It is, ironically, the Islamic wish for an authentically erotic, a properly sensual, culture that has led to its endorsement of severely scrupulous, almost puritanical, attitudes towards the abuse of the sexual instinct. Traditional Islam's notorious 'extreme' (*hudood*) ordinances for sexual offences cannot be properly understood without a compelling sense of the scripture's own high estimate of the sexual office.

The veil is no doubt an apt symbol for the sexual culture the Koran sanctions and encourages men and women to cultivate. For it well captures the idea of a reverent invitation that, variously, in the hands of female adventurism or male-sponsored desires, may deteriorate into what is irreverently suggestive, even base. The invitation is also a liability, just as in the case of Nature whose religious significance may well be lost in the more superficial invitation to seek control and technological dominion. The veil could enslave, cramp or distort even valid sexual ambition; or it could successfully serve as an index to the truly erotic culture.

VI

In that largely unaccountable desire for immortality which is a unique feature of our species, religious believers may claim a distinctively rational ground. Theism offers, through its faith in the immortality of the soul, important hopes and distinctive ambitions. Though many conceptual difficulties beset this religious belief in survival beyond the grave, it is not clear that it is incoherent. At any rate, acceptance of this conviction has given an overriding purpose to countless human beings throughout history. Certainly, by standing robust witness to an after-life, Islam has produced an impressive record of zestful bravery and purposeful courage in the context of holy struggle against militant forms of evil.

The Koran is alert, on multiple levels, to the fact of transience. All things, including human generations, pass away. Only 'thy Lord, full of majesty' is exempt from the indifferent ravages of time. As for the rest of us, God has decreed time as an index to the fragility of all, especially the sinful, society.

In these meditative contexts, where the koranic mood is in dangerous proximity to the forbidden impulse of tragedy, there is a peculiarly moving beauty in the language which translation drastically reduces. It is a language, at any rate, that indelibly impressed those in the contemplative traditions of Islamic theism. For the Arabs, the Koran is the first document to impose a specifically religious significance on the facts of human impermanence and mortality. No adequate philosophy of man and his place in the titanic immensity called the universe could conceivably omit references to this centrally relevant truth of our condition. The pre-Islamic Arabs were naturally impressed by the transience of all things mortal; most entertained tragic notions. In the event Islam was destined to frustrate the will to tragedy while radically satisfying the residual desire for a conclusive triumph over the limitations of physical extinction.

That there was in Muhammad's Arabia a national longing for some successful transcendence of the natural and human order is amply evidenced in pagan poetry. The Koran offers in conscious opposition to such pagan poetry, a new approach to physical extinction. For Islam, like every responsible metaphysic of man, accepts and psychically reckons with the fact of death. It completely changed its significance for the Arabs. The Koran distances itself from the martial ethos of pre-Islamic Arabia with its strong traditions of *muru'ah* (virility) displayed in courage and recklessness. But, in a manner typical of its religious genius, it effectively transformed the protest against death by recruiting the old recklessness for a new cause, thereby dignifying the recklessness while ensuring the cause.

If Islamic history overflows with episodes of courageous sacrifice of life for the cause of faith, it is at least partly because a due recognition of the greatness of God, according to the Koran, necessitates such dramatic gestures. Though there are many, including unspectacular, ways of pleasing God, martyrdom is, according to all learned authorities, unquestionably the best. Tradition has confidently maintained that martyrs for the cause of Islam are the only exceptions to the rule of strict reckoning on the awful day of judgement. (Muhammad, incidentally, will be judged like anyone else since he died a natural death.)

The Koran takes martyrdom seriously. It denies that martyrs are dead; rather, believers are instructed to say, martyrs are living in the presence of God, satisfied and rejoicing in their new state. This is no reductionist sentimentalism that merely allows the dead to live in the memories of the living – with good and evil leaving some permanent heritage while its agents have long left the scene. The Koran has a strikingly robust doctrine about an after-life, with contrasted fates awaiting the good and the bad. Those who endorse the greatness of God may validly entertain high hopes of entering Paradise. As for the rest, for whom their own whims were greater (*akbar*) than God, the sacred volume has a clear message. Their destination is Hell, which is, Sartre notwithstanding, by no means just other people.

VII

'Every path,' declared the late Ayatollah Khomeini, 'can lead to Hell.' Some paths much quicker than others, one might immediately add. (The comment is as true, if not more so, than the maxim that inspires it.) Khomeini himself goes on to list science, mysticism, theology, ethics and, surprisingly, even monotheism as all capable of leading to perdition. It is an apt observation for our purposes here, intimating as it does the dangers of abusing powerful and profound faiths. The potential threat of 'political religion', for want of a better phrase, is all too obvious, especially when it strikes alliance with human arrogance and lust for domination.

There can be no easy complacency these days, arguing as we do for the necessity of religion to generations that barely care. There are many today who have no wish to be 'saved', to be 'successful' in the eyes of God. Islam offers spiritual success to those who prefer failure. It is no small paradox; but there we have it. It is a religious puzzle we must accept on faith and move on. But it is always right and unequivocally just to seek, no matter how painful, a full and permanent controversy with those who reject Islam without adequate basis, who disbelieve in its inspiration while cynically exploiting it for purely political or personal ends.

Such an engagement with the rejectors, however, does not allow us to impose upon them any militancy of our own persuasion. That way lies Hell and alienation. For the interests of Islam are not properly served by encouraging the hypocritical element, already extremely large among the educated and secularised classes in the House of Islam. In such a rendezvous, painful as it is to the committed Muslim, God has the last word. For them their works, and to us ours.

VIII

'What should it profit a house in the night that a lamp is set forth on its roof – when all is dark within?' Sheikh Abu Hamid al-Ghazzali's rhetorical question, attributed to Jesus of Nazareth,[6] brings us to the last turn on the road to Mecca. I have already remarked in the Preface that Muslims have clearly failed to interpret and appropriate Islam properly for the needs of the modern age. There are many reasons for this failure; the chief ones are the shallowness of intellectual responses to the challenges of modernity and an increasing shallowness in the life of faith.

Al-Ghazzali's question well catches the problem. A little religion is a very dangerous thing. Within the House of Islam, there is today a great need for self-criticism and introspection, both severely jeopardised by the emphasis on a purely external, somewhat legalistic, religious observance. Muslims are religiously obliged to turn inward, to take the full measure of their own failings, and try to effect social and personal criticism in the larger attempt to seek the mercy of God. Islam may well be the best religion with the worst followers.

The pen may be mightier than the sword; but prayer is certainly so. Muslims need to develop, deepen the life of faith. A deeper spirituality, with prayer at its core, will constitute an important part of the characteristically *religious* reckoning with secularity. Religions are not saved by mental efforts alone. We must live as faithful people; we must strengthen our style of dealing with modernity by living within the parameters of faith, by actively striving for a genuine religiosity that seeks and finds resources for honest, including intellectually honest, living in a difficult age. There are many theological puzzles on our hands; the silence of God is increasingly oppressive, heavier each day on the heart of every reflective believer. And yet here too prayer has its place: 'Our Lord, burden us not with what we have not the strength to bear' (K:2:286).

Faith needs to move mountains: the mountains of doubt, hesitation, unclarity, weakness of will. The opening chapter of the Koran well captures the flavour of this religious imperative, one that underlines one entirely indispensable mood of the authentically religious temper. 'Thee alone we worship, Thee alone we ask for help', says the *surah*. Could there be a better way of imposing an embargo on every false ideal, an operative veto on any attempt to seek support from purely human sources? This indeed is the voice of the truly iconoclastic conscience. But to attain here the right kind of trust in God – an effortless trust – requires effort, sustained labour. 'Guide us in the straight path', the *surah* continues. The mood for submission (*islam*) is well captured in the imperative *ihdena* (Guide us!) – gracefully requesting the grace of God, yet enjoining human effort in the making of the plea.

There may be certainties and consolations when we get to the heavenly city – but there are few left on the road to it. It will be a difficult journey; and we have miles to go before we sleep. But I hope Muslims can improve on these admittedly rudimentary beginnings.

It is a revealing feature of the Muslim mind that, though the Muslim calendar has put an end to it, the fourteenth century still lingers on. There is a curious kind of finality about this century in the voice of the simple believer as well as in that of the sophisticated religionist. There is a very keen sense of an impending crisis in this world, heightened by prophetic warnings of imminence of judgement.

The Muslim fourteenth century has, however, ended; and the fifteenth has already reached a tenth of its span. Islam is now fully in a modern world of competing ideologies and penetrating scepticisms, mostly of Anglo-American provenance, that look with justified suspicion on any exclusivist dogmatic claim. Trust in God is no longer enough; we must tie the camel first. Muslim destinies today need to be shaped partly by conscious choice and struggle. We must earn the right to a future.

Notes

Chapter 1: The Fateful Vision

1 These words form the first five verses of the ninety-sixth chapter (*surah*) of the Arabic Koran in its present arrangement. References to the Muslim scripture are henceforth given in parentheses in the body of the text with the number of the *surah* followed by the number of the verse, thus (K:96:1–5). It is customary, incidentally, for Muslim writers to place the pious expression 'Peace be upon him' after every mention of the name Muhammad, especially in devotional contexts. I hope it does not seem unduly irreverent to omit this expression in a primarily philosophical work.

2 A.H. or *Anno Hegirae* from the word '*hijrah*' meaning 'to sever kinship ties'. All dates in this book refer to the Christian Era unless otherwise stated.

3 According to most religious authorities in Islam, Adam – the first man – was himself a minor prophet.

4 The Arabic word *ummi* is variously interpreted by translators as 'the common people' (Arberry), 'the unlettered ones' (Pickthall), and so on. I have used several different translations of the Koran; where translators differ significantly I have chosen one meaning in the text of the chapter while alerting the reader in a note to other possible meanings.

5 Although the Muslim creed consists only of the double testimony of faith in Allah and acceptance of Muhammad's prophethood, the claim that the office of prophethood is permanently abolished after the advent of the Arabian Prophet is held, by all orthodox authorities, to be a defining feature of Islam. This explains, incidentally, the extreme hostility shown by Muslims towards the group known variously as the Ahmadis or Qadianis, founded in nineteenth-century India by Mirza Ghulam Ahmad, who claimed to be a 'satellite' prophet deriving his status from Muhammad. Even though the Qadianis denied that their founder brought a new religious law which superseded the koranic dispensation, they were, recently, condemned as apostates.

6 The word 'Allah', written without emphasis throughout this work, is a contraction of *al* (the) and '*ilah* (god), hence, 'the [only] god'. I use the words 'Allah' and 'God' interchangeably here. Both are meant to denote indifferently the unique being who created the world *ex nihilo* (or rather, more accurately, after a period of time during which nothing existed) and whose nature and actions are in dispute among Jews, Christians and Muslims. Christian Arabs, incidentally, use the word 'Allah' to refer to God.

7 The Arabic word here (*yaum*) can denote various periods of time, even years and centuries. It should be read as one reads English expressions such as 'the Day of Judgement' – which need not suggest any specific duration. See K:32:5

where one such day (*yaum*) is said to be equivalent to 'a thousand years of your reckoning'. See also K:7:54; 10:3, etc.; cf. K:41:9 where the world is said to have been created in two 'days'.

8 The Koran rejects the biblical view that Satan (*Shaitan*) is a fallen angel. Iblis, to use the proper name of the supreme evil being, is said to be a member of a class of elemental agencies – the *jinn* – who, unlike men, are made of fire but who, like men, have the free will to accept or reject God. See K:15:26ff and K:38:71ff. Angels, according to the Koran, do not have the free will to obey or disobey God: they invariably do as they are told, and are, in consequence, not in a position to 'fall'.

9 Some orientalists have rightly argued that later Islam has exaggerated the depravity of the pagan Arabs before the coming of the new faith. Some Arab nationalists have recently even hinted that the pre-Islamic Arabs were indeed an inherently 'great' people (whatever that may mean) already suited to the task of receiving Allah's final message. Whatever the independent merits of such a view, it is religiously suspect. Leaving aside the fact that God may choose a people as much for their rectitude as for their depravity, the religious point of course is that God does not choose a nation because it is already great: the fact that God chooses a nation itself makes it great. Whatever the exact truth of the matter, it is safe to assume that God would not choose any nation whose members thought, like the Arab and Israeli nationalists, that their nation was actually great.

10 The Muslim scripture is properly known as *al-Koran* (or phonetically more accurately, *al-Qur'ān*) which literally means 'the lecture' or 'the recital'. I have deliberately dropped the definite article.

11 It is unwise here to make too many generalisations, not to mention predictions. There are sizeable groups of extremely strict Jews in Israel; and many young Jews in the Middle East are increasingly attracted to their orthodox Hebrew roots. As for western Christianity, Keith Ward has recently argued that Christianity is neither dead nor dying in modern Britain. See his *The Turn of the Tide: Christian Belief in Britain Today* (London: BBC Publications, 1986); see also *In Search of Christianity* (London: Firethorn Press, 1986), edited with an introduction by Tony Moss, for a similarly optimistic assessment of Christianity's future in England. In America and Canada, Christian evangelism is alive and well, especially in 'the Bible Belt'. Even in western intellectual circles, there are many highly distinguished scientists and philosophers who are also orthodox Christian (or Jewish) believers. Perhaps it is too sanguine for the humanist critics of theism to think that theism is on its deathbed – even in intellectual culture. Certainly, Kai Nielsen's 'mopping up operation' after the big scrub by the Enlightenment may be a little premature. See his *Philosophy and Atheism* (New York: Prometheus Books, 1985) and his *God, Scepticism and Modernity*.

12 *Jesus and the Muslim: An Exploration* (London: Allen and Unwin, 1985), p.296.

13 *The Sea of Faith: Christianity in Change* (London: BBC, 1984, paperback 1985), p.7. This is an eloquent account of the problems of modernity and of their roots in the nineteenth-century intellectual culture of Europe. For another (and similar) assessment of the relevance of modernity to Islam, see Hans Küng, *On Being A Christian* (London: Collins, 1977), pp.106–7. The English translation is by Edward Quinn.

14 The most impartial accounts of Islam are, it seems to me, not those proffered by Jews and Christians, nor, for that matter, by ordinary Muslims, but rather by those non-Muslim theists who convert to Islam. See, for example, Suzanne

Haneef's excellent *What Everyone Should Know About Islam and Muslims* (Chicago: Kazi Publications, 1979).

15 For a thoroughly biased, indeed more or less wholly false, interpretation of Islam, see the works of D.S. Margoliouth, sometime Laudian Professor of Arabic at Oxford. The Anglican clergyman and Arabist Montgomery Watt admits, unduly weakly, what is actually entirely indisputable, that western religious thought has, in the past, completely failed to make a fair estimate of Islam. See his 'Islam and the West', in *Islam in the Modern World* (London: Croom Helm, 1983), edited by Denis MacEoin and Ahmed al-Shahi, pp.1–8.

16 In view of this, orientalist literature by non-Muslim hands can *only* be recommended in default of serious rivals from the Islamic camp. These western writings are often avoidably biased, almost all of them betraying a deep-rooted malice towards Islam and its Prophet. For further discussion, see chapter 9.

17 It could be said in mitigation of this last criticism that the Christians of the Middle Ages knew little about the world of their Muslim enemies. But surely if the West could acquire the secular learning of the Arabs (and, through the Arabs, of the Greeks), it is difficult to see why the Christians should have remained ignorant of the *religious* beliefs of their opponents. Given what we know of the character of medieval Christendom, it is, I believe, not too conspiratorial to suspect a cynical explanation for the West's ignorance of Islam.

18 Christianity alone among the universal faiths continues to generate reforming self-accusation, a trait particularly pronounced in a rather neglected book entitled *Objections to Christian Belief*, edited with an introduction by A.R. Vidler (London: Constable, 1963), in which four Christian thinkers from Cambridge engage in a rigorous examination of their own faithful convictions. It is, however, disturbing to note that Christians are, in general, remarkably reluctant to accept even valid criticisms if these happen to come from *Muslim* quarters.

19 Two such Christian writers deserve special praise: Terence Penelhum and Peter Berger. Penelhum, it seems to me, sees more clearly the problems of secular modernity than any other modern religious thinker whether Christian, Jewish or Muslim. See especially his *God and Scepticism: A Study in Scepticism and Fideism* (Boston: Reidel, 1983). For some criticisms of Penelhum's philosophy of religion, see my *The Light in the Enlightenment* (London: Grey Seal Books, 1990), chapter V. Berger's views can be found in his insightful *The Heretical Imperative: Contemporary Possibilities of Religious Affirmation* (London: Collins, 1980). For some powerful criticisms of Berger's thought, see Lesslie Newbigin's *Foolishness to the Greeks: The Gospel and Western Culture* (London: SPCK, 1986).

20 Part of the reason for this is of course that Christian clergymen often receive mainstream university education in addition to their purely religious training for the ministry.

21 Leszek Kolakowski, *Religion* (London, Glasgow: Fontana Paperbacks, 1982), p.135. The book is concerned mainly with natural theology although the title, like the sub-title, suggests all-encompassing concerns.

22 This Christian sub-culture is, however, characterised by wealth, influence and privilege, particularly in the United Kingdom. Its members have, notwithstanding their avowal to be indifferent to the desire for worldly power, actually shown remarkable political acumen in defence of their traditional position.

23 A word here about modern Jewish theology would surely not be out of place. Since Judaism is not a proselytising faith, its religious thinkers have not had the usual reasons for developing a sophisticated argumentative apologetics. To be sure, there have been specifically Jewish reactions to the modern world. But

many of these have been inspired, understandably enough, by a desire to come to terms with the massive twentieth-century destruction of European Jewry and the theological puzzles both about the moral nature of God and the alleged infidelity of Israel – as the original People of Covenant – that such a circumstance invites Jews to ponder. For a discussion of the problem of overwhelming evil, see Rabbi Dr Norman Solomon's stirring piece, 'Jewish Responses to the Holocaust', delivered as an address to the Polish Bishops' Conference in April 1988 and available from the Centre for the Study of Judaism, Birmingham, England. The development of a post-Holocaust theology, however, is, while a clearly legitimate concern, obviously a much narrower one than the problem of a full-scale confrontation with secular modernity. The latter supplies a task for all theists.

24 There are many twentieth-century commentaries on the Koran, often massive works of scholarly industry. See, for example, the commentaries by the late Abul Ala Maududi; Abdullah Yusuf Ali's commentary enjoys great popularity especially with those who have mystical (Sufi) leanings; commentaries by Marmaduke Pickthall and Muhammad Asad, both converts to Islam, rightly enjoy much prestige among Muslims. All these commentators, except Abdullah Yusuf Ali, betray the deep influence of past exegetical masters and traditionalists of the early centuries of Islam.

25 Islam has never had any shortage of theologians. I list only a few influential recent books and collections here – *Islam and Contemporary Society* is a collection edited by Salem Azzam and issued under the auspices of the Islamic Council of Europe (founded in 1973). It contains articles by eminent hands, including Seyyid Hossein Nasr and the late Ismail al-Faruqi. Unfortunately, modernity is not felt to be a genuine problem; like all ideological literature, it manages to preach, with clarity, but only to the converted. Another recent collection whose contributors betray a similar indifference to secularity is edited by Khurshid Ahmad and entitled *Islam: Its Meaning and Message*. This volume contains works by famous hands, including the distinguished exegetes Muhammad Asad and Abul Ala Maududi. The reader should also consult some of the recent works of Muhammad Hamidullah, especially his *Introduction to Islam*. The writings of Hossein Nasr enjoy great prestige but are unfortunately very obscure – indeed obscure beyond any rational excuse. Nasr, a former Gifford Lecturer, may reasonably be compared, given the lack of clarity of his claims, to Paul Tillich. Like Frithjof Schuon, Nasr has Sufi leanings which sometimes encourage both a departure from the norms of logic and a liberty to use exalted phrases of unclear meaning. Schuon, who is a convert to Islam, is the author of the widely known *Understanding Islam*. It is worth adding here that the periodicals issued by centres of Islamic learning (such as the Islamic Foundation, the Cambridge Academy of Islam, the Muslim Institute and so on in the United Kingdom) provide, with few exceptions, the usual and predictably stale orthodox diet. Unsurprisingly, Christian critics find in these publications impressive evidence of the current *trahison des clercs* by Muslim intellectuals and, accordingly, refuse to take their work seriously. (Where the works mentioned here are discussed in any detail, full publication details are, naturally, given.)

26 There is of course no extant philosophical tradition in Islam. The only twentieth-century figure who can be classed as a truly Islamic philosopher is Dr Muhammad Iqbal, the Indian religious theoretician often cited as one of the architects of modern Pakistan. Iqbal was educated at various places including Cambridge and Munich; he wrote mainly in Urdu and Persian. His views continue to act as an incubus on any new theoretical departures in Muslim thought in Pakistan.

There is a vast industry devoted to the publishing of Iqbal's works to supply the needs of Pakistani higher education. (Think here of the publishing industry producing St Thomas Aquinas's works in some Thomist circles.) For a general picture of Iqbal's life and work, see Syed Abdul Vahid's *Studies in Iqbal* (Lahore: Shaikh Muhammad Ashraf, 1967) and Masud-ul-Hasan's huge *Life of Iqbal* (Lahore: Ferozsons, 1978), in two volumes. My own view is that we today both need to recognise Iqbal's versatile genius and yet also go beyond him in the larger attempt to meet the challenges of modernity. For further discussion of the philosophical tradition of Islam, see chapter 2.

27 I have in mind the work of the late Fazlur Rahman of the Chicago Divinity School. He left Pakistan in part because of hostility from the more orthodox religionists. See his *Islam and Modernity: Transformation of an Intellectual Tradition* (Chicago: University of Chicago Press, 1982, 1984). Although the title is very promising, the book is in effect a sociological survey of Islam's confrontation with modernity in various Muslim lands: there is, in my view, no serious theoretical engagement with the problems that secularity and ideological pluralism bring in their train.

28 Many of the writings in this category are brilliant but imbalanced. See, for example, some of the writings of Kalim Siddiqui of the Muslim Institute in London. During the 1980s, Siddiqui and his colleagues produced a great deal of literature in praise of the Iranian Revolution. In itself, this is perfectly legitimate but indignation at the West should not blind us to the true nature of secularity as a universal challenge to theism. See the regular output from the Open Press, the publishing organ of the Institute. See also some of the writings of Maryam Jameelah, an extraordinarily courageous Jewish lady who converted to Islam, married a Muslim and settled in Pakistan. Though the context of her work is only partly related to the current political resurgence of Islam, her writings are a good example of powerful but imbalanced condemnations of the West. Both *Islam and Modernism* (Lahore: Mohammed Yusuf Khan, 1968) and *Islam versus the West* (Lahore: Mohammed Yusuf Khan, 1968) are from her pen.

29 Riffat Hassan, a Muslim scholar working at the University of Louisville in Kentucky, has even taken to heart the problem of religious pluralism. See her 'Messianism and Islam', in *Journal of Ecumenical Studies*, vol.22, no.2, Spring 1985, pp.261–91; see also her 'The Basis for a Hindu–Muslim Dialogue and Steps in that Direction from a Muslim Perspective', in *Religious Liberty and Human Rights in Nations and in Religions* (New York: Hippocrene Books, 1986), edited by Leonard Swidler. Hassan encourages Jews, Christians and Muslims to engage in religious 'trialogue'. It is also worth noting here that some of the Muslim contributors to *Islam and the Contemporary Muslim World* (New Delhi: Light and Life Publishers, 1981), edited by Anwar Moazzam, show an atypical concern to come to terms with modernity.

30 Compare *umma muslima* i.e. the Muslim community. There are two importantly different senses of the word 'Muslim' in Islamic vocabulary. In the narrower sense, those who give allegiance to the Arabian Prophet are Muslims; in the broader sense, anyone who submits to the divine will is a Muslim. ('Islam' means 'submission to the will of God'.) Thus, the Koran often refers to the Jews and Christians as submitters i.e., as Muslims in the broader sense. Correspondingly, *islam* is the act of submission while Islam is the name of the historical religion inaugurated by Muhammad, which interprets *islam* as its central imperative.

31 The Koran (33:40) contains the influential comment that Muhammad is 'the

Seal of the Prophets' – a claim which is interpreted by all orthodox authorities as in effect a declaration of the end of the age of revelation. This doctrine is held to be a defining feature of Islam: those who deny it are condemned as apostates and not merely as heretics. Hence the recent expulsion of the Ahmadis from the House of Islam. The Ahmadis argue in their defence that if the age of revelation has indeed come to an end, there is no warrant for the orthodox Muslim claims about the coming of the Expected One (*al-Mahdi*) and of Jesus in the latter days for the final battle with the anti-Christ. Conflicting theological opinions on such details abound among the Muslim sects.

32 This is Berger's point in *The Heretical Imperative*, op.cit. The Greek word for heresy (*hairesis*) means, as Berger points out, choice; in that sense, urges Berger, we are all heretics today for we are, whether we admit it or not, choosers. Even traditional faith is one heresy among others. But, as Newbigin argues in his *Foolishness to the Greeks* (which is a useful corrective to Berger's claims), while we may all be heretics today, our heresies are committed only with respect to values and religious doctrines, not with respect to what are taken as scientific facts and accepted norms. It is not all a matter of choice. See Newbigin, op.cit., p.16. (See also note 19 above.)

33 Think here of Muhammad's dealings with the disaffected hypocrites and rejectors. The Koran strongly counsels Muhammad simply to part ways with his detractors. Thus K:109:6 well expresses the correct sentiment: 'For you your religion, and for me my religion.' 'Option, not compulsion' is the right slogan here.

34 I have explored the theme of religious freedom in my *Be Careful with Muhammad! The Salman Rushdie Affair* (London: Bellew Publishing, 1989).

35 This legislation does not seem to find any support in the Koran itself which restricts the death penalty to those apostates who engage in active hostility towards the Islamic state. However, there is some equivocal support for this Draconian ruling in the traditional sayings attributed to Muhammad – the literary materials known as the *hadith*. In 1968, at a meeting of the Islamic Research Academy, Sheikh Abu Zahra demanded the death penalty for apostasy. If this ruling were to be enacted, the Ahmadis would be executed although second-generation Ahmadis – born to Ahmadi parents – would escape punishment on account of having been born outside the House of Islam.

36 This is St Paul's idiom in 2 Thess. 3:6. Certainly Muslims do not turn a blind eye. For the average Muslim, meeting an Ahmadi is far more dramatic than meeting any ordinary heretic or even non-Muslim. Recently, even in a secularised and religiously free United Kingdom, there were some violent clashes between Islamic orthodoxy and the Ahmadis.

Chapter 2: A Change of Masters

1 *Handbook of Early Muhammadan Tradition*, XXXVI, 1. References to the traditions (*hadith*) of Muhammad will be given according to the system used by Wensinck in the *Handbook*. For a discussion of this system of recording traditions, see Martin Lings's *Muhammad: His Life Based on the Earliest Sources* (London: Unwin Paperbacks, 1986), p.330.

2 Al-Ghazzali was severely criticised as a 'free-thinker' in his own day. Some time after his death, as is often the lot of great men, he was hailed as a defender of the faith.

3 There have always been some minor movements attempting, especially in recent

centuries, to revive the rational philosophical tradition of Islam. But none has had the character of the ancient Muslim rationalist (*muta-kallim*) tradition. The aim has generally been to 'update' Islamic legal regulations for the needs of a given age. Even so, there are potentially philosophical insights in the writings of several nineteenth-century writers, such as Shah Wali Ullah and Sir Syed Ahmad Khan, both of India, and Muhammad Abduh of Egypt. Dr Muhammad Iqbal tried to revive a philosophical tradition in our century but his philosophical writing is not taken seriously either by western writers or by his co-religionists. See his *The Reconstruction of Religious Thought in Islam* (Oxford: Oxford University Press, 1934). Iqbal is regarded as a religious reformer for the twentieth century – a view restricted largely to Muslims from the Indian sub-continent.

4 Many *surahs* of the Koran are named without warrant of dominant theme or content. The naming, sometimes multiple, settles on any incident or feature which amazed the original audience in Muhammad's Arabia.

5 The view that (academic) philosophy is a temptation may be familiar to Christian readers too. In his *Paradise Regained*, Milton has Greek philosophy as one of the temptations offered by Satan to Christ during his sojourn in the desert. The suggestion fails to find a warrant in the New Testament. cf. Luke 4:1–13 and Matt. 4:1–11.

6 For an account of my reservations about extending the charge of idolatry (*shirk*) to modern rejectors, see chapter 5.

7 Sir Karl Popper, *Unended Quest: An Intellectual Autobiography* (Glasgow, London: Fontana-Collins, 1976), p.18.

8 I am unhappy with the term 'intermittent' here because of its connotations of an 'on-and-off' kind of commitment, like a switch that floods a room with light or darkness. But it is the best word I could find.

9 See Penelhum's insightful *God and Scepticism* (Boston: Reidel, 1983), pp.169–82 and his *Problems of Religious Knowledge* (New York: Herder and Herder, 1971), pp.112–48.

10 This is famously true of the prophet Jacob according to the koranic narrative (K:12:4ff). Jacob *knows*, according to *surah* 12, that his son Joseph is not actually dead and that God will cause Joseph to return to his father and family. The biblical narrative in Genesis would suggest that Jacob is convinced that his favourite son has indeed been murdered or killed. Both narratives concur that a pious man's faith is on trial while differing on the question of Jacob's knowledge of his true circumstance.

11 The goal of the Islamic life is, strictly speaking, not salvation but rather triumph: men are not so much 'saved' as attain entry into Paradise and win, partly through effort, God's favour.

12 There is, of course, to cite a parallel, an obvious measure of exclusivism in the Islamic law that prohibits non-Muslims from entering Mecca, on account of the city's peculiar sanctity in Muslim eyes.

13 This claim about the impossibility of a genuinely theoretical interest in a significant or momentous theme is found also in secular thought. Many radical social theorists deny the possibility of any value-free or purely objective interest in socio-political reality: any intellectual position at all, it is thought, conceals some ideological posture or other.

14 *The Light in the Enlightenment* (London: Grey Seal Books, 1990), chapters II and VI.

15 Many of the humanist critics of religion are totally unsympathetic to the religious vision. See especially the writings of Antony Flew and Kai Nielsen. Nielsen seems to me to be losing all sympathy with the religious outlook. See

his *Philosophy and Atheism* (Buffalo: Prometheus Books, 1985), pp.33–40, for a revealing autobiographical sketch.

16 The Koran rejects the doctrines of the Fall and original sin, seeing Adam's disobedience in Heaven as a single self-contained act of transgression. If anything, the Koran suggests that the saga of human history begins with the 'Rise' rather than the Fall of man.

17 This discussion raises fascinating issues beyond the compass of this book. Is the content of faith intrinsically rational but merely appears contra-rational to those uninfluenced by grace? Is the content of faith contra-rational – only this feature is welcome to the believer influenced by grace, unwelcome to the rejector? At any rate, faith (*iman*), according to Muslims, remains, notwithstanding its rationality, a gift of supernatural grace.

18 I have elsewhere argued that these assumptions are indeed plausible. See my *The Light in the Enlightenment*, chapter II. I fear, however, thát my arguments there may well seem, to the religionists, to be based on question-begging assumptions.

19 One of the great benefits of academic philosophy pursued long and well by able opponents is that ultimate conflicts can be identified and question-begging assumptions exposed.

Chapter 3: 'Poetry from Heaven'

1 This is why Muslims reject the appellation 'Muhammadanism'. It is unfortunate that some Christian and non-Muslim critics resolutely refuse to see the excellent reasons for this rejection. In an attempt to justify the label 'Muhammadanism', an Arabist as distinguished as the late Professor Sir Hamilton Gibb allows himself to remark: '[I]n a less self-conscious age Muslims were proud to call their community *al-umma al-Muhammadiyya*.' See his *Mohammedanism: An Historical Survey* (London: Oxford University Press, 1969), p.2. Now, surely Muslims are still proud of that title; they merely resent the unwelcome implication that there is, between Islam and Muhammad, a generic relationship akin to that between Christianity and Christ. It is true that many Muslims, especially Sufi mystics, have in their devotions praised Muhammad in a way that suggests that he is much more than a human guide commissioned to deliver a message. But such praise has never, with impunity, spilled over into worship. Certainly, while Muslims view Islam as the primordial faith inaugurated by Allah himself at the very beginning of human history, such a view cannot reasonably be entertained by the non-Muslim. For those who reject the divine inspiration of the Koran, Islam begins in Arabia in the seventh century: it is simply the faithful conviction that informed the ministry of a certain Muhammad ibn Abdullah. Even so, however, one cannot ignore the fact that those who embrace Islam have clearly and emphatically, from the earliest times, repudiated the opinion that they worship the founder of their faith, that their faith is actually centred in the personality of Muhammad. It is indeed difficult to resist the suspicion that Gibb and his like-minded companions prefer, in this matter, falsehood to truth.

2 The Prophet himself and, in consequence, the subsequent Muslim tradition, have sternly distinguished the Koran from the recorded actions and sayings of the messenger. The prophetic traditions (*hadith*) complement the Koran, serve, like the Talmud *vis-à-vis* the Torah, as a kind of commentary on the revealed text. They are written in a diction recognisably less impressive than the Koran,

sometimes reflecting the Prophet's Qureishi dialect. Although no canon of these traditions has won universal acceptance among Islamic scholars (the materials are based, like the New Testament, on an unreliable oral tradition) they are seen by many as authoritative. But no one regards them as constituting the literal word of Allah. Some scholars within Islam regard them as spurious; debate about their status continues. The *hadith* were collected using criteria that are sometimes stricter, sometimes looser than those employed by western students of historiography and critical scriptural scholarship. For an excellent and fair account, see Solomon Nigosian's *Islam: The Way of Submission* (Crucible Press, 1987), pp.122ff.

3 Questions about the nature of the Koran – is it eternal? is it uncreated? – have justly been compared to questions about the nature of the Christ. These worries considerably exercised the ingenuity of classical Islam. For a summary of traditional Muslim views about this, see A.S. Tritton's insightful 'The Speech of God', in *Studia Islamica*, vol.33, 1971, pp.5–22.

4 Many commentators endorse the implication, somewhat unnecessarily extravagant in my view, that classical Arabic is the language of Heaven.

5 For a brief characterisation of this significant if rather obvious distinction, see my *The Light in the Enlightenment* (London: Grey Seal Books, 1990).

6 A fierce debate about the Prophet's own role in the writing of the Koran has always been one of the many bones of contention between Muslims and their detractors. It is fair to speculate, I trust, that Muhammad was no more an established creative artist than the producers of the Synoptic Gospels were professional writers. Muslim biographers have certainly exaggerated the extent of the Prophet's literary impoverishment, no doubt in the interests of emphasising the miraculous nature of the Koran. It is quite possible that Muhammad could write and read as much as an ordinary merchant of his time; this, however, would give no reasonable grounds for expecting him to produce a work of incomparable literary genius after his fortieth year.

7 Professor Gibb openly begs this question in his inaptly named *Mohammedanism: An Historical Survey*. (See note 1.)

8 Many modern Christians see their scripture as divinely inspired in some sense but not as the infallibly dictated literal word of God.

9 Friedrich Nietzsche's view of inspiration, to list a rather discrepant ally, is strikingly similar to the Muslim view of Muhammad's prophetic experience. The idea seems to be that both concepts and the appropriate language are imposed from outside on the person during the period of inspiration, he himself being merely an involuntary mouthpiece or, if you like, a robot. During the period of trance, all human contribution is in abeyance. See Nietzsche's profound *Ecce Homo* (Harmondsworth: Penguin Books, 1979), translated by R.J. Hollingdale, pp.102–3. For a detailed discussion of the Islamic conception of revelation (*wahy*) see my *The Way of the Crescent* (London: Grey Seal Books), forthcoming.

10 The translation is by A.J. Arberry. What is meant could be either that the speech is foreign or simply not of sufficient literary quality.

11 The greatest Arab poet among the Qureish at the time of Muhammad is generally thought to be a certain Labid bin Rabi'ah who apparently abjured poetry altogether in his later years in recognition of the literary superiority of the Koran.

12 The two towns are Mecca and Ta'if. And there was no shortage of candidates for self-confessed greatness, although the occasion of the revelation of the verse is probably specific. Muhammad ibn Ishaq in his celebrated *Sirat Rasul Allah*

(*Life of the Messenger of God*) claims that the verse refers to one al-Walid ibn al-Mughirah who listed himself along with Amr bin Umayyah ath-Thaqafi as being men greater than Muhammad and hence better claimants to Allah's favours. See p.238 of the Wustenfeld edition of the *Sirat*.

13 Arthur J. Arberry comes closest to the truth of the matter in saying that 'the Koran is neither prose nor poetry, but a unique fusion of both'. See his *The Koran Interpreted* (Oxford: Oxford University Press, 1964), p.x.

14 Arabists concede that in the original Arabic, the sacred scripture of Islam has a unique literary structure – a kind of rhymed prose – which defies fully satisfactory translation. The English 'translation' of the Koran which is generally thought to have the greatest literary distinction is that by the late A.J. Arberry, Professor of Arabic at Cambridge. Arberry concedes, in his title, that the Koran is untranslatable: see his *The Koran Interpreted*, p.xii.

15 It is noteworthy that while the Gospels are rightly seen as literary masterpieces, no Christian has seriously argued that their linguistic excellence entails divine origin. Jews see the Torah and the Psalms as being sacred writings but not on account of their literary qualities. The claim, then, that literary excellence can imply divine provenance is peculiar to Islam.

16 Apart from the existence of strange Arabic words and idioms, the cryptic initials (*muqataat*) at the beginnings of many *surahs*, such as *surah* 2, 3, 7, etc., have long baffled Muslim and non-Muslim students alike. The hostile explanations for these initials, such as the offensive orientalist conjecture that Muhammad probably stuttered these letters before the text began to flow smoothly, can all safely be dismissed as the unworthy residue of Christian fanaticism. Muslims themselves have surmised that the letters are uninterpretable but probably have something to do with the miraculous nature of the book.

17 Recall here Thomas Carlyle's famous verdict, in his discussion of the heroic in history, that the Koran appears, on first reading, at least to a European, as haphazard and confused. But Carlyle's considered judgement is that the sacred volume is so strikingly sincere in the quality of its conviction that any juxtaposed peculiarity in literary design pales into insignificance. Carlyle is, incidentally, still worth reading even though his Victorian style is, to us, florid if not somewhat *rococo*.

18 It is customary for western critics to discern a change in Muhammad's moral character on the basis of this modification in the Koran's literary emphasis. The claim is that the Arabian iconoclast changed from being a sincere God-seeker and passionate reformer at Mecca to being a political opportunist and debauched sensualist at Medina. This view, though clearly laughable, continues to enjoy much support and will concern us at length in chapter 9.

19 Ahmad ibn Muhammad ibn Hanbal, vol.IV, pp.133–4, using Wensinck's system of reference for recording traditions. For an explanation of this system, see chapter 2, note 1.

20 It is an essential impulse of the religious imagination to attempt to relate the aesthetic and the moral forces within civilisation.

21 Mohammad Marmaduke Pickthall's *The Meaning of the Glorious Koran: An Explanatory Translation* rightly enjoys a prodigiously massive prestige among Muslims since many non-Muslim translators often deliberately employ a style of expression that masks cynicism, personal prejudice and theological bias.

22 In order to see that, one needs to look at the manner in which the Koran was

originally received. The revelation was originally like a running conversation with the community of faith; the spiritual tension was built up from an almost brooding and ruminative inception to an emotionally active close. The Koran today, as a written record, says everything at once since a book, unlike a (coherent) conversation, asserts all its claims simultaneously, as it were, rather than in sequence – since one can read it anywhere at random. For purposes of public worship, the Koran is usually recited on the principle of crescendo: a slow, almost lethargic, opening gives way eventually to a powerful culmination.

23 The *jinn* are an important part of Muslim thought throughout the history of Islam. They receive significant mention in the Koran (72:1ff.; 46:29ff.) which is unsurprising once we remember that the Devil is a *jinn* who, out of arrogant self-will, freely rejected Allah's sovereignty. Muslim religionists have assigned to certain verses of the revealed canon an apotropaic power: in many traditional Islamic societies these verses are still recited, in the original Arabic, in the presence of rebellious *jinn* thought to have taken possession of a person.

24 The Sufi mystics have famously read many layers of significance into the sacred text, though their interpretations are, to the extent that they are religious, quite defensible if rather adventurous.

25 Zaid is mentioned by name in *surah* 33, v.37; *surah* 111, v.1 condemns Abu Lahab (whose real name, incidentally, was Abdul 'Uzza).

26 Examples abound: Muhammad's staunch companion Abu Bakr is referred to as 'the companion in the cave' (K:9:40); the wandering mystic identified as Khidr by later Islam is referred to simply as 'one of our servants' (K:18:66); and so on.

27 Words such as *jehad* (meaning struggle or effort, often translated as holy war), *taqwa* (meaning piety inspired by fear), *iman* (meaning a faith grounded in confirmed knowledge), and so on, are familiar examples.

28 Maurice Bucaille, *The Bible, the Qur'an and Science* (Paris: Seghers, 1983), 10th edition, translated from the French by A.D. Pannell and Maurice Bucaille. See also his *What is the Origin of Man?* (Paris: Seghers, 1984), 3rd edition. For Aisha Abd-ar-Rahman at-Tarjumana's views, see some of the old output from the Diwan Press run by the Norwich group of Sufis once headed by Sheikh Abd-ul-Qadir as-Sufi ad-Darqawi. For Wadud's views, see his *Phenomena of Nature and the Qur'an* (Lahore: Sayed Khalid Wadud, 1971).

29 This is Bucaille's argument in the works by him cited in note 28 above.

30 Theism can of course tolerate at best a secondary kind of ultimacy for Nature. Modern science has taken the final step in the desacralisation of Nature: it has eliminated God as well on the grounds that a transcendent being active in the spatio-temporal continuum may, through miraculous interventions, especially surreptitious ones, render difficult the scientific task of discerning the normal regularities in the natural world. For a development of such a contention, see Christine Overall's 'Miracles as Evidence Against the Existence of God', in *The Southern Journal of Philosophy*, vol.XXIII, no.3, 1985, pp.347–53. I take Overall to task in my 'Miracles as Evidence for the Existence of God' in *Scottish Journal of Religious Studies*, 1990.

31 This is probably the Koran's version of the traditional story of the Seven Sleepers of Ephesus at the time of the Decian Persecution (K:18:9–27).

32 K:18:22; Arberry's translation. Christian writers often deride the Koran's condemnation of speculative curiosity as a form of specifically Islamic provincialism. Yet an identical attitude towards enthusiasm in the pursuit of secular

knowledge can be found in Christian religious circles – prominently in the Miltonic seventeenth century.

33 To say, for instance, that 'Joseph was sold for a paltry price' (K:12:20) in preference to 'Joseph was sold for twenty shekels of silver' (Gen. 37:38) is highly characteristic of the Muslim scripture. Jewish and Christian critics discern in such vagueness Muhammad's ignorance of the relevant factual and historical details that abound in the Old Testament and, to a lesser extent, in the New. Such a cynical attitude ultimately discredits only those who entertain it.

34 Thus, for example, the Jewish rabbis of Yathrib (Medina), sceptical of Muhammad's claim to heavenly inspiration, had challenged him to apply to Allah for esoteric information about the itinerary of the traveller referred to in *surah* 18 (vv.83ff.) as Dhul Qarnayn (literally, 'he of the two horns'), identified by most commentators as the Macedonian adventurer Alexander the Great. Even here, the Koran characteristically builds a religious intent into a story that can be read purely for its historical, indeed geographical, interest.

35 Salman Rushdie has dramatically referred to the affair of 'the Satanic Verses' in his recent novel of the same name.

36 Some of the moral attitudes of such men as Abraham, Moses, Jesus and Muhammad certainly seem offensive to modern ethical sensibilities. Although western critics are usually very eager to cite Muhammad as the best example of the unworthy side of religious morality, my own view is that the moral deportment of *all* the seminal religious figures of the Judaeo-Christian-Islamic tradition, including Jesus, is subject to valid secular criticism. Christians would have a difficult time in accepting some of the harsher remarks attributed to Jesus if it weren't for the tendency to slip into moral doublethink at a crucial juncture.

37 The incident is related in *surah* 37, v.102. Compare the biblical version.

38 Muslims argue that John 14:26 is foretelling the advent of Muhammad, not the Holy Ghost. The Koran claims that the prophethood of Muhammad was confirmed by Jesus in the Gospels and by those to whom the Torah was given (K:7:157; 61:6). For further discussion, see Abdul Ahad Dawud's *Muhammad in the Bible* (Sarawak: Angkaton Nahdhatul-Islam Bersatu, 1978) and Maurice Bucaille's *The Bible, the Qur'an and Science* (Paris: Seghers, 1983). This theological controversy is beyond the scope of our concerns. Christians who seek clues about the ministry of Jesus in passages of Isaiah in the Old Testament will be only too familiar with the impulse here. It is in debates such as these that one is impressed by the problematic nature of scripture given its tendency to make allusions and cryptic remarks elastic enough to cover the aspirations of many contending parties.

39 Nietzsche, of all people, catches the Koran's sentiment when he remarks: 'Wisdom sets bounds even to knowledge.' See his *Twilight of the Idols* (Harmondsworth: Penguin Books, 1968), translated by R.J. Hollingdale in one volume along with *The Anti-Christ*, p.23.

40 The Koran concedes that the scriptures given to previous communities of Jews and Christians were (religiously) all-sufficient (K:6:154), a concession which the contemporary Jews and Christians quickly made into a basis for their refusal to convert to Islam.

41 Think here of some of the statements, especially the opening ones, in Ludwig Wittgenstein's *Tractatus*. The claims are made *ex cathedra* with a genuine lack of nuance or fear of contradiction.

42 The Koran mentions, it would seem, only three. The institution of the five canonical daily prayers was established by the Prophet himself.

43 Most of the incidents in the Prophet's personal life, such as the slander against

his young wife, Ayeshah, mentioned in *surah* 24, vv.11ff., had a general import for all believers at all times. However, there are occurrences, such as the incident related in *surah* 66, vv.1ff., which seem to have no universal significance and hence could perhaps have been omitted.

44 For such an understanding and its anthropological underpinnings, see David Hume's masterly *The Natural History of Religion* (London: Adam and Charles Black, 1956), edited with an introduction by H.E. Root.

45 The Roman Catholic scholar G.K. Chesterton *argued* for the religious view in his highly original *The Everlasting Man* (Burns and Oates, 1974), originally published in 1925. See especially pp.21ff.

46 Some commentators think that Luqman was not a prophet but merely a sage. Most identify him with the African slave-fabulist Aesop. Traditional Islam puts the estimate of the total number of religiously inspired teachers at 124,000. Presumably, so large a number is capable of covering the possibility that all religions (before the coming of Islam in the seventh century) were divinely ordained whatever falsehoods may have crept into them at a later stage.

47 See also my *The Light in the Enlightenment*.

48 Quoted by Frithjof Schuon in his *Understanding Islam* (London: Allen and Unwin, 1976; Mandala edition, 1986), p.139, n.1.

49 It is perhaps worth mentioning here one charge of anachronism which has an even weaker basis than the usual question-begging reliance on the authenticity of the Bible. Some non-Muslim critics have argued that the Koran identifies, by a truly astonishing anachronism, Mary, the Mother of Jesus, with the sister of Moses and Aaron (K:3:32; 3:34; 19:38). This charge is based on a straightforward ignorance of Arabic idiom. Mary, the mother of Jesus, is rightly referred to as 'the sister of Aaron' (K:19:28) in recognition of her priestly lineage. Such a description, like 'sons of Abraham' or 'Children of Adam', typically does not, indeed cannot without absurdity, imply or presuppose direct physical consanguinity. If a claim such as 'All Muslims are the sons of Abraham' or 'All of us are the Children of Adam' is taken literally, it is untrue and outrageously so. The tendency to interpret scripture literally is, in such cases, clearly unjustified. It is this kind of uninformed and unworthy criticism of Islam that leads Muslims to engage in bitter polemical exchanges with non-Muslims, especially Christians. A Muslim may be tempted to say to a Christian that literalism in scriptural interpretation is to blame for a colossally consequential blunder (committed by Christians) with respect to the expression 'the Son of God'. Polemic inspires further polemic.

50 Some critics of Islam have sought to deny the Koran's textual purity. It may safely be said that there are motives but no grounds for the denial.

51 The 'theological revisionists', as I call them, are a group of secularised 'sophisticated' Christian thinkers. The most prominent members of the group are Terence Penelhum, John Hick, Basil Mitchell and Richard Swinburne. For some criticisms of theological revisionism, see my *The Light in the Enlightenment*, chapter V.

52 Many secularised modern Christians believe that scripture contains some purely human (and hence fallible) elements.

53 Lesslie Newbigin, *Foolishness to the Greeks* (London: SPCK, 1986), p.43.

54 There are of course many differences, some significant, between the koranic and the biblical accounts of creation but none affects the point being made here.

55 Richard Swinburne, *Faith and Reason* (Oxford: Clarendon Press, 1981), p.182.

56 Ibid., pp.181–3.

57 I should say incidentally that I am a realist as indeed are all the writers whose views are being criticised here. Realism is the philosophical view, as I understand it, according to which there is an objectively correct way of seeing the world since there is an independent world out there – a world independent of human thought and language. Language is, in other words, the servant, not the master, of reality. I make explicit this controversial metaphysical assumption because the problems of realism and anti-realism are live ones for contemporary analytical philosophers.

58 I have argued elsewhere that Swinburne's own way of drawing this distinction rests on a *petitio principii*. See my 'Religious Messages and Cultural Myths', in *Sophia*, vol.25, no.3, October 1986, pp.32–40.

59 The writings of the Christian theologian Karl Barth exemplify the neo-orthodox response to modernity.

60 Psalms 7:9.

61 Swinburn, op.cit., p.182.

62 Such a concession opens up the possibility of rejecting the Bible in favour of a related rival scripture – say, the Koran. I argue this point in my *The Light in the Enlightenment*. Given that the object of our devotion is God, not our beliefs about God, one is morally obliged to distinguish truly revealed doctrine from teaching that is falsely claimed to be revealed.

63 Some Christian writers have argued that they can avoid these standard criticisms of scripture by an appeal to a different model of revelation. Revelation, it is urged, is not, for a Christian, primarily informational. God reveals himself in gracious relationship with his creatures. For Jews and Muslims, divine revelation is primarily in the form of a written record in a sacred language; for Christians, the argument runs, revelation finds its primary locus in the experience of relationship with Christ. It is not the message but the messenger, it is concluded, that really matters. I have elsewhere argued that the move to an alternative model of revelation is misguided and cannot, in any case, shield the Christian against the criticisms I have outlined. See my *The Light in the Enlightenment*.

64 The rule, rather unhelpful in practice, is, in the first instance, about the distinction between the literal and the allegorical in scripture.

65 The charge of evasion is, particularly in religious contexts, a deeply problematic one. Religious writers have always contended that if there is a God, it is only to be expected *a priori* that in regard to a great deal of what he is alleged to be doing in the world, we should be puzzled. The God of faith, as opposed to the God of the thinkers, is a *deus arcanus*. Unsurprisingly, therefore, the theologian cannot resolve each and every theological puzzle; and to accuse him of evasion on the sole ground that he cannot resolve them may, in this context, be illegitimate. For further discussion, see my *The Light in the Enlightenment*.

Chapter 4: The Silence of Allah

1 Some learned authorities dispute this interpretation since the Last Supper is associated, by Christians, with the Eucharist, an institution whose theological foundations the Koran vehemently rejects. It is clear, however, that the gathering headed by Jesus in this passage (K:5:112ff.) is in some way of great and terminative significance.

2 This is incidentally a most characteristic feature of sacred literature in the Hebraic tradition. We get the same sentiment in Christ's reported sayings.

Though it is not sinful to be merely inquisitive, blessed are they that believe *without* knowing, says Jesus, after dispelling the doubts of the sceptical disciple.

3 The Ahmadi sect notoriously denied this in claiming that Mirza Ghulam Ahmad was a prophet sent to the modern world. The Ahmadis were recently declared to be outside the pale of orthodoxy and condemned as non-Muslims. Given the Ahmadi concern with Christ and his ministry, it is now, incidentally, both possible and judicious for the Ahmadis to see their faith as a *Christian* rather than *Islamic* heresy. This option should particularly appeal to second-generation Ahmadis who were born as Ahmadis.

4 Iqbal's *Message from the East*, published in Persian in 1923, was written in friendly response to Goethe's pioneering *Der West-ostliche Divan (The Western-Eastern Divan)* of 1819.

5 It is an established fact in the sociology of intellectual life that many distinguished thinkers and scientists are often surprisingly orthodox religious believers. Examples from the Jewish and Christian households of faith are unnecessary. Professor Abdus Salam, a recent Nobel Prize winner in Physics, deserves mention here although, unfortunately, he belongs to the Ahmadi sect which has recently been excluded from the House of Islam.

6 It is fair to say that much of the credit for this achievement and for the associated birth of a truly modern science must go to western man although Islam did contribute greatly to the creation of the Renaissance in Europe.

7 For a powerful and clear statement of the problem of coherence, see the voluminous writings of Professor Kai Nielsen. Nielsen, himself a committed Marxist, is one of our leading philosophers of religion. See especially his *Scepticism* (London: Macmillan, 1973), *An Introduction to the Philosophy of Religion* (London: Macmillan, 1982), *Contemporary Critiques of Religion* (London: Macmillan, 1971) and *Philosophy and Atheism* (Buffalo: Prometheus Books, 1985). For some familiar criticism of Nielsen's radical atheism, see my *The Light in the Enlightenment* (London: Grey Seal Books, 1990), chapter VI.

8 The quotation is from a private correspondence dated 16 June 1987, between the Rev. Cragg and the present author. The author wishes to thank the Rev. Cragg for a series of gracious letters notwithstanding fundamental differences of opinion about the Crescent and its rivalry with the Cross.

Chapter 5: The Wisdom of the Fool

1 Among nineteenth-century English novelists, Thomas Hardy's works give the best picture of the gradual encroachment of science and agnosticism on a traditional rural existence. See especially his *Tess of the D'Urbervilles, Far from the Madding Crowd* and *The Return of the Native*; his hugely neglected poetry also offers perceptive observations on our theme.

2 Some orthodox Muslim writers have argued that all prophets were sinless but this view finds no basis in the Koran. Although the Koran vindicates certain prophetic figures – Lot and David among them – against some biblical accusations, the divine forefinger is raised, on one occasion or another, at all God's envoys, including Muhammad. The only exception is Jesus, whose behaviour is never criticised either in the Koran or in the *hadith*. Some commentators hold the unverifiable view that some prophets were caused, by God, to commit certain kinds of sins for purposes of educating themselves and their communities about the consequences of disobeying God. Opinions abound concerning what

kinds of lapses in behaviour and thought count as sinful in the case of prophetic figures.

3 Jean-Paul Sartre, *Existentialism and Humanism* (London: Eyre Methuen, 1948, 1973), translated from the French by Philip Mairet, p.56.

4 Although some nineteenth-century English literature – that by Hardy, for example – prefigures modern sentiments about the sordidness of life in a world without providence, it is only in twentieth-century imaginative writings that these sentiments have found full expression. Part of the reason for this of course is that the traditional literary convention which authorised only the use of soft and domesticated language, even in describing harsh and ugly realities, is now largely rejected.

5 A well-attested tradition (*hadith*) of the Prophet tells us that every newborn infant is a Muslim, a natural submitter to the will of Allah; nurture alone turns him into an adherent of any non-Muslim conviction.

6 The only exceptions, presumably, are those who are invincibly or congenitally ignorant of the existence of God.

7 Compare here Reinhold Niebuhr's strikingly Islamic sentiment in the famous passage in *The Nature and Destiny of Man* (New York: Charles Scribner's Sons, 1949), vol.1, pp.165–6: '[T]he reason which asks the question whether the God of religious faith is plausible has already implied a negative answer to the question because it has made itself God and naturally cannot tolerate another.'

8 It is worth noting, in this context, the sheer crudity and literalness of paganism during the age of revelation. Azar, Abraham's father, sold idols made of wood and stone (K:6:75); part of the Meccan prosperity in pre-Islamic days depended upon guardianship of the central sanctuary housing many famous idols, a fact which largely explains incidentally the Qureish's hostility to Muhammad's iconoclasm.

9 cf. Col. 3:5; Eph. 5:5.

10 There are countless examples both from the Christian and from the Muslim camp. A prominent instance is Muhammad Iqbal in his *Khizr-e-Rah* (Lahore: Pan-Islamic Publications, 1965), translated into English by Abdur-Rahman Tariq and Aziz Ahmad Sheikh as *The Guide*. This short book is in the form of imaginary questions put to the unnamed personality of *surah* 18 (vv.60–82), referred to simply as 'one of our servants whom we had taught', to whom Moses applies for apprenticeship in esoteric learning. Commenting on the chaos in the human world, this personality, identified as the wandering mystic Khizr by most commentators, attributes it to the implicit idolatry of our modern age.

11 I have in mind here not orthodox or neo-orthodox Christian writers (like Karl Barth or Reinhold Niebuhr) but rather secularised Christians and those concerned to come to terms with modernity. One of the discrepant weaknesses of so much writing by Christian writers immersed in the ethos of modernity is the lack of awareness of the fact that the accusation of idolatry cannot be made without great reservation in this increasingly secular age. Thus, to take just one example, the Rev. Kenneth Cragg in his insightful *The Mind of the Qur'an: Chapters in Reflection* (London: Allen and Unwin, 1973) seems unalert to the need for this reservation.

12 This must surely be the reason for the amazingly frequent discussion of the clash between Moses and the sorcerers (K:7:103–26; 10:75–81; 20:56–76; 26:10–51). Note particularly Moses' condemnation of the behaviour of the magician-idolater As-Samiri (K:20:85–97), probably an Egyptian immigrant who had sought to mislead the Children of Israel.

13 I assume that the satanist in question believes in the existence of God – and of the Devil, presumably – but merely refuses to worship God.

14 Other paradigm cases of idolatry include the famously tragic case of the two lovers Laila and Majnun – the Romeo and Juliet of the East – one of whom, in his passion, took his lover, in preference to Allah, to be the referent of the Muslim prayer.

15 Some of the ideas in this section were originally presented in a paper entitled 'Faust and the New Idolaters: Reflections on *Shirk*', given in 1987 at the Selly Oak Centre for the Study of Islam and Christian–Muslim Relations, Birmingham. The author wishes to take this opportunity to thank the Rev. Dr Sigvard von Sicard for the invitation and the hospitality.

16 For further discussion, see Kai Nielsen, *Contemporary Critiques of Religion* (London: Macmillan, 1971), Antony Flew, 'Theology and Falsification', in *The Philosophy of Religion* (Oxford: Oxford University Press), edited by Basil Mitchell, pp.13–22.

17 The term *jehad*, which has recently been alarming so many westerners, actually means 'to strive' or 'to struggle', although 'holy war' is not an altogether inappropriate rendering. Although the Koran recommends fighting against certain groups (K:2:190; 2:217–18; 2:246; 4:75), such military effort to promote the cause of Islam (*qatelu-fi-sabillillah*, literally, fighting in the way of Allah) is not precisely equivalent to *jehad* – which is often, particularly nowadays, identified, wrongly, with the normal exigences of the moral life and religious piety.

18 Indifference is more or less foreign to the Koran though hypocrisy (*nifaq*) has connotations of lukewarm allegiance. The closest we get to indifference within the scriptural world is in Rev. 3:15–16 where a group known as the Laodiceans receive a brief mention.

19 It may surprise some readers to note that in Exod. 16:9–10, Yahweh is said to reveal himself directly to a whole community, not just to their prophetic representative.

Chapter 6: The Brave New World

1 *Twilight of the Idols* (Harmondsworth: Penguin Books, 1968), translated by R.J. Hollingdale, p.45. Emphasis in original. Few contemporary analysts have shown any great interest in Nietzsche's philosophy of religion. Part of the reason for this is the conviction that Nietzsche's aphoristic style sets undue limits to the detailed development of his insights. A careful study would show, however, I believe, that there is a full and coherent intellectual reality behind the pithy remarks. My aim in this chapter is not, incidentally, to expound the details of a specifically Nietzschean humanism – a separate and complex task.

2 *Ecce Homo* (Harmondsworth: Penguin Books, 1979), translated by R.J. Hollingdale. Some writers have dismissed Nietzsche's anti-theistic fury as merely a presage of his incipient madness; some religionists have even hinted that Nietzsche's powerful critique of the religious mentality is happily nullified by his eventual insanity. It is unfortunate that even Iqbal, one of Nietzsche's contemporaries, declined to engage in a serious debate with his atheistic rival, contenting himself with a few hostile satirical remarks in verse.

3 *Ecce Homo*, p.66.

4 I should record a couple of terminological points here, points which are not merely verbal, springing as they do from serious and substantive concerns. I

take 'atheism' and 'humanism', both blanket terms, to be roughly equisignificant and implying at once the non-existence of the divine and the self-sufficiency of the human. To be sure, there may be a species of humanism that is compatible with theism; and our definition is adopted for convenience rather than out of any wish to beg the question concerning such a possibility. It is also worth recording here that atheism, as generally understood, is compatible with more or less all political opinions (other than theocracy of course). Thus, Nietzsche was an inegalitarian, some would say (not without reason) a kind of Fascist; Marx, like many modern atheists – Kai Nielsen comes to mind – was radical in political persuasion; and there are some conservative atheists too of whom Antony Flew is perhaps the most famous in the Anglo-American philosophical community.

5 The term *dahariyya* is not itself koranic, the closest in the scriptural lexicon being *kafir* deriving from *kufr*. A speculative atheist (*dahariyya*) is one who denies the very existence of God – a phenomenon apparently quite alien to the age of revelation.

6 I say 'arguably' of course not on account of any doubts about Spinoza's moral uprightness but because of unclarity about his views. It is an undisputed fact that he was expelled from the Jewish community because of heresy; we also know that his radical views about the Bible excited hostility from Christian quarters. But it is not clear that he was an atheist since his 'atheism' has been described controversially as anything from outright disbelief in a personal deity to God-intoxicated pantheism. Incidentally, although I think Voltaire was a virtuous man, I do not list him here since, I suppose, he was really a deist, perhaps an agnostic, rather than an out-and-out atheist.

7 The infancy of the tradition partly explains the circumstance that there is no generally accepted standard of merit or accusation used in judging the behaviour of an atheist. One does not say accusingly, 'You are not really an atheist' in quite the same way (or nearly as often) as one says, 'You are not really a Christian'.

8 It is clear that Nietzsche rejected Christian ethics; it is arguable whether or not he rejected all forms of theistic morality and it is highly improbable that he rejected morality altogether.

9 For some powerful expressions of the malaise of men in the brave new world of post-Christian culture, see *Robert Lowell's Poems: A Selection* (London, Boston: Faber and Faber, 1974), edited with an introduction and notes by Jonathan Raban.

10 Think here of the kind of deeply felt fear of divine judgement that informed the daily lives of the Jewish Patriarchs, the early Church Fathers and the Companions of Muhammad.

11 Friedrich Nietzsche, *Ecce Homo*, p.44.

12 I am not unaware of some theists, particularly Christian theists, who talk with great confidence about God, the divine will, and the attainment of personal salvation. Now, while it may be a piece of capital infidelity to be excessively pessimistic about one's chances of salvation or of ultimate success, it is none the less important for us to note the religious caveats implicit in cautionary formulae such as 'by the grace of God' or 'if Allah wills'. Clearly, such religious phrases are empty unless one recognises that it is *God* who has the last word in the affair. The Koran rightly and strongly condemns all purely human expressions of undue optimism about the attainment of success in the religious life (K:2:111; 62:6).

13 By 'polemic', I mean 'unworthy criticism of alien conviction'. Given the current

deadlocks between faith and rejection, and between one faith and its religious rivals, the concept of polemic is very badly in need of investigation. We need to know what precisely polemic amounts to, why it is unacceptable in responsible exchange, and how it differs from fair criticism. The problem of polemic in inter-religious dialogue will concern us, indirectly, in chapter 9.

14 'Of Atheism', in Bacon's *Essays*. I have modernised the spelling of a few words.

15 For an exploration of these issues, from a poetic angle, see my 'Union of Modern Misanthropes (UMM)', in my *The Mother of Judas Iscariot and Other Poems* (London, New York: Regency Press, 1988).

16 Apart from *Ecce Homo* and *Twilight of the Idols*, see also *The Anti-Christ*, *Thus Spoke Zarathustra* and *Beyond Good and Evil*.

Chapter 7: The Kingdom of God

1 The standard interpretations of *fanin* are 'perishing' (Arberry) and 'passing away' (Pickthall).

2 The Koran frequently advises men to 'fear' God; the Arabic word for fear of God (*taqwa*) is rarely used for describing fear of other beings or entities. See also note 11.

3 Friedrich Nietzsche, *Ecce Homo* (Harmondsworth: Penguin Books, 1979), translated by R.J. Hollingdale, p.44.

4 In his *The Revival of the Religious Sciences*, al-Ghazzali had managed to effect an admittedly uneasy alliance between legalist Islam and Sufi mysticism. But Sufi pantheism, often associated with the thirteenth-century Spanish Muslim mystic al-'Arabi, had at its core an extravagant monism – the view that there is nothing but God – which once again estranged Islamic orthodoxy. Al-'Arabi's monism may well, however, have influenced some Christians (perhaps St John of the Cross among them) and some Jews (possibly even the Jewish heretic Baruch Spinoza).

5 Such a view introduces so many intolerable complications. For one thing, it effectively denies freedom of the human will, which in turn makes a mockery of the historic struggle between good and evil, and may sometimes be subversive of orthopraxy. For another, it implies that even Muhammad, the prophet of Allah, was an illusory being, not to speak of the Sufis themselves, though they were eager to obliterate the distinction between themselves and God.

6 We can appreciate the religious enthusiasm that inspired such a remark. But, in a sober mood, one should note its strange implications. The Sheikh's own social life must have suffered on account of remarks like 'Only God lives at this address'. Indeed it wasn't long before an outraged orthodoxy arrived at his house to interrogate him about his true identity. The tenth-century mystic-saint Mansur al-Hallaj suffered much more drastically. He had, in a moment of ecstasy, exclaimed 'I am the truth', effectively identifying himself with the Deity (cf. John 14:6). In 922, al-Hallaj was publicly executed for offences against the dignity of God.

7 It is questionable to what extent Iqbal's ideas have influenced Muslims outside Pakistan and India. Owing to the resurgence of Islam in post-revolutionary Iran, some Iranian writers have recently shown interest in Iqbal's work; he, incidentally, also wrote in Persian.

8 This view is also stated or implied in New Testament teaching about salvation and damnation although many modern Christians find it difficult to swallow. See Matt. 18:6–9.

9 This is not to deny, *contra* Christian critics of Islam, that a life of faith begun out of the fear of the Deity may eventually lead to one in which love was a motive or even a dominant motive.

10 See also K:59:18–21 for some atypically gentle remarks the mellow and edificatory tone of which invites comparison with Rom. 13: 'Let every soul . . . '

11 Arberry's translation. In the quoted passage, two different Arabic words are indifferently translated as 'fear'. For fear of the people, the word is *khawf*; the fear of God is called *taqwa*. Strictly speaking, *taqwa* means 'due or just observance of one's creaturely duty to Allah'. (See Pickthall's translation.) Although *khawf* can be directed towards God (K:5:23; 5:28), *taqwa* cannot properly be directed towards any non-divine entity.

12 There can be no fully moral relationship unless the parties in question respect some common ethical rules. Think here of the *partial* moral reciprocity in relationships between adults and children, adults and mentally handicapped people, and between human beings and animals. In the last case, the relationship is totally one-sided: we have moral obligations with respect to animals but they have none towards us.

13 Masud-ul-Hasan, *Life of Iqbal* (Lahore: Ferozsons, 1978), Book II, first edition, p.238.

14 See my *The Light in the Enlightenment* for a discussion of Christian neo-orthodoxy.

15 'Thy kingdom come, Thy will be done' in the Lord's Prayer expresses a milder form of the sentiment implicit in 'He is the dominant'. The characteristic sentiments of Jewish piety are, unsurprisingly, well-nigh identical to those of Islam.

16 W.B. Yeats, 'Sailing to Byzantium'. The original line is: 'Gather me into the artifice of eternity.'

Chapter 8: The Riddle of Man

1 This passage is variously interpreted as 'Man is born impatient and miserly' (Sher Ali), 'fretful' (Arberry) and 'anxious' (Pickthall).

2 This is Arberry's rendering. Sher Ali has 'to face hardships'; Pickthall has both 'in affliction' and, curiously, 'in an atmosphere'. Kenneth Cragg also has 'in trouble' in his recent translation *Readings in the Qur'an* (London: Collins, 1988), p.109. The original phrase itself has built into it the connotations of tension and endurance in the face of adversity.

3 Greek philosophical views about knowledge and the moral life have enjoyed great popularity with Muslims – who, of course, transmitted Greek learning to the West. The Socratic-Platonic doctrine of *anamnesis* has a clear affinity with the koranic view about the need for recollecting a truth of which one is heedless (*ghafil*). Of all the Greek thinkers, Muslim writers have a marked preference for Aristotle partly because of the Koran's predilection for the doctrine of the mean and the implied emphasis on the need for balance and equilibrium in the ethical life.

4 The classical Arabic word for knowledge is *'ilm*; it usually denotes religious knowledge, i.e. a kind of pious rationality. Knowledge, in Islamic thought, is more or less identical to the Greek notion of *sophia* (rational wisdom) as opposed to *techne* (awareness of technique).

5 Allah does not, incidentally, wager with Satan concerning the outcome of the

struggle between good and evil. Such an attitude would be considered immoral in Islam.

6 The Sufis are fond of quoting an apocryphal *hadith* to the effect that 'God is a treasure' and takes delight in men discovering or 'knowing' him. (The metaphor of knowing also denotes sexual information in sacred writing as in 'Abraham knew his wife'.) This emphasis on the aesthetic significance of man for God's diversion, however, directly contradicts the Koran's repeated insistence on the primacy of man's moral vocation.

7 The Koran frequently warns believers about Satan's enmity to man – both hidden (K:7:27) and manifest (K:2:168; 2:208; 12:4; repeated often). Milton unwittingly catches the koranic sentiment in his *Paradise Lost*, Book 1, lines 159–65.

8 The Christian reader is irresistibly reminded of Gerald Manley Hopkins's lament: *Quare via impiorum prosperatur?* (Why do sinners' ways prosper?)

9 The Socratic belief in the efficacy of 'knowledge' in the pursuit of the good is surely questionable although knowledge is, for Socrates as for Muslim thinkers, properly to be seen as a kind of practical wisdom, not merely theoretical cognisance.

10 The Invocation is the opening declaration, usually not numbered, that is affixed to each *surah* of the Koran and uttered by Muslims when they begin any (significant) act. *Surah* 9 uniquely lacks the Invocation because, according to some authorities, it contains unusually harsh passages so that a prefatory announcement of divine mercy would seem out of place. This explanation is, it seems to me, entirely unconvincing since countless harsh passages occur throughout the rest of the Koran.

11 A convenient barometer of enthusiasm is the rate at which heresy is created. The Early Church witnessed countless heresies within a few centuries; Christianity has not produced a genuinely novel heresy for several centuries now. Islam has produced a number of heresies within the last century or so.

12 Critics of Gandhi wonder if he even conquered his sexuality in view of accusations of morally questionable 'chastity experiments', involving young women, conducted in his later years.

13 The closest equivalent to sinfulness, within the koranic lexicon, is *zulm*. *Zulm* is self-wronging i.e., men's proclivity to be treacherous towards their own higher nature. This is of course the Koran's favourite *motif*.

14 It could be that conspicuous wickedness is rarer than conspicuous virtue in human history. At any rate, most of us are morally mediocre – neither morally excellent nor depraved.

15 One of the unintended results of the development of modern hagiography has been the realisation that genuine virtue is rarely achieved – indeed far less often than had traditionally been supposed.

16 *Confessions*, book X, chapter 29.

17 XLIX, 2; according to Wensinck's system of reference for recording *hadith* literature.

18 For some remarks on the nature of *zulm*, see note 13.

19 Hence, of course, that penetratingly educational but clearly unfair witticism about Christians praying for one another on Sundays and preying upon one another on weekdays. Jews and Muslims, one supposes, do much the same, albeit on a different day. I have explored this theme from a poetic angle in my 'A Ghetto for Christ' and 'Friday Afternoon with Allah' in my *The Mother of Judas Iscariot and Other Poems* (London, New York: Regency Press, 1988).

20 According to all orthodox religious authorities within Islam, the fulfilment of

practical religious obligations, such as daily prayer, is *not* a condition of being a Muslim. A public recitation of the creed suffices to place a man within the ambit of Islam.

21 Sheikh Muhammad ibn 'Isa at-Tirmidhi, XXXI, 79; Wensinck's system.

22 There is a sense in which this is clearly false: in life we often bear each other's burdens. What is meant, presumably, is that with respect to salvation, no one is in a position to lighten his own burden by transferring it to someone else. The Koran warns that on the Last Day, the normal bonds of human community will disintegrate: each person will be so preoccupied with his or her own salvation that brothers will fail to recognise each other, mothers will show no sympathy for their own offspring, and so on.

23 Christian critics have often insisted that Islam is a predestinarian faith – 'Calvinism overheated'! – that denies the autonomy of the human creature; and yet Islam actually has a far greater stress on the freedom and autonomy of man than a Christianity that centrally relies on salvation seen as man's external rescue by God. This is one of the many instances of the absurdity into which even intelligent critics are led by *a priori* theological prejudices.

24 I take this to be the Christian view though there are Christians who deny the claim that Jesus intended to abolish the law. They appeal to Matt. 5:17–18 in support of their view. But this passage sits ill with St Paul's claim in Rom. 10:4 ('Christ is the end of the law') and in Gal. 3:24–5. It is unclear, as usual, what Jesus himself believed. For further discussion, see chapter 9.

25 The quotation is from a private correspondence dated 7 September 1987, between the Rev. Cragg and the present author. For Cragg's views, see his *The Mind of the Qur'an* (London: Allen and Unwin, 1973), *Muhammad and the Christian* (London: Darton, Longman and Todd, 1984) and *Jesus and the Muslim* (London: Allen and Unwin, 1985).

26 The capacity of a religion to excite pathos increases as faith declines – as practical piety and serious acceptance reach a low ebb. The significance of this remark in the case of western Christianity hardly needs comment.

27 For further discussion of the doctrine of the Incarnation and of how it creates a radical rift between Islam and Christianity, see chapter 9.

28 It is indeed paradoxical that Christians should seek to dispense with law given that the impulse behind the Atonement is itself starkly legalistic: the divine judge must be satisfied. In fact, of course, here is indeed a sovereignty with a ruthlessness that neither mercy can fully mitigate nor a misguided impulse to domestication completely soften.

29 Martin Luther King made this famous comment at a political rally.

30 One welcomes the Christian emphasis on interiority and the purity of inner motivation; but to suggest that, for instance, adultery is committed even in the lustful glance is tantamount to the imposition of an extremely unrealistic demand on human nature. Ironically, Christians have replaced some already strict Jewish regulations with even stricter ones. Unsurprisingly, in practice, most have usually failed to live up to either.

31 'The world is justified only as an aesthetic phenomenon' is possibly the most tragic remark in the entire Nietzschean corpus.

32 It is for this reason that the Koran contains nothing parallel to something like the Book of Job. To see this as a deficiency within the spiritual resources of Islam is to beg an important question about the nature of an authentic religiosity. In fact, of course, the lack of a theory of tragedy within Islam is not accidental, being as it is a deliberate feature of a characteristically Islamic religious vision.

The minority *Shi'ah* view is indeed heretical, incidentally, precisely because its *temperament* is so radically opposed to that of orthodox Islam.

33 For a detailed discussion of the differences between Christianity and Islam, from a variety of angles, see chapter 9.

Chapter 9: Choice and Destiny

1 The annual pilgrimage to Mecca, the *Hajj*, is in every other sense a tribute to Islam's complete lack of racism. As the second largest religious assembly in the world, it welcomes Muslim believers of all races and tongues. For an impression of this remarkable event, see the autobiography of Malcolm X.

2 I restrict my remarks to intellectual, as opposed to popular, western culture. In the latter, the recent rise of evangelical Christianity, especially in North America, has tended to emphasise an isolationist attitude that discerns exclusive privileges in being a 'true' Christian.

3 There will no doubt be a complex pattern of family resemblances among religions and ideologies.

4 Could there be a single overwhelming affiliation? Or will there be many different ones? Will these affiliations be inspired by religious conviction or merely reflect pragmatic political need?

5 *Now I See* (London: Sheed and Ward, 1933; reprinted, 1946), p.101.

6 Nietzsche alone among nineteenth-century western thinkers noted the significant differences between the three heavenly religions. Thus, for example, he saw that the attitude towards power implicit in Judaism and Islam was radically different from that implicit in Pauline Christianity. See especially *The Anti-Christ* (Harmondsworth: Penguin Books, 1968), translated by R.J. Hollingdale in one volume along with *Twilight of the Idols*. For Nietzsche's views on Islam, see sections 59 and 60 of *The Anti-Christ*.

7 Islam as a tradition has within it all the usual elements – silence, poverty, solitude – that form part of a contemplative or mystical asceticism. But these elements are not generally held to be central though they are often highly esteemed.

8 In practice, of course, Christians have rarely, if ever, been passive in the face of persecution, although, I would argue, the posture of passivity is entailed by any serious attempt at the imitation of Christ.

9 The revival of militant Islam, particularly in Iran, is an obvious case in point.

10 It is not in vain that Buddhism has been called 'the Christianity of the East'.

11 It has to be conceded, in fairness, that many Muslims have and do identify Islam with the dominant political power in the land, often seeing it and its interests as being entailed by Allah's providence. Muslims have, at times, been reactionary, obscurantist and unnecessarily conservative in their attitudes, thereby supplying hindrances to some kinds of social progress.

12 The details are of great significance, however, to any Jews and Christians who decide to convert to Islam (and vice versa, of course).

13 But Islam is certainly not simply 'Judaism for the Arabs', although this myth is taking a long time to die. Charles Torrey popularised the view that Islam was essentially Jewish. More recently, Michael Cook and Patricia Crone have argued, using non-Muslim texts, that Islam was originally a variety of Jewish messianism! See their *Hagarism: The Making of the Islamic World* (Cambridge: Cambridge Unviersity Press, 1977). At any rate, as I have already indicated in chapter 3, Islam has, from its very inception, yearned, unlike Judaism, for

universal scope. Judaism has never successfully freed itself from a nationalist taint – a circumstance now pronounced on account of the existence of the state of Israel.

14 A standard text on Jewish–Muslim relations, political and religious, is S.D. Goitein's *Jews and Arabs: Their Contacts Through the Ages* (New York: Schocken Books, 1974), third revised edition. The book is now slightly dated in view of recent developments in Israel and the Middle East.

15 A word here about the complex political rivalries in the Middle East is not out of place. Many Muslims remain ambivalent about the Zionist state of Israel. To be sure, the Hebrew peoples certainly need and deserve, it is thought, a state within the Middle East. The Koran declares that the Promised Land is the rightful property of the Children of Israel (K:5:21; 7:137). The only real problem is that of delineating the piece of land that can legitimately be seen as 'promised'. Certainly, as many orthodox Jews concede, there is no scriptural warrant for Israel to extend its borders indefinitely. (In fact, some extremely strict Jews regard the state of Israel as anathema.) For some fair and well-thought-out remarks, see Professor Moshe Ma'oz's 'The West Bank: An Israeli View', in *Arabia: The Islamic World Review*, vol.6, no.62, October 1986, pp.10–11. What I find disturbing is the tendency of the western media to engage in moral doublethink when covering the Arab–Israeli conflict. No western commentator has, to my knowledge, noted the discrepancy in allowing Israel to use Old Testament prophecy to justify the capture of various lands while disallowing Khomeini from using the relatively modern seventh-century prophecy to justify the capture of Jerusalem. Perhaps, it would be best to leave religious texts out of the aspirations of political expansionism, from whatever source, Jewish or Muslim, such aspirations emanate.

16 For a summary of the theological issues at stake here, see John Sawyer's 'Islam and Judaism', in *Islam in the Modern World* (London: Croom Helm, 1983), edited by Denis MacEoin and Ahmed Al-Shahi, pp.27–35. Sawyer makes some questionable claims about the motives behind the anti-Jewish 'polemic' in the Koran. A failure to draw a distinction between valid criticism and uninformed prejudice vitiates part of Sawyer's analysis.

17 The Koran confirms the Virgin Birth (K:19:16–21); the Immaculate Conception is also confirmed though only as an implication of the Koran's general denial of original sin. The Muslim scripture refers to the allegedly apocryphal miracle of Jesus's speech, in the cradle, in confirmation of his mission (K:19:29–30). Christians usually disown this particular miracle on the grounds that it is too fantastic to be worthy of credence. For a faith that is, on any estimate, so full of incredible and amazing occurrences, this seems a surprisingly weak argument.

18 The denial of the Crucifixion, which entails a rejection of the Resurrection as superfluous, is quite problematic. It is difficult, for obvious reasons, to verify the truth of the koranic claim that God, within human history, secretly translated Jesus's soul and, presumably, his body. At any rate, the denial of the Crucifixion has startled both Christian and Jewish students of Islam, leading some even to question whether or not the character called 'Isa in the Koran is to be identified with the character known as Jesus in Christian perspective.

19 There are countless opinions about Jesus among Muslim writers. The Ahmadi sect, recently expelled from the Islamic community, has a highly original view of the status and ministry of Jesus. For details, see Mirza Ghulam Ahmad's well-argued Urdu treatise *Masih Hindustan Main*, translated into English as *Jesus in India* (London: The London Mosque, 1978).

20 Jesus, according to the Koran (K:3:50), relaxed certain laws that had been imposed on the Children of Israel on account of their sins.

21 For an account of Jesus and his ministry that resembles the standard Islamic one, see the writings of Geza Vermes, the renowned Jewish scholar of the New Testament. Vermes argues, with insight and clarity, that Jesus's teaching can only be understood against the larger religious milieu of first-century Palestinian Judaism. In frequently contrasting the Jesus of history with the divine Christ of the Church, Vermes has come in for bitter criticism from Christian quarters. For a summary of Vermes' views, see his *Jesus and the World of Judaism* (London: SCM Press, 1983) which contains the Riddell Memorial Lectures and the provocative 1974 Claude Goldsmid Montefiore Lecture.

22 This is an unclear charge. It could mean anything from wilful misinterpretation to deliberate negligence or even actual textual deletion. The Koran reserves an exceptionally pointed piece of sarcasm for those who reject the signs of God while already possessing a scripture: their case, says *surah* 62 (v.5) is as the case of a donkey carrying books.

23 Paul – Bulos in Arabic – is apparently not mentioned in the Koran. It is possible that there may be some indirect allusion to him in some obscure verse.

24 Nietzsche, especially in *The Anti-Christ*, also excoriates Paul for distorting the original message of the faith, though Nietzsche's emphasis is on the moral rather than doctrinal aspect of the alleged distortion. Hence, of course, the questionable witticism: 'There has only been one Christian – and he died on the Cross.'

25 The Christians are not alone, incidentally, in failing to preserve their scriptures. Loss or distortion of scripture seems to be an occupational hazard of divine tuition: the Scrolls (*suhuf*), revealed to Abraham (K:2:129; 53:36–7), are now completely lost. Hence, incidentally, Islam's passionate concern to preserve the Arabic Koran.

26 The New Testament has, not without reason, been compared to the *hadith* – the literary materials that are supposed to be records of Muhammad's actions and words. Muslims have always sternly distinguished the Koran from the *hadith*.

27 Islam's insistence on a strictly identifiable corpus of canonical scriptures is, I believe, integrally tied up with its character as a 'political religion'. The more 'politicised' a faith, the greater the emphasis on a defined body of revealed insight as the only source of fully authoritative guidance. It is noteworthy that Hindus, Jews, Buddhists and Christians all have a relatively relaxed attitude towards the delimitation of sacred canon.

28 'Associationism' is, in one important way, a very misleading term, particularly as a translation of *shirk*. Both Christians and Muslims agree that God does indeed graciously associate himself with mankind and the natural universe. The quarrel is over the extent and nature of this association. While the pagan mind misunderstands the nature of God's involvement with creation – and, in doing so, commits idolatry (*shirk*) – the religious mind, whether Christian or Muslim, attempts to grasp the true nature of the divine concern with man and the world and, having done so, expresses gratitude.

29 Christianity differs from Islam in its stance both on the character of God and on man's relationship to God. Here my emphasis is on the different pictures of God in the two monotheisms. For an account of the corresponding differences in human nature, see chapter 8.

30 One consequence of this juxtaposition, contends Nietzsche in *The Anti-Christ*, is that a full-blooded Old Testament humanity – living, dying, killing, fornicating,

repenting – suddenly appears domesticated, 'castrated' in the New Testament with its radical rejection of power and sexuality.

31 Preaching to the Gentiles is of course the occasion for the proverbial 'wasting pearls before swine' (Matt. 7:6). That the churches can square even such a manifestly isolationist claim with their commitment to religious universalism in mission perhaps best exposes the extent to which the clergy deliberately cultivates a psychological immunity to the charge of contradiction.

32 It is worth adding here that the Trinitarian church, favouring Pauline doctrine, persecuted the group known as the Unitarians – who, like the Muslims, incidentally, accused the Trinitarians of corrupting their scripture. Some modern Christians dismiss the Unitarians as not being 'real Christians'. Such a claim is, historically considered, utterly self-indulgent. For if anyone has the right to claim Jesus as a leader, the Unitarians do.

33 To be sure, as much can be – indeed has been – said, by radical critics, about *all* central theistic claims, whether Christian, Jewish or Muslim. But Christianity suffers, when all is said and done, from certain problems, conceptual in character, that are peculiar to it.

34 A Muslim is bound to risk the appearance of bias when examining a religiously rival Christian vision.

35 The idea of an ordained clergy is, in principle, foreign to an Islam that originally consisted of simple doctrines accessible to all adherents. In fact, of course, a religious class developed soon afterwards, one concerned to create, and occasionally solve, problems connected with the interpretation of law and dogma.

36 Was it some such suspicion that led Professor John Hick to reject the Incarnation while claiming to remain a Christian?

37 Two points are worth noting here. Does God need to learn about human suffering – by first-hand experience? This is the first and foremost question here. Secondly, the Incarnation offers *one* particular picture of divine humility; and we can imagine even humbler postures. Nietzsche writes: 'A god come to earth ought to *do* nothing whatever but wrong: to take upon oneself, not the punishment, but the *guilt* – only that would be godlike.' See his *Ecce Homo* (Harmondsworth: Penguin Books, 1979), translated by R.J. Hollingdale, p.45. Emphasis in original.

38 See my earlier discussion, in chapter 3, of the Muslim, particularly Arab, proclivity to regard the Koran as authentic solely on account of its perceived beauty.

39 The Rev. Kenneth Cragg's *Jesus and the Muslim* (London: Allen and Unwin, 1985), a work of the fully committed Christian imagination, remains painfully silent about the central problem of the *coherence* of the doctrines of the Incarnation and the Trinity while offering admittedly powerful arguments in support of the rich moral potential of such orthodox Christian claims. It is noteworthy that even St Thomas has to fall back on mystery when it comes to the Incarnation and the Trinity. Canon Brian Hebblethwaite's *The Incarnation: Collected Essays in Christology* (Cambridge: Cambridge University Press, 1987) came to hand at a late stage in the writing of this book. Hebblethwaite's discussion does not seem to call for any radical revision of opinion about the (alleged) incoherence of the doctrine.

40 Though the royal 'We' occurs in koranic verses, God is said to be strictly unique; his numerical unity is often affirmed. The Trinitarian doctrine is vehemently rejected as being incompatible with this kind of unity.

41 The Unitarian Church is, of course, to some extent, an exception here.

42 It is not clear, however, that Christians would necessarily welcome such an accomplishment. Again, though Christians often complain that Muslim groups never sponsor inter-faith work, Christians do recognise the benefits of retaining this monopoly of inter-religious concerns.

43 This view is held, even today, with varying degrees of subtlety, by almost all Christian critics, including sympathetic ones.

44 Maxime Rodinson's well-known and acclaimed *Mohammed* (Harmondsworth: Penguin Books, 1971), translated into English by Anne Carter, first published in French in 1961, is essentially a propagandist biography. Written from a Marxist perspective, it merely records a few of the Prophet's virtues while expatiating on his alleged vices.

45 *Christianity and the World Religions* (London: Collins, 1987), p.5, edited by Hans Küng et al., translated from the German by Peter Heinegg.

46 Kenneth Cragg's sympathetic *Muhammad and the Christian* (London: Darton, Longman and Todd, 1984), is, in the last analysis, marred by Christian theological preconceptions that militate against impartial inquiry. I take Cragg to task in some detail in my *The Way of the Crescent* (London:Grey Seal Books), forthcoming.

47 John Laffin's *The Dagger of Islam* (London: Sphere Books, 1979) is typical of recent western literature about Islam. Some parts of this book come close to hate literature; the book would almost certainly be banned if the object of its abuse were some non-Islamic group. While Laffin's work has the virtue of frankness, the proclivity to prejudice often seeks more devious means. One popular strategy involves the promotion of the work of non-western black writers solely because of their anti-Islamic turn of mind. Take, for instance, V.S. Naipaul's *Among the Believers: An Islamic Journey* (London: André Deutsch, 1981), which is much praised by western critics. Yet it is at best a work of fictional journalism, taking all the usual liberties of that profession, based as it is entirely on anecdotal evidence, casual conversations with Muslims, and fugitive incidents. What, then, is the source of its authority as a book about contemporary Islam and the Muslims? One cannot explain the popularity of Naipaul's book until one searches for motives – which is, of course, precisely where one finds the correct explanation. Naipaul, himself not a Muslim, betrays certain psychological dislocations when commenting on the spectacular wealth of a tiny number of Arab Muslims, who, like all upstarts, tend to display it in a vulgar fashion. I was not altogether surprised to note recently that most of the literature about Islam is, in my local library, classed under 'Terrorism and Crime'.

48 The Koran insists that Jesus, like other envoys, performed miracles by the permission (*izn*) of Allah. Unfortunately, later Islam attributed many miracles to Muhammad in order to make sure that he did not appear inferior to Christ – thereby falling victim to the same temptation that the Christians have experienced when they effected comparisons between the two figures, claiming that Muhammad had not performed any miracles at all.

49 LXV; Wensinck's system of *hadith* reference.

50 Many Muslims have failed to take their Prophet seriously on this score. Some have even pontificated that he was a supernatural light – *nur* – a view that contradicts the Koran's unequivocal claim that he was merely human.

51 In any case, the comparison is, from an Islamic perspective, uninteresting: the historical Jesus would be in radical agreement with his successor, the historical Muhammad, both men confirming each other's spiritual credentials. After all, both Jesus and Muhammad are, according to the Koran, austerely monotheistic

in outlook. To be sure, the Jesus of the Christian churches would certainly not view Muhammad as a legitimate successor.

52 The only notable exception here is H.A.R. Gibb who has tried to justify the label 'Muhammadanism' as legitimate. See chapter 3, note 1.

53 Looking for 'Christ figures' in a religion like Buddhism is, for obvious reasons, perfectly justified.

54 Hans Küng's sincerity and honesty surely deserve recognition. Küng is one Christian writer who has not tried to evade criticisms of the predominant Christian attitude towards Islam. It is because the Church manages to produce men like Küng that opponents are forced to recognise the humility of the Christian clergy. See Küng's 'Christianity and World Religions: The Dialogue with Islam as One Model', in *The Muslim World*, vol.LXXVII, no.2, April 1987, pp.80–95. Hossein Nasr has a good response to Küng in the same issue of the journal, pp.96ff.

55 Much the same applies to inter-faith centres set up to serve multi-cultural communities in the United Kingdom. These centres are essentially missionary organisations. A Christian policy-maker directs the centre; people of other faiths, including a few Muslims, are hired to fill subordinate positions. Strategically significant positions of influence remain in Christian hands; and this is justified in a Christian country. But, if so, how are such centres religiously liberal?

56 I recognise that Islamic universities in most countries would not countenance Jewish or Christian teachers of Islam. But such closed societies make no claim to being liberal in their religious attitudes. Christians sometimes complain that despite the presence of Muslims in large numbers in the liberal West, there is no school of religious or philosophical thought, reared in a western ethos, that may be labelled 'Islamic' in perspective. If my observations are near to the mark, this state of affairs is to be expected.

57 Certainly, to recognise the integrity of religiously plural perspectives, as we all must in the modern world, may require a general concession to other faiths – a concession that implies *inter alia* a concession to Christianity.

58 For further discussion of apostasy in Islamic thought, see my *Be Careful with Muhammad! The Salman Rushdie Affair* (London: Bellew Publishing, 1989), Chapter 4.

59 Many conversions to Roman Catholicism have, however, also had a markedly strong element of intellectual reasoning. There are probably few instances of Muslims converting to Catholic Christianity.

60 The fact that a religion offers one precisely what one desires is not in itself a reason for thinking it true (or false). The Koran fiercely condemns all unduly optimistic assessments of the likelihood of success in the religious life.

61 In this respect, the scripture of Islam is far superior – in its honesty and directness of mood – to the papers presented at inter-faith conferences. In the Koran, friendly references to the Jewish and Christian societies co-exist along with hostile remarks about some of their members – a feature that has baffled Jewish and Christian commentators, leading some to conclude, wrongly and hastily, that the koranic stance is self-contradictory. In fact, of course, this circumstance of tension is only to be expected in an area of more or less sectarian disagreement itself underlined by native anxieties about issues of moment.

62 In the Muslim camp, Hasan Askari deserves mention as a *Shi'ah* scholar committed to the attainment of a genuine community of sentiment and doctrine among adherents of the three theisms. His attempts to have trialogue and, more

ambitiously, a global theology, both strike me as being wildly naïve. See *Inter-Religion: Journal of Spiritual Quest*, edited by Hasan Askari, vol.2, no.1, July 1987, for the usual diet of poorly argued claims about 'universal mysticism' mixed with inferior poetry. For somewhat more realistic hopes, see the *recent* writings of Hossein Nasr. My own view, like that of the Koran, is, predictably, pessimistic. The Koran does not encourage dialogue beyond a certain point, recognising the fact that deadlocks created by dogma cannot easily be broken. There is a hint in the sacred volume that men will carry these disputes beyond the grave and contend in front of 'thy Lord on the Day of Resurrection who will decide touching their differences' (K:2:113). The Koran regards debate between Jews and Christians as being entirely baseless: 'And the Jews say the Christians have nothing to stand on and the Christians say the Jews have nothing to stand on; and yet they both read the same scripture!' (K:2:113).

63 No Christian account of this event has been traced.

64 This is of course a version of John Hick's famous view known as 'eschatological verification'. The claim is that death is, as it were, an argument: it serves to prove or disprove a given faith. For details, see John Hick, 'Theology and Verification', in *The Logic of God: Theology and Verification* (Indianapolis: Bobbs-Merrill, 1975), edited by Malcolm Diamond and Thomas Litzenburg, pp.188–208.

65 For a discussion of the Christian attitude towards the law of God, see chapter 8.

66 All authorities regard this as a very early Meccan revelation, possibly the second.

67 Some scholars – famously, Ibn Khaldun – claim that v.39 of *surah* 8 is the first one to sanction militant conflict. It is significant that this is a Meccan verse albeit in a largely Medinan *surah*.

68 The context of revelation of this verse is probably the breaking of a treaty between the Muslims and their pagan adversaries. The Muslims, it seems, were in general quite averse to militant struggle; *surah* 2 (v.216) exhorts them to fight 'though it be hateful unto you'.

69 The aim of Islamic conquest, incidentally, is indeed conquest, not conversion. The vanquished communities may normally retain their faiths on condition that their members acknowledge their subjugation and pay a nominal tax in return for protection under the 'political' wing of the House of Islam.

70 This is the essence of the Rev. Kenneth Cragg's critique of the Islamic involvement with power in his *Muhammad and the Christian* and *Jesus and the Muslim*. I take Cragg to task in detail in my *The Way of the Crescent* (London: Grey Seal Books), forthcoming.

71 It is ironic that the Koran is the only scripture in the monotheistic tradition to contain a relatively detailed discussion of the phenomenon of hypocrisy (*nifaq*) in the religious life. Why should a scripture be concerned with, disturbed by, hypocrisy if not in an attempt to take the full measure of the interior self? This is, once again, one of the many instances of the palpable absurdity into which even intelligent critics are led by the over-subtleties of *a priori* theological prejudice.

72 And, in practice too, Muslims have usually been far more willing than their Christian opponents to effect peaceful reconciliation, especially in the Holy Land. Let us not forget the belligerence of the Crusaders in the heyday of Christianity as a political force.

73 In fact, of course, power is the name of the game here. And Christians know that as well as (if not better than) their rivals. Once a group is in a position to safeguard its own interests effectively, it can not only afford to ignore the nasty

graffiti scribbled here and there, it can even afford to talk about turning the other cheek.

74 For a more nuanced account, see my *The Way of the Crescent* (London: Grey Seal Books), forthcoming.

75 To be sure, one should ultimately judge a faith by its ideals, not by the practice of those who profess it: it would be unfair to hold Islam and Christianity responsible for the failings respectively of Muslims and Christians, themselves often merely the failings of our common humanity. But, even so, one should not ignore the practice of the adherents of a religion since no religion exists apart from the actual implementation, however inadequate, of its constitutive principles. Moreover, unless one examines the practice of the faithful, one cannot resolve the important problem concerning the practical viability – realism – of the demands made by a faith.

76 The Christian ruler of Abyssinia, however, displayed exemplary tolerance at a crucial hour in the history of Islam when a party of exiled Muslims took refuge – from Meccan persecution – in Christian Abyssinia. They were honourably treated by the ruler who, many scholars claim, may well have remained a Christian while respecting the koranic account of Jesus and his mother contained in *surah* 19.

77 It is still relatively common for allegedly impartial Christian critics to accuse Muslims of having forced their faith on many Jews and Christians. Oddly enough, the *exact* opposite was often the case. Since non-Muslim monotheists had to pay a nominal tax (*jizya*) to the Muslim state in return for protection and the right to autonomy (K:9:29) (an obligation from which Muslims were exempt) many corrupt Islamic rulers *prevented* conversion to Islam as a means of keeping the treasury in good order.

78 See Robert Caspar's thoughtful remarks in 'The Permanent Significance of Islam's Monotheism', in *Concilium*, special issue entitled *Monotheism* (Edinburgh: T. and T. Clark, 1985), edited by Claude Geffre and Jean-Pierre Jossua, pp.67–78. Caspar's piece is translated by Francis McDonagh.

79 Note the larger context of the exclusivist claim in *surah* 3 (v.85): Islam is the religion of *all* the prophets who preceded Muhammad (K:3:84) whatever their respective communities may have actually done with it.

80 Some Christians, however, restrict salvation to Christians on the authority of Mark 16:15–16. The authenticity of this passage (Mark 16:9–20) is disputed.

81 The possibility of universal damnation is a Pickwickian one since Allah has enjoined mercy upon himself when dealing with his creatures.

82 For Hick's views on religious pluralism, see his *Arguments for the Existence of God* (London: Macmillan, 1971), pp.117–20 and his *God and the Universe of Faiths* (London: Macmillan, 1973).

83 I myself have criticised Hick's view of non-Christian faiths, showing how an orthodox Christian is likely to find it unpalatable. Hick is, of course, familiar with these kinds of criticisms. For details, see my *The Light in the Enlightenment* (London: Grey Seal Books, 1990), chapter 5.

Chapter 10: The Road to Mecca

1 *The Everlasting Man* (Burns and Oates, 1974), originally published in 1925, p.9.

2 *Diary of a Genius* (London: Pan Books, Picador edition, 1976), p.52, translated from the French by Richard Howard.

3 Kenneth Cragg, *The Pen and the Faith* (London: Allen and Unwin, 1985), chapter 7.
4 'The Great Perhaps' in *Resurgence*, no.137, 1990, pp.47–8.
5 The term is koranic. A man and woman are said to be like garments for each other.
6 *The Revival of the Religious Sciences*, Book III, section 198, Cairo edition. Compare the passage in Matt. 23:27.

Index

Abraham, 4, 30, 61, 153, 185, 198
Abu Lahab, 96, 105
Adam, 4, 5, 144, 147, 154–5, 198
Addison, Joseph, 77, 81
adoptionism, 182
Adorno, Theodor, 8
Afghanistan, 170
Africa, 64
agnosticism, 86, 108
al-Ahmad, Jalal, 8
Allah *see* God
Americas, 64
angels, 52, 58–9, 101, 143, 144–5, 147, 200
animism, 108
Anselm, St, 95
Answer to the Complaint (Iqbal), 132–3
anthropology, 206
apathy, 111
apologetics, 116
apostasy, 21, 22
Aquinas, St Thomas, 30, 34, 73, 95
Arabic language, 18, 44, 50–1
Arabs, 39, 50–2
Aramaic language, 177
archaeology, 148
al-Ash'ari, 25
al-Ashraf, Ka'b bin, 44
astronomy, 53
atheism, 65, 89–98, 104–5, 111–12, 115–22, 125–8
Auden, W. H., 23
Augustine, St, 34, 71, 95, 152
Aurelius, Marcus, 117
authorship of the Koran, 41–2
Averöes (Ibn Rushd), 26
Avicenna (Ibn Sina), 25

al-Azhar, 22, 28

Bacon, Francis, 125, 126
Badr, Battle of, 52
Bakunin, Mikhail, 95
Barth, Karl, 34, 69
beauty, 47
Bedouins, 39
belief, 36–7, 48–9, 85
Benares, 165
Bible, 57, 67, 68, 69–71, 177–8; Old Testament, 30, 90, 172, 176, 177, 183; New Testament, 68, 158, 173, 176–7
biology, 53
al-Bistami, Sheikh Abu Yazid, 131
British Humanist Association, 125
The Brothers Karamazov (Dostoyevsky), 94
Bucaille, Maurice, 53
Buddhism, 40, 108, 167, 168, 169, 185
al-Bukhari, 186
Byzantines, 149

Cairo, 8
calligraphy, Islamic, 47
Caspar, Father Robert, 197
Chesterton, G. K., 202
Children of Israel, 64, 133
China, 64
choice, freedom of, 20–1
Christianity, 6, 7, 40, 49, 108; as an apolitical faith, 169; attitude to Islam, 59; attitudes to the law, 155–6, 158; attitudes to scriptures, 69–73; decline of, 120, 127; and disbelief, 90–1; as a distortion of Islam, 171–4, 181–2; 'Divine Command' school, 117; doctrine of

the Incarnation, 156–7, 174–5,
179–80, 182; doctrine of the Trinity,
174, 179, 180, 182, 186; ecumene,
167; The Fall, 154–5; fideism, 34;
God in the Old and New Testaments,
176–7; God's engagement with
creation, 176; and idolatry, 99–100;
Islamic reservations about central
claims of, 177–82; Islamic–Christian
dialogue, 181–92, 196–7, 206;
Marxist rejection of, 170–1; mention
in the Koran, 64; messianic hopes,
160; and modernity, 12–13, 15; and
morality, 138; perceptions of Islam,
182–7; piety, 197–8; and power,
193–4, 195–6; relationship with
Islam, 171–4; rivalry with Islam,
165; and secularity, 9, 10–11,
13–14, 16; tolerance, 166–7; tragic
instinct, 160–1
circumcision, 62–3
clergy, 9
The Complaint (Iqbal), 132
conversion, 190, 201
Cordoba mosque, 129
Cragg, Rev. Kenneth, 10, 85, 156, 157,
206, 209
creation, 70, 71, 176
Crusades, 13, 140
'ulama, 9
Cupitt, Rev. Don, 11
cynicism, 127

Dali, Salvador, 204, 205
Darwin, Charles, 12, 69, 73
Darwinism, 73
David, 4, 57, 61, 64, 185
death, 149–50, 200, 211–12
Deliverance from Error (al-Ghazzali),
26
demons, 58–9, 101
Descartes, René, 185
Devil, 5, 59, 92, 103, 106, 144–5, 146
Dhul Nun, 132
dialogue, Islamic-Christian, 181–92,
196–7, 206
*Dialogues Concerning Natural
Religion*, 81
'Divine Command' school, 117
Divino Afflante (Pius XII), 71
dominance of God, 129–42

Dostoyevsky, Fyodor, 94, 119

ecumene, 165, 167–8, 170
Eden, 4, 5, 6, 155
Egypt, 122
elemental beings, 52
emotions, appeal to, 47
Enlightenment, 7, 12, 69, 70, 73, 126,
127, 128, 139
Ess, Josef van, 185
Europe, 64
evolution, 73
exclusivism, 199
Ezra, 99

fact-value distinction, 82
faith, 34–5, 38, 48–9, 85, 95
The Fall, 154–5
fanaticism, 189, 203
Far East, 64
al-Farabi, Abu Nasr, 25
fear of God, 135
Feuerbach, Ludwig, 10, 141
fideism, 34
Francis, St, 151
Frankfurt School, 8
free choice, 20–1
fundamentalism, 74

Gabriel, 3, 36, 40, 41, 52
Galilee, 177
Gandhi, Mahatma, 150
Gehenna, 6
Genesis, 70, 72
ghaflah (heedlessness), 5, 91, 110, 143
al-Ghazzali, Sheikh Abu Hamid, 26,
34, 37, 95, 213
God: and the authorship of the Koran,
40, 41–2, 43; creation, 176;
differences between Old and New
Testaments, 176–7; dominance,
129–42; and faith, 34; and human
nature, 143–7, 151–2, 157–8;
Incarnation, 156–7, 174–5, 179–80,
182; indifference to, 111; man's
status in relation to, 145–7; in
Muhammad's preaching, 4–5; and
Muslim objections to philosophy,
27–8; rejection of, 89–112;
revelation through Nature, 77–80;

silence of, 81, 83–6, 106–11; wrath, 5–6
Goethe, J. W. von, 44, 103
Gospels, 30, 59, 90, 92, 157, 173
Greece, 123, 160
Greek philosophy, 25, 34–5

Hanifs, 64
Hardy, Thomas, 95
al-Harith, Nadir ibn, 44
Hebrews, 198
heedlessness (*ghaflah*), 5, 91, 110, 143
Hejaz, 6, 39, 149
Hell, 135, 136, 149, 150, 212–13
Hellenic philosophy, 25, 34–5
Hemingway, Ernest, 124–5
heresy, 15, 21, 22, 166
Hick, John, 199–200
Hinduism, 99, 108, 123, 185, 196
Hira, Mount, 3, 52
history, 148
Holy Spirit, 36, 85, 157
Hopkins, Gerard Manley, 105
Horkheimer, Max, 8
Hud, 57, 64
human nature, 143–61
humanism, 10, 12, 97, 100, 102, 105, 115–16, 118, 125–8, 137–8, 141, 160, 165; *see also* Marxism
humanitarianism, 127
Hume, David, 47, 81
hypocrisy, 91, 153

Iblis, 144
Ibn Rushd (Averröes), 26
Ibn Sina (Avicenna), 25
ideology, 165–6, 204
idolatry (*shirk*), 28, 98–104, 130
immortality, 211
Incarnation, 156–7, 174–5, 179–80, 182
The Incoherence of the Incoherence (Ibn Rushd), 26
The Incoherence of the Philosophers (al-Ghazzali), 26
India, 55, 64, 196
indifference, 111
Industrial Revolution, 10
innovation, 15, 17–19
intolerance, 195–6
Invocation, 149

Iqbal, Dr Muhammad, 45, 77–8, 81, 129, 132–3, 137, 139
Iran, 14
Issac, 4
Ishmael, 4
Israelites, 198

Jacob, 64
Jeremiah, 185
Jerusalem, 165
Jesus Christ, 4, 28, 30, 59, 61, 64, 99, 103, 155, 157, 160, 172–5, 177–8, 181–2, 185–7, 194
Jews *see* Judaism and Jews
jinn, 52, 58–9
Job, 133, 176
John, St, 178
Jonah, 132, 186
Joseph, 183
Judaism and Jews, 6, 7, 40, 108, 167, 196; attitude to Islam, 59; attitudes to the law, 155, 158; and disbelief, 90–1; and idolatry, 99–100; mention in the Koran, 64; messianic hopes, 160; and modernity, 15; piety, 198; relationship with Islam, 171
justice, 159

Kant, Immanuel, 141
Khomeini, Ayatollah, 8, 212
Kierkegaard, Søren, 33, 34
al-Kindi, Ya'ub, 25
Kishk, Sheikh, 8
Kolakowski, Professor, 13
Koran, 6, 15; as 'an explanation of all things', 62–3; Arabic character, 50–2; authorship, 41–2; Christian attitudes to, 183; on the Devil, 103; on freedom of choice, 21; God's mercy, 135–6; on human nature, 143–54, 158; on hypocrisy in religious life, 91; importance to Muslims, 40–1, 48; interpretation, 53, 75; Jesus in, 172–3, 181–2; justifies use of force, 193; literary status, 43–7; on morality, 117; on mortality, 211–12; and the natural world, 78–9, 81; need for critical scholarship, 66–8; and objections to philosophy, 26, 28, 31–2, 35–6;

omissions, 56–7, 62–3; origins of Islam, 198; preoccupation with justice, 159; recitation of, 203; references to sexuality, 209; on rejection, 89–92, 94, 96–7, 100, 102, 104; relevance to modern man, 39–40, 49–55, 57–8, 75–6; role as final arbiter, 27; support for peace and reconciliation, 195

language, Arabic, 18, 44, 50–1
Last Day, 6, 106, 147
law, Muslim and Christian attitudes to, 155–6, 158–9
Letters Concerning Toleration (Locke), 115
life, purpose of, 93–4, 114–15
literature, Koran as, 43–7
Locke, John, 115
logical positivism, 84
Luke, St, 178
Lunn, Arnold, 168
Lutheran church, 201

madrasah, 67
Magians, 64
magic, 55
Maimonides, 95
Marcuse, Herbert, 8
Mark, St, 178
martyrdom, 212
Marx, Karl, 10, 69, 73, 95, 97, 117, 166
Marxism, 12, 49, 102, 165, 167, 168–71
Matthew, St, 178
Mecca, 165, 184, 193
Medina, 3, 184
mercy of God, 135–7
Messiah, 172
Middle East, 8, 14, 184
militant struggle, 193
Milton, John, 42, 45, 83
miracles, 84, 108
Mirza Ghulam Ahmad, 191
missionaries, 13
modernity, 11–13, 14–15, 17, 22–3, 204
Moghul Empire, 196
monotheism, 55, 56–7, 63–4, 65
morality, 116–21, 134, 138

More, Sir Thomas, 118
mortality, 209, 211–12
Mosaic Law, 172
Moscow, 165
Moses, 4, 26, 30, 59, 100, 112, 118, 133, 166, 185, 186, 194
Muhammad, Prophet, 3–4, 15, 100, 118, 148, 165, 166; and the authorship of the Koran, 41–2; Christian perception of, 183–6, 192; death, 212; detractors, 58–61, 67; greatness, 151; and Islam as a political faith, 169; in Islamic–Christian dialogue, 191–2; and the Koran, 40–1; preaches partial intolerance, 196; Tabuk expedition, 149; use of political power, 193–4

Nature, 77–84, 93, 94, 98, 127, 140, 208–9
neo-Darwinism, 73
New Covenant, 155, 177
New Testament, 68, 158, 173, 176–7
Nietzsche, Friedrich, 10, 28, 69, 95, 97, 114, 117, 120, 125, 128, 150, 177, 185
Noah, 133, 183

obscurantism, 112
orthodoxy, 7–8, 108
Orwell, George, 101

pacifism, 195
paganism, 55, 56, 100, 102
Palestine, 177
Paradise, 199, 200, 212
Pascal, Blaise, 107
Patriarchs, 198
Paul, St, 69, 117, 123, 173, 175–6, 178
peace, 195
Penelhum, Terence, 30
penitence, 151
'People of the Book', 59
Pharaoh, 133, 148
philosophy: basic presuppositions, 36–7; objections to, 24–6
physics, 53
physiology, 53
Pickthall, Marmaduke, 48
piety, 146, 147, 149–51, 154, 197–8

Pilate, Pontius, 169
Pius XII, Pope, 71
Plato, 47, 118
pluralism, 14, 165, 166, 197–201, 204
poetry, 39, 43, 52, 77, 132
political faith, Islam as, 168–70
polytheism, 55, 64, 196
Popper, Sir Karl, 29
pornography, 210
positivism, 84
power, 169–70, 193–7
prayer, 63, 213
preachers, 203, 204
prophets, 59, 64, 83, 185, 186; false prophets, 58
propositions, theological, 109
Protagoras, 128
Protestantism, 12, 138, 158, 166–7, 177, 206

Qadiani sect, 191
al-Qushayri, Sheikh Muslim ibn al-jajjaj, 152

radio, 202, 203–4
Ramadan, 48, 123, 151, 202
reason, 35, 37–8
reflection (*taddabur*), 203, 204, 205, 209
rejection, 89–112, 139, 148–9
relevance, 19
revelation, 58–61, 64, 74, 75–6, 112
The Revival of the Religious Sciences (al-Ghazzali), 26
Roman Catholic church, 7, 47, 85, 111
Roman Empire, 122, 123
Rome, 165
Rumi, Jalal al-Din, 45, 110
Russell, Bertrand, 97, 117

Sabians, 64
saints, 151, 152, 153
Salih, 57, 64
salvation, 199–200
Sartre, Jean-Paul, 93, 95, 212
Satan, 5, 59, 92, 103, 106, 144–5, 146
Saudi Arabia, 165, 201
Saul, 61
scepticism, 10, 11, 14–15, 23, 37, 58–61, 93
Sch'aib, 64

Schleiermacher, Friedrich, 13
Scholastics, 131
science, 52–5, 57–8, 209
secularity, 9–11, 13–17, 23, 56–7
self-deception, 95–6
seminaries, 67, 188
sexuality, 131, 150, 151, 209–10
Shakespeare, William, 44, 45
Shi'ah, 160
shirk (idolatry), 28, 98–104, 143
as-Sijistani, Abu Da'ud, 25–6
Sikhism, 40, 108, 196
sin, 153–5, 169
Socrates, 114, 185
Solomon, 4, 57, 61, 64, 185
sorcery, 59
South Africa, 170
sovereignty of God, 129–42
Spain, 196
Spinoza, Baruch, 117
spirits, 52
Strauss, Johann, 98
submission, 32–3, 145, 148, 153
Sufis, 77, 98, 131
sunna, 15
Sunnis, 111, 201
supernatural, 51–2, 101, 139–40
Sweden, 201
Swinburne, Richard, 70, 72, 73
Syria, 67, 149

Tabuk expedition, 149
at-Tamini, Hanzalah, 152
at-Tarjumana, Aisha Abd-ar-Rahman, 53
teachers, 155
technology, 208–9
Tess of the D'Urbervilles (Hardy), 95
Thomas, Dylan, 121
Thomism, 13
tolerance, 166–8, 195–6
Torah, 59, 66, 92, 157, 158, 172, 176
tragedy, 160–1, 211
trial by imprecation, 191–2
Trinity, 174, 179, 180, 182, 186
triumphalism, 188–90, 207

unbelief, 89–98, 101; *see also* atheism; humanism

veils, 80, 210

virtue, 144, 147, 150

Wadud, S. A., 53
warfare, 195
Western culture, 8, 13, 127

Wittgenstein, Ludwig, 50, 180
women, segregation, 210

Yahweh, 176
Yathrib, 3

A NOTE ON THE AUTHOR

Shabbir Akhtar was born in Pakistan but has long been
settled in Bradford, England. He was educated at St.
Catharine's College of Cambridge University and at the
University of Calgary, Alberta. He received a Ph.D. in the
philosophy of religion. Mr. Akhtar has worked as a community relations officer in Bradford, where he is also a
member of the Bradford Council of Mosques. His writings
include articles on religion for a variety of journals and
periodicals, and a widely praised book about the Salman
Rushdie affair, *Be Careful with Muhammad!*